Iceland

Norway

Sweden

Finland

Denmark

Estonia

Latvia

Lithuania

Netherlands

Poland

United
Kingdom

Germany

Ireland

Belgium

Czech Republic

Slovakia

Luxembourg

Liechtenstein

Austria

Hungary

Romania

Switzerland

Slovenia

Croatia

France

Bosnia and
Herzegovina

Serbia

Bulgaria

San Marino

Montenegro

Kosovo

Andorra

FYR Macedonia

Turkey

Monaco

Italy

Albania

Portugal

Spain

Vatican City

Greece

Malta

Cyprus

THE SOCIAL ATLAS OF EUROPE

DIMITRIS BALLAS, DANNY DORLING AND BENJAMIN HENNIG

First published in Great Britain in 2014 by:
Policy Press
University of Bristol
6th Floor, Howard House
Queen's Avenue
Clifton
Bristol, BS8 1SD
UK

Tel +44 (0)117 331 5020 / Fax +44 (0)117 331 5367
pp-info@bristol.ac.uk / www.policypress.co.uk

North American office:
Policy Press
c/o The University of Chicago Press
1427 East 60th Street
Chicago, IL 60637
USA

Tel +1 773 702 7700 / Fax +1 773-702-9756
sales@press.uchicago.edu / www.press.uchicago.edu

British Library Cataloguing in Publication Data
A catalogue record for this book is available from the
British Library.

Library of Congress Cataloging-in-Publication Data
A catalog record for this book has been requested

ISBN: 978 1 44731 353 3 (hardcover)

Typeset and cover design by Soapbox, www.soapbox.co.uk

Printed and bound in Great Britain by Gomer Press Limited,
Llandysul, Ceredigion

The Policy Press uses environmentally
responsible print partners

DEDICATED TO

Jean Monet,
one of the founding fathers of
the European Union

Janos Szego,
who created human cartography
in Europe

Pavlos Fyssas,
murdered in Athens in
September 2013

CONTENTS

ACKNOWLEDGEMENTS

We are very grateful to our publishers and in particular to the Director of Policy Press, Alison Shaw, for all her great encouragement, feedback and support from the very early stages of this project, and also to Laura Vickers, as well as the anonymous reviewers who provided constructive comments on the early drafts and book proposal. We are also extremely grateful to the Production Editor, Jo Morton, who meticulously read through and corrected several versions of the proofs and provided very helpful comments and suggestions, and to Katherine James, who copy-edited the typescript. We are also very grateful to the design and typesetting team for all their hard and excellent work and support and in particular to Dave Worth, Paulien Hosang, John Schwartz and Rachel Bray. Thanks are also due to Susannah Emery, Kathryn King, Victoria Pittman and to all staff in Policy Press – it has been really great working with them on this project.

We would also like to thank Laurent Chalard for his constructive comments and very helpful suggestions and Álvaro Martinez-Perez for comments, advice and help with some of the data sources.

Thanks are also due to all providers of the data used in this book (listed in the Appendix giving sources of data). We would also like to acknowledge that the EU-SILC data set was provided by Eurostat. The results of all data processing and analyses we conducted and interpretations are ours and not those of Eurostat, the European Commission or any of the national authorities and other organisations whose data we have used. Any remaining errors or misunderstandings are, of course, our own responsibility.

Dimitris Ballas is extremely grateful to Vicky Yiagopoulou for all her constant support and encouragement. Danny Dorling would like to thank Alison Dorling for allowing him not yet to slow down. Benjamin Hennig is deeply grateful to Tina Gotthardt who has built many bridges over the borders that are mapped in this book.

GLOSSARY OF TERMS AND ABBREVIATIONS

AGE-STANDARDISED MORTALITY RATE the ratio of the number of observed deaths in a study to the number of expected deaths in a population.

CBS Centraal Bureau voor de Statistiek (Statistics Netherlands).

CIA (United States) Central Intelligence Agency.

DESTATIS Federal Statistical Office of Germany.

DG REGIO European Commission's Directorate-General for Regional Policy.

DG RTD European Commission's Directorate-General for Research and Innovation.

EFGS European Forum for Geostatistics.

EQLS European Quality of Life Surveys.

EU European Union.

EUROSTAT the statistical office of the European Union.

EU-SILC European Union Statistics on Income and Living Conditions.

FDI foreign direct investment.

FYR MACEDONIA Former Yugoslav Republic of Macedonia.

GDP gross domestic product.

GINI INDEX a measure of inequality showing the extent to which the distribution of a variable (such as income) deviates from a perfectly equal distribution.

ICIS International Centre for Integrated Assessment and Sustainable Development (at Maastricht University).

ILO International Labour Organisation.

IMF International Monetary Fund

ISCED International Standard Classification of Education, dividing educational attainment into the following levels: Level 0 – Pre-primary education; Level 1 – Primary education; Level 2 – Lower secondary education; Level 3 – Upper secondary education; Level 4: Post-secondary non-tertiary education; Level 5 – Tertiary education (first stage); Level 6 –Tertiary education (second stage). For more detailed information see: http://epp.eurostat.ec.europa.eu/statistics_explained/index.php/Glossary:International_standard_classification_of_education_%28ISCED%29

JRC (European Commission) Joint Research Centre.

MODIS Moderate Resolution Imaging Spectroradiometer.

NASA National Aeronautics and Space Administration.

NORDREGIO Nordic Centre for Spatial Development.

NUTS Nomenclature d'Unités Territoriales Statistiques. This is the Eurostat classification system for dividing up the economic territory of the EU for the purpose of the collection, development and harmonisation of EU regional statistics, and socio-economic analyses of the regions. It is divided into three levels: NUTS 1 (major socio-economic regions – essentially country level); NUTS 2 (basic regions for the application of regional policies – major region level); NUTS 3 (small regions for specific diagnoses – county level). For more information see: http://epp.eurostat.ec.europa.eu/portal/page/portal/nuts_nomenclature/introduction

OECD Organisation for Economic Co-operation and Development.

PPCS /PPS purchasing power consumption standard /purchasing power standard. This is a measure that helps in making valid comparisons of consumption power between regions by adjusting monetary values. For more information see: http://epp.eurostat.ec.europa.eu/statistics_explained/index.php/Glossary:Purchasing_power_consumption_standard_%28PPCS%29

SEDAC Socio-Economic Data and Applications Center of the Columbia University, New York.

UK United Kingdom.

UN United Nations.

UN-CTS United Nations Surveys on Crime Trends and the Operations of Criminal Justice Systems.

WHO World Health Organisation.

WORLDCLIM a world database of global climate layers with a spatial resolution of about 1 square kilometre, developed by Robert J. Hijmans, Susan Cameron, and Juan Parra, at the University of California, Berkeley, in collaboration with Peter Jones and Andrew Jarvis (International Center for Tropical Agriculture) and Karen Richardson (Cooperative Research Centre for Tropical Rainforest Ecology and Management).

1

INTRODUCTION

A NEW WAY OF LOOKING AT EUROPE

The EU has delivered half a century of peace, stability, and prosperity, helped raise living standards and launched a single European currency, the euro and is progressively building a single Europe-wide market in which people, goods, services, and capital move among Member States as freely as within one country.
European Commission, 2012a

This is one of the declarations made on the European Union (EU) official website. The motto of the EU – the largest, most populous, political union of separate countries in the world – is 'United in diversity', signifying the intentions and efforts of Europeans to work together for peace and prosperity, while at the same time highlighting the idea that the many different cultures, traditions and languages of Europe are a key asset, benefit and legacy.

The EU website suggests that the history of the EU can be divided into six major periods as follows:

• *1945–59: A peaceful Europe – the beginnings of cooperation*

• *1960s: The 'Swinging Sixties' – a period of economic growth*

• *1970s: A growing Community – the first Enlargement*

• *1980s: The changing face of Europe – the fall of the Berlin Wall*

• *1990s: A Europe without frontiers*

• *2000s: A decade of further expansion*
(European Commission, 2012b)

However, at this stage it cannot be predicted how the current, seventh (2010s) decade might be labelled. In the aftermath of the financial crisis, will it be known as the decade of ever-closer union and pan-European identity, salvation and solidarity? Or will it be the decade of austerity and the revival of old divisions,

national stereotypes and hatred? Will it be the decade of sustainability, 'green growth' and social cohesion? Or will it be the decade of rising mass poverty, gross inequality, social exclusion and environmental degradation? On one hand there have been some optimistic signs, including a recent report by the European Commission suggesting a reduction in health inequalities between European regions and, in particular, a narrowing of gaps in life expectancy and infant mortality (European Commission, 2013a). However, there are also suggestions, from evidence such as that presented in a recent Red Cross report, that '*Europe is sinking into a protracted period of deepening poverty, mass unemployment, social exclusion, greater inequality, and collective despair as a result of austerity policies adopted in response to the debt and currency crisis of the past four years*' (Traynor, 2013).

The aim of *The Social Atlas of Europe* is to offer a human geography perspective on the above issues by bringing together maps and facts on a wide range of topics affecting Europe and its people.

Our approach is underpinned by the view that Europe is something much more than just a world region or a collection of nation states: a hope that we are moving towards the conception of a 'European people' instead of a 'Europe of nations'.[1] In this book we argue that the EU needs to be thought of as an entity that is more than just a union of member states, more than just a common market or just a potential monetary or fiscal union. There is a need to rethink European social identity. What does it mean to be European today? To what extent do the citizens of EU member states feel that they are citizens of something larger than their own country?

It is hoped that this atlas may enhance a perception of European identity and solidarity, and the feeling of affiliation and belonging to something larger than the nation-state.

One way to move towards a 'European people' instead of a 'nation-states' mentality and to bolster European identity further is to think of Europe and its economy, culture, history and human and physical geography in

terms of a single large land mass. This may already be happening to some extent, especially among the rapidly increasing numbers of Europeans who live, study and/or work in a member state other than their country of birth, including two of the authors of this atlas (the third having returned home to work within a mile of where he was born).

Europe is also often increasingly presented in terms indicative of a place of diversity and delight by popular travel publications: '*Few places pack the punch of Europe. From its Northern Lights to its Southern shores, this drama queen keeps on thrilling, surprising and confusing with her extraordinary wealth of sights, sounds, peoples and parties*' (Lonely Planet, 2013). However, the history of Europe has a far darker flipside to the tale of ever greater enlightenment and understanding. It is also where the spoils of conquest were first landed and where both world wars began.

The maps presented in this atlas show just how different are the separate countries, regions and great cities of this continent, but also how often they are so similar. Looking at the maps in this atlas you can begin to believe that you are looking at the cartography of a single large group of people.

THE COUNTRIES REPRESENTED IN THIS ATLAS

It is often claimed that European identity is underpinned by common European values and ideals, such as the establishment of democratic institutions, respect for human rights (including the far too little-celebrated abolition of the death penalty) and the protection of minorities. These rights and aims are all included in the so-called 'Copenhagen criteria' that need to be met before the accession of a country to the EU will even be considered (European Commission, 2013b).

---

1 One day even this idea may appear quaint and outmoded as people all around the world start to see themselves as part of one entity; but that day is still hard to imagine.

This atlas maps those countries that currently meet those criteria or come very close.

We include in this atlas all states that have demonstrated a strong commitment to a common European future by their close association with the EU, either as current members or as official candidate states (or official potential candidates for EU accession) and/or those that have signed up to the European Economic Area, the Schengen Zone (a group of countries that have abolished border controls for travel between them) or the European Monetary Union.

THE MAPS

This social atlas highlights the notion of Europe as a single entity by looking at its physical and population geography simultaneously in new ways, using state-of-the-art Geographical Information Systems (GIS) and new human cartography techniques, building on recent developments and innovative Worldmapper applications (these are described in more detail in Dorling et al, 2008; Worldmapper, 2009; Hennig, 2013; Views of the World, 2013). In this atlas we present nearly two hundred maps and illustrations, painting a picture of Europe, its people and its environment in relation to a wide range of themes and using data from a variety of sources such as the European Values Survey, Eurostat (including data from such surveys such as the European Union Statistics on Income and Living Conditions), the International Labour Organisation, the World Bank and the World Health Organization. All the maps are accompanied by a commentary and in some cases by graphs showing additional complementary information. The atlas may be read in the sequence that it is written, chapter by chapter, but it is also possible to just refer to particular chapters or maps of interest. We hope that you will enjoy this atlas, or, at the very least, find it interesting to see Europe in a way you've probably not seen it before.

Mapping techniques

The maps here differ from traditional maps because here area is made proportional to particular social statistics rather than reflecting land area. Often traditional map projections do not even reflect land area accurately because they may, for example, maintain compass directions, which has the effect of making the North of Europe appear much larger than it really is.

The new maps shown in this atlas often use the population of Europe as the key variable that is represented by the area of each country and region. Alternatively in most of the country-level maps a different variable relating to the population is used and this can result in some very unusual maps being created. In some ways these country-level 'cartograms' are a little like pie charts, where the size of each slice of the pie is proportional to the number of people in each country having a particular characteristic. However, unlike pie charts, the countries on these maps still always touch their original neighbours and so it is far easier to get an overview of the entire distribution in one glance. When population is used as the basic variable, other variables can be used to determine how to shade each region on these maps. The reader then has their attention automatically drawn to the places where there are most people.

HOW TO IDENTIFY THE COUNTRIES

All the maps in this atlas include all European states that currently meet at least one of the key criteria detailed above. A list of these states is given in Table 1, with their estimated population in 2012. Figure 1 shows a land area map of these countries, using a colour scale, starting with shades of dark red to demarcate those countries with the most recent association with Europe, moving through the rainbow to a shade of violet for the oldest members of the EU. This colour scheme is followed throughout this atlas so that on all the country-level maps the same country is always shown in the same colour. A European identity may well be forming but

many Europeans have little idea of how many countries there are in Europe, let alone being able to identify them, and that is before we begin to stretch and twist these maps.

There are three different types of maps in this atlas:

• Country cartograms

• Population cartograms with thematic mapping showing the geographical distribution of a variable of interest

• Gridded-population (Hennig) cartograms with thematic mapping.

FIGURE 1
Land area map of Europe

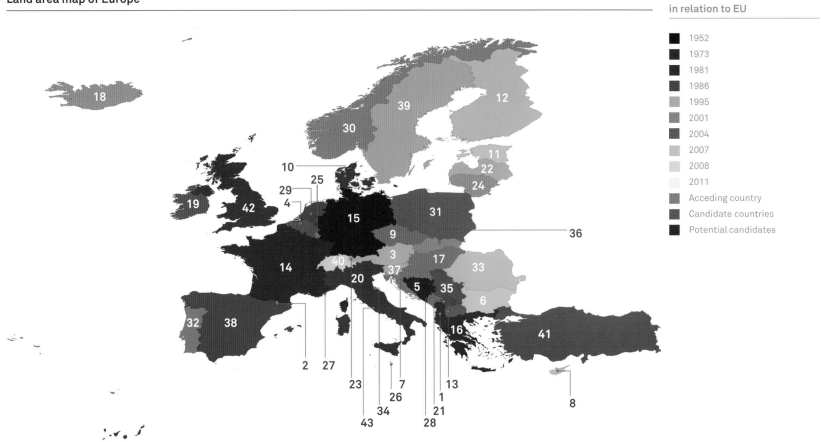

Colours denote years of
accession or current status
in relation to EU

- 1952
- 1973
- 1981
- 1986
- 1995
- 2001
- 2004
- 2007
- 2008
- 2011
- Acceding country
- Candidate countries
- Potential candidates

Table 1

The European states included in this atlas

	OFFICIAL NAME	POPULATION			OFFICIAL NAME	POPULATION
1	Republic of Albania	2,831,741		22	Republic of Latvia	2,041,763
2	Principality of Andorra	85,015		23	Principality of Liechtenstein	36,475
3	Republic of Austria	8,443,018		24	Republic of Lithuania	3,007,758
4	Kingdom of Belgium	11,094,850		25	Grand Duchy of Luxembourg	524,853
5	Bosnia and Herzegovina	3,839,265		26	Republic of Malta	417,520
6	Republic of Bulgaria	7,327,224		27	Principality of Monaco	33,085
7	Republic of Croatia	4,398,150		28	Montenegro	621,240
8	Republic of Cyprus	862,011		29	Kingdom of the Netherlands	16,730,348
9	Czech Republic	10,505,445		30	Kingdom of Norway	4,985,870
10	Kingdom of Denmark	5,580,516		31	Republic of Poland	38,538,447
11	Republic of Estonia	1,339,662		32	Portuguese Republic	10,541,840
12	Republic of Finland	5,401,267		33	Romania	21,355,849
13	Former Yugoslav Republic of Macedonia	2,059,794		34	Republic of San Marino	32,166
				35	Republic of Serbia	7,241,295
14	French Republic	65,327,724		36	Slovak Republic	5,404,322
15	Federal Republic of Germany	81,843,743		37	Republic of Slovenia	2,055,496
16	Hellenic Republic	11,290,067		38	Kingdom of Spain	46,196,276
17	Republic of Hungary	9,957,731		39	Kingdom of Sweden	9,482,855
18	Republic of Iceland	319,575		40	Swiss Confederation	7,954,66
19	Republic of Ireland	4,582,769		41	Republic of Turkey	74,724,269
20	Italian Republic	60,820,696		42	United Kingdom of Great Britain and Northern Ireland	62,989,551
21	Kosovo (under UN Security Council Resolution 1244/99)	1,800,000		43	State of the Vatican City	800

Country cartograms

This type of map uses the rainbow colour scheme shown in Figure 1 but with each country resized on the basis of a variable of interest. Rather than showing land area, Figure 2 shows the countries resized according to their total population (listed in Table 1): the larger the population of a member state the larger the area it occupies on the map. Germany, the largest country and home (at the time of writing) to 82 million people, occupies the largest area, followed by Turkey, France, the United Kingdom and Italy, whereas the space occupied by relatively sparsely populated countries like Iceland and the Scandinavian countries is much smaller on the population cartogram in Figure 2 than it is on the land area map in Figure 1.

The cartographic technique used to create the map shown in Figure 2 applies the density-equalising approach proposed by two physicists (Gastner and Newman, 2004). This technique is increasingly seen as the most appropriate way to visualise geographical data in the social sciences[2] if you are interested in mapping people rather than land, especially if you do not wish to concentrate on empty land.

What the technique does is to iteratively alter the original map so that areas of high density slowly expand and areas of low density shrink in such a way that eventually all areas are of, say, equal population density, in which case an equal population cartogram is created. The algorithm behind the technique does this using a method that is minimally distorting and which attempts to preserve conformality at all points. A conformal map projection is one in which angles are preserved locally. The technique is an approximation so as not to produce results that are too hard to interpret. Thus, areas with a value of zero shrink but do not disappear entirely, and countries should still be generally recognisable from their shape and position even after their size is changed.

In this atlas we have typically used this type of map when there was data available for all our reference states (with the exception of Chapter 12, where this type of map is used to explore variables for current EU members only) and that data added up to a meaningful total at the European level. This usually involved a count of people (e.g. the number of people unemployed) but it could also be any other number adding up to a meaningful total (e.g. total Gross Domestic Product in euros or total carbon dioxide emissions in kilotons).

Population cartograms with thematic mapping

This type of map is based on the cartogram shown in Figure 2, but shaded accordingly to show the variation of the variable mapped. This type of map was used when data was not available for all the states that were selected to be mapped in this atlas (e.g. the total number of people working in different kinds of occupations, using data from the EU Statistics on Income and Living Conditions: see Maps 6.051 to 6.059) and/or when the variable mapped was not adding up to a meaningful total at the European level (e.g. income inequality measures: see Maps 11.135 to 11.137).

This is still a population cartogram, but the cartogram is now simply a base map, and it is the shading in the cartogram which represents the distribution that is being discussed. It can be difficult to understand this abstractly but it becomes clear as you read through the atlas which kind of map is which and when the variable of interest is being used to shade areas rather than size them.

Gridded-population cartograms with thematic mapping

Another way that countries are mapped in this atlas is by applying the same density-equalising approach to create a gridded-population cartogram, meaning that the underlying projection onto which the map has been transformed is one where people are equally distributed on a grid stretched so that each grid cell has an area proportional to the population within that cell.[3] The size of each of the grid cells therefore reflects the number of people living in this area; the projection means that the base map itself reflects the real population distribution on a coherent geographical reference (and not the population based on artificial administrative units like the nation states used in Figure 2). Figure 3 shows a gridded-population cartogram of the countries mapped in Figures 1 and 2. This cartogram uses finer-level geographical information about where people live and gives an even better representation of the distribution of Europe's population than Figure 2, as it shows more clearly where most people are concentrated – in cities. For instance, Madrid, Paris, Istanbul and London are huge, while the whole of Scandinavia is small. Countries and regions that are more densely populated (for example most of the UK, Italy, Poland, Romania) are more visible on the map whereas the large rural areas in the north of the Europe appear considerably smaller. The Rhine-Ruhr metropolitan region in Western Europe, including the areas of Cologne, Dortmund and expanding towards the Netherlands, is much more prominent than it is on a conventional map.

2 For more details on the technique, as well as examples of applications to date, see Gastner and Newman, 2004; Dorling et al, 2008; Dorling and Thomas, 2011.

3 For more details on the technique and applications see Hennig, 2013; www.viewsoftheworld.net

FIGURE 2
Population cartogram of Europe

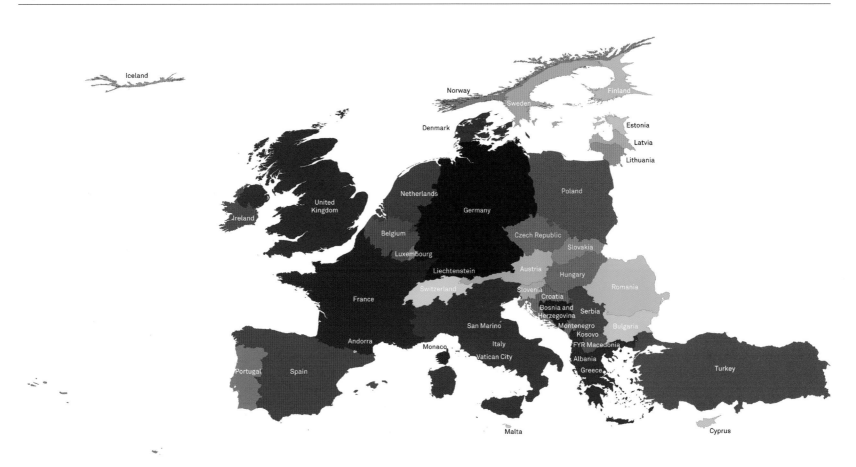

FIGURE 3
Gridded-population cartogram of Europe
Basemap: Hennig Projection Gridded Population Cartogram

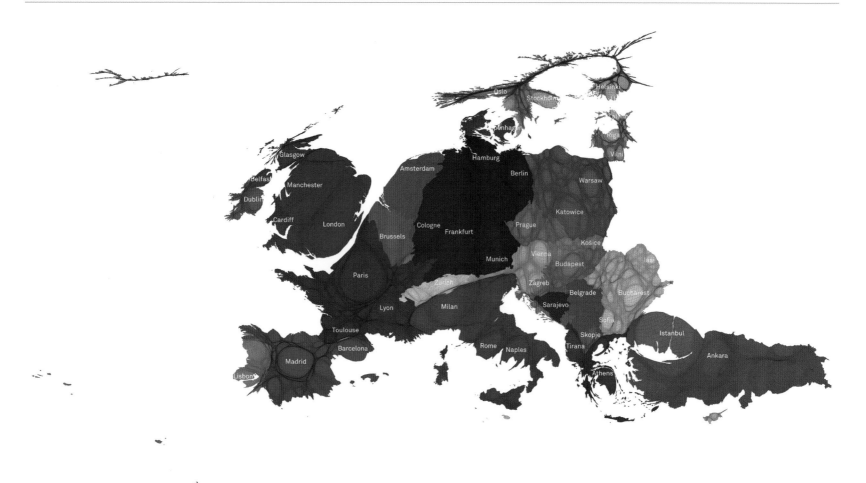

More information can be represented on gridded-population cartograms by added shading. Figure 4 is the topographic version of the map shown in Figure 3, with the area being drawn proportionally to population but coloured by altitude. Thus physical geography and human geography can both be shown on the map. In a way this can be thought of as the inverse of a traditional physical geography map, displaying cities: this is a new, human geography map, depicting mountains and valleys. European mapping needs to change if an entity as complex and diverse as the human geography of this continent is to be shown in all its detail, in a way in which a map may be able to fire up imaginations, certainly of its younger citizens who are more used to seeing the world graphically in ways their grandparents could have hardly imagined.

In order to make better sense of the human cartographic approaches used in this atlas we provide some further examples projecting physical features onto gridded-population cartograms in Figures 5, 6, 7 and 8.

First, the issues of cold, of heating, of insulation, of a sustainable energy future, are made stark in Figure 5. All that the figure actually shows is where was coldest in the cold winter of 2010, but the extent to which this cold impacted on the population will have depended on all those other factors. However, before those issues can be considered it is important simply to see who was most affected, and to see that we need a population cartogram that highlights where the largest numbers suffered the coldest temperatures. This map shows the difference between the temperature of the land surface for the week 3–10 December 2010 and the average temperature for the same week in the years 2002–09. Clearly a divide settled across Europe between people living in those parts to the south and west that were less frozen and those in parts of the UK, in France just south of Paris, in much of Scandinavia and the interior of the European mainland – while in Athens it was only just a bit nippy.

Next we show on population cartograms the normal patterns of rainfall across the continent first monthly (Figure 6) and then annually (Figure 8). Rain, like much else, does not respect national borders. We are also a little less interested in the rain that does not fall on our heads as compared to that which does. But who in Europe experiences the most rain and at what times of the year?

These maps show Europe as a land mass, stretching from Iceland to Turkey, that is both arid in places and, at different times in different areas, soaked. These maps matter because they show the actual experience of the people living in Europe. To understand these maps it may help to imagine that they are the product of a satellite hovering in stationary orbit over the continent but containing a special lens which magnifies the cities and minimises the wilderness just to the extent to give everyone equal representation. It is also a satellite with a camera that can detect far more than simply physical properties such as vegetation, heat and moisture.

Animals are moved about Europe as if there are no borders. Pigs, for instance, begin life in one country, are fattened up in Denmark, and are then taken to Catalonia in huge numbers for slaughter (to the extent that it pollutes the water supply). This may appear not of great relevance to rainfall, but large amounts of rainfall are needed if the slurry from industrially produced pigs is to be washed away without also polluting water stocks. What you see in Figures 6 and 8 is the rain as it falls on people; what you see in Figure 7 is the rain as it falls on land.

It can be argued that visualising and mapping Europe in the ways shown in these maps[4] makes it easier for Europeans not only to make more sense of their home area's physical and human geography but also to think of Europe as a single entity – the place they belong to or their 'homeland' (rather than their nation state). The boundaries defining nation states are, after all, often not much more than the historic boundaries of the realms of royal houses with particular religious affiliations that became fossilised at particular moments in time. Natural and man-made disasters (e.g. the Chernobyl radiation cloud), however, show no regard for state borders.

The adoption of the mapping approach employed in this book may make it more likely for people to care about an environmental disaster or social unrest or hardship affecting others elsewhere in Europe: in other words to feel solidarity with other people and places and to enhance a sense of common identity.

4 In this book we present an alternative visualisation of Europe, which can complement the land area maps that may be found in conventional atlases and other sources that have been extensively used to map Europe.

FIGURE 4
Gridded population cartogram representation of the topography of Europe
Basemap: Hennig Projection Gridded Population Cartogram

Altitude

■ Low-land
▦ Mid-altitude
■ High-land

FIGURE 5
Europe's 'Big Freeze'
Basemap: Hennig Projection Gridded Population Cartogram

Land surface temperature
anomaly
(°C)

15

0

-15

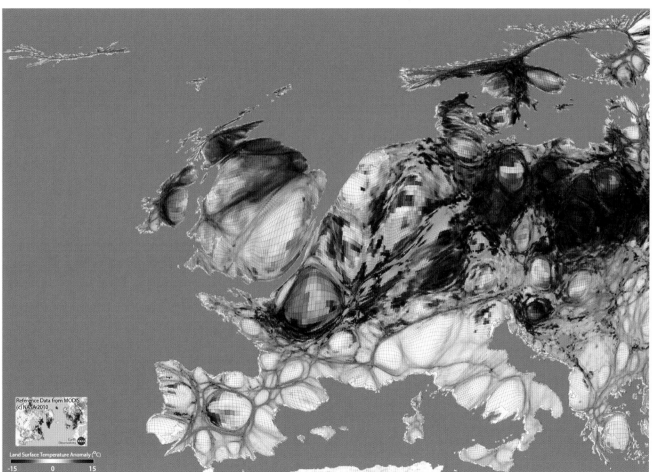

FIGURE 6
Monthly precipitation in Europe – population cartograms

JANUARY

FEBRUARY

MARCH

APRIL

MAY

JUNE

JULY

AUGUST

SEPTEMBER

OCTOBER

NOVEMBER

DECEMBER

(mm)

< 15	40–50	90–100	130–140	170–180
15–20	50–60	100–110	140–150	180–190
20–30	70–80	110–120	150–160	190–200
30–40	80–90	120–130	160–170	>200

FIGURE 7
Monthly precipitation in Europe – land area maps

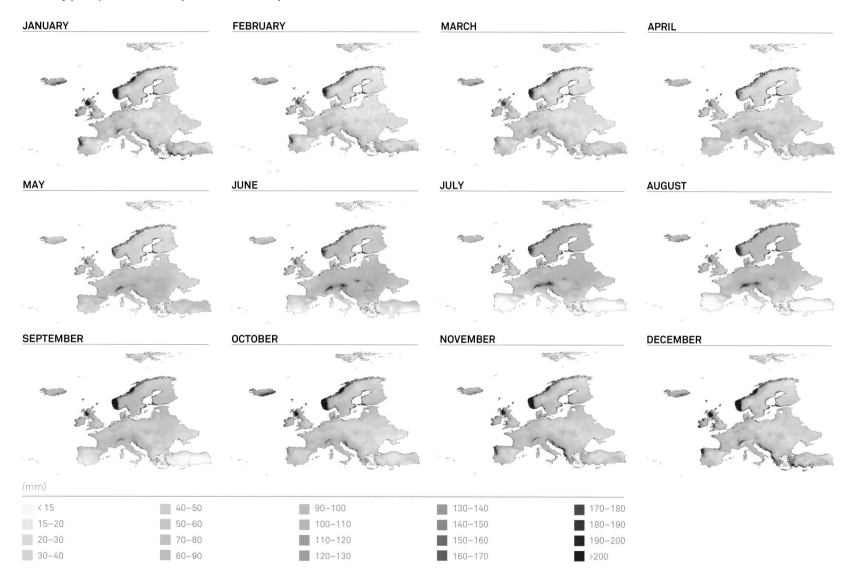

JANUARY FEBRUARY MARCH APRIL

MAY JUNE JULY AUGUST

SEPTEMBER OCTOBER NOVEMBER DECEMBER

(mm)

< 15	40–50	90–100	130–140	170–180
15–20	50–60	100–110	140–150	180–190
20–30	70–80	110–120	150–160	190–200
30–40	80–90	120–130	160–170	>200

FIGURE 8
Annual precipitation in Europe
Basemap: Hennig Projection Gridded Population Cartogram

Annual precipitation in Europe
(mm)

- <400
- 400–450
- 450–500
- 500–550
- 550–600
- 600–650
- 650–700
- 700–750
- 750–800
- 800–850
- 850–900
- 900–950
- 9500–1000
- 1000–1250
- 1250–1500
- 1500–1750
- >1750

Area drawn in proportion to population

2

IDENTITY AND CULTURE

MAP 2.001 – CAN THE DEATH PENALTY BE JUSTIFIED?
Distribution of Europeans stating they would 'never' accept the death penalty as justifiable
Source: European Values Survey, 2008

CAN YOU JUSTIFY THE DEATH PENALTY?
Note that '5' is the option most favoured by those who say they are unsure

| 45% | 7% | 6% | 4% | 12% | 5% | 5% | 5% | 3% | 8% |

NEVER (1)   ALWAYS JUSTIFIABLE (10)

Article 2 Right to life
1. Everyone has the right to life.
2. No one shall be condemned to
the death penalty, or executed.
*Charter of Fundamental Rights of the European
Union, 2007/C 303/01*

The protection of human rights and, most importantly, of the right not to be executed, is considered to be one of Europe's principal contemporary values. It is one of the key 'Copenhagen criteria' that needs to be met before any country can be considered as a potential member of the European Union.

According to the latest data from the European Values Survey, on a scale of 1 (never) to 10 (always), 45% of all Europeans answered 'never' when asked if they agree with the death penalty; just 8% answered 'always'.

It's possible that where the memory of executions is recent, or continues to be kept alive, opposition to the idea of execution being reintroduced is strongest. The largest number opposed to the idea is observed in Kosovo (87%), followed by Malta (68%), Turkey (67%), Italy (63%) and Bosnia and Herzegovina (60%). Countries where the fewest people say the death penalty should never be reintroduced include the Czech Republic (15%), Lithuania (21%), Latvia (21%), Hungary (22%), Estonia (24%) and the United Kingdom (25%).

MAP 2.002 – HOW IMPORTANT IS RELIGION IN YOUR LIFE?

Estimated distribution of people who believe religion is 'very important'

Source: European Values Survey, 2008

The Convention on the Future of Europe's deliberations over the EU Constitution has thrown into relief the role of religion in defining 'Europeanness' ... The debate over whether Christianity should be seen as constitutive of European identity has been framed by wider concerns about collective identities and memories in Europe.

Schlesinger and Foret, 2006, p 59

There have long been debates about the importance of religion in shaping European identity – in particular of Christianity, Islam and Judaism, which are often described as the 'great religions of the West'. But how important is religion in the life of Europeans?

According to the most recent data from the European Values Survey, 27% of all Europeans consider religion to be very important and another 27% as 'quite important', whereas for 22% it is 'not at all important'.

In Turkey, 80% of the surveyed population believe that religion is very important in their lives, followed by Cyprus (59%), Malta (59%) and Romania (55%). The smallest percentages are observed in Estonia (5%), the Czech Republic (6.3%), Germany (7.8%) and Sweden (8.3%).

HOW IMPORTANT IS RELIGION IN YOUR LIFE?

Europeans are almost perfectly divided into four groups by religious belief

| 27% | 27% | 24% | 22% |

VERY IMPORTANT

NOT AT ALL IMPORTANT

MAP 2.003 – DO YOU BELIEVE IN LIFE AFTER DEATH?
Distribution of Europeans who do not believe in any form of an afterlife
Source: European Values Survey, 2008

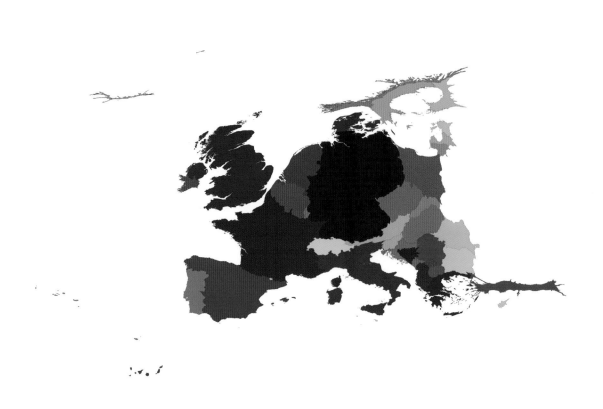

Believing in life after death is a key aspect of many religions. This map shows estimates of people who do not believe in any form of an afterlife (44% of all Europeans). The map reflects how important, or unimportant, religion is in the lives of Europeans.

Albania is at the top of the list of non-believers, with 74.3% not believing in life after death. This may be due to the heritage of the strong anti-religious policies of the former Maoist Albanian leader Enver Hoxha. It is closely followed by countries which, like Albania, were formerly members of the communist bloc – countries such as Montenegro (71.0%), the Czech Republic (69.8%) and Bulgaria (68.3%). Next highest is Germany (68.1%), part of which was also in the communist bloc. Among the countries with the lowest number of non-believers are Turkey (5.7%), Malta (12.7%), Kosovo (24.4%), Romania (26.5%) and Poland (27.7%). It is interesting to note that in Poland Catholicism was a leading force in the contestation of communism.

Across Europe, an estimated 56% of the population believe in life after death, while 44% do not. The question appears to have been phrased in a way that would encourage people not to express the agnostic belief – that is, that there may be a life after death but they have no way of knowing.

DO YOU BELIEVE IN LIFE AFTER DEATH?

56%   44%

YES   NO

MAP 2.004 – HOW IMPORTANT IS POLITICS IN YOUR LIFE?
Distribution of Europeans stating that politics is 'very important' in their life
Source: European Values Survey, 2008

Conscious of its spiritual and moral heritage, the Union is founded on the indivisible, universal values of human dignity, freedom, equality and solidarity; *it is based on the principles of democracy and the rule of law.* It places the individual at the heart of its activities, by establishing the citizenship of the Union and by creating an area of freedom, security and justice.

Preamble to the Charter of Fundamental Rights of the European Union (Official Journal of the European Union, 2007), emphasis added

The country with the largest estimated proportion of its population believing that politics is very important in their lives is Sweden (47%). When the latest survey was taken, in 2008, this country also stood out not just in relation to the rest of Europe but also compared with its Scandinavian neighbours, as being especially convinced of the importance of politics. The second largest proportion is observed in Turkey (20.3%), followed by Kosovo (19.4%), Cyprus (16.2%) and FYR Macedonia (16.2%). The lowest rates of agreement that politics is important in life are found in Lithuania (2.6%), Slovenia (2.7%), Estonia (2.9%), Albania (3.3%) and Croatia (3.5%).

The word 'politics' can mean different things in English (in that it can relate to personal strategies of behaviour as well as to public administration or government) and may be interpreted differently in different languages. This question is a good example of where the precise translation of the word may have an effect on the answers given.

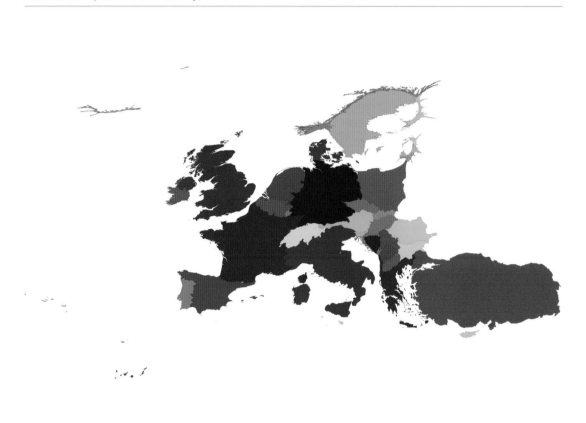

HOW IMPORTANT IN YOUR LIFE IS POLITICS?
Answers to this question may be influenced by when it is asked

11%	30%	35%	24%

VERY IMPORTANT

NOT AT ALL IMPORTANT

MAP 2.005 – HOW IMPORTANT IN LIFE IS LEISURE TIME?
Distribution of Europeans stating that leisure time is 'very important' in their life

Source: European Values Survey, 2008

... the real measuring rod of human freedom ... is leisure time, not in the sense of 'time for doing nothing' but in the sense of time freed from the iron necessity to produce and reproduce material livelihood, and therefore disposable for all-round and free development of the individual talents, wishes, capacities, potentialities, of each human being.

Ernest Mandel Internet Archive, 2005, referring to Marx and Engels

The country with the highest share of its population believing in the importance of leisure to life is FYR Macedonia (70.2%), followed by Cyprus (54.5%), Ireland (54.4%), the Netherlands (53.5%) and Denmark (53.0%). By contrast, the lowest proportions believing that leisure is very important are seen in Sweden (7.2%), Albania (14.8%), Lithuania (19.9%), Latvia (24.6%) and Croatia (26.2%).

As with other questions on values, the precise translation of the word 'leisure' may well influence the results. Where the translated word more strongly implies 'partying', fewer may agree; where it implies 'having a rest', more may agree that it is important to life.

With no common language used across Europe, and different nationalities having different conceptions of words such as 'leisure', this map could simply be a representation of different verbal interpretations.

HOW IMPORTANT IN YOUR LIFE IS LEISURE TIME?
A large majority of Europeans (86%) see leisure as important

39%	47%	12%	2%

VERY IMPORTANT   NOT AT ALL IMPORTANT

MAP 2.006 – HOW IMPORTANT IN LIFE IS WORK?
Distribution of Europeans stating that work is 'very important' in their life
Source: European Values Survey, 2008

HOW IMPORTANT IN YOUR LIFE IS WORK?
Most Europeans (89%) see work as important

60%   29%   6% 5%

VERY IMPORTANT   NOT AT ALL IMPORTANT

When asked to rate the importance of work in their lives on a 4 point scale (ranging from 'not at all important' to 'very important'), 60% of respondents said that it was 'very important'.

The largest percentage of people who say work is very important is found in Sweden (92%), followed by Turkey (83%), FYR Macedonia (79%), Cyprus (76%) and Malta (71%). The smallest percentages are in Finland (34%), Lithuania (42%), the Czech Republic (43%), the United Kingdom (45%) and the Netherlands (45%). It's interesting to note that two neighbouring countries, Sweden and Finland, seem to be at the opposite ends of this spectrum. Although they are similar in many ways, their respective languages come from very different origins, so it is likely that translated words have different connotations in the two countries.

Work can be seen as very important if the issue is whether you have work or not, and need the money earned from work in order to survive. Some people believe that work is important in imposing some kind of discipline on life, and that without people working, society could not function. Where things that are essential to life, such as child care, are not counted as work, then work is seen as less important. Some paid work is viewed as being 'unnecessary work' – an example might be employing in a shop an extra member of staff whose main purpose is to persuade people to buy things they do not wish to buy!

MAP 2.007 – HOW IMPORTANT IN LIFE IS FAMILY?
Distribution of Europeans stating that family is 'very important' in their life
Source: European Values Survey, 2008

HOW IMPORTANT IN YOUR LIFE IS FAMILY?
In Europe, 98% of people agree that family is at least 'quite important'

VERY IMPORTANT   NOT AT ALL IMPORTANT

The specific boundaries of different family systems are often not crystal clear, and subregional differences abound. For example, in some respects Ireland does not fit well into northern European family patterns, northern and southern France often appear to walk divergent paths, and the southern fringes of Spain, Italy, or Portugal often show characteristics distinct from the northern parts of those same countries.

Reher, 1998, p 203

When Europeans were asked in the most recent European Values Survey, how important family is in their lives, 86% answered that they consider it to be 'very important'. The highest percentages of all are in countries at the geographical extremities of Europe: in Turkey and Iceland (96%), followed by FYR Macedonia, Cyprus, Malta, Montenegro, Italy, Hungary, Luxembourg and Slovakia. In all these countries more than 90% of people agreed that family is very important in their lives.

The smallest percentage is observed in Sweden (55%). Sweden is also the country in the world where the highest numbers of people are known to live alone: 'Single adults almost occupy a majority (47 per cent) of all Swedish dwellings, but they are still far from being a majority of all Swedish people' (Dorling, 2013, p 229).

MAP 2.008 – HOW IMPORTANT IN LIFE ARE FRIENDS AND ACQUAINTANCES?

Distribution of Europeans stating that friends and acquaintances are 'very important' in their life

Source: European Values Survey, 2008

HOW IMPORTANT IN LIFE ARE FRIENDS AND ACQUAINTANCES?

50% 43% 6% 1%

VERY IMPORTANT   NOT AT ALL IMPORTANT

What is a friend? A single soul dwelling in two bodies.

Aristotle, quoted by Diogenes Laertius in Lives of the Philosophers (Hicks, 1972)

Half of all Europeans consider that friends and acquaintances are very important in their lives. This map shows how these estimated numbers are distributed across Europe.

FYR Macedonia has the highest percentage (76%) of people valuing friends and acquaintances as very important, followed closely by Turkey (74%) and Ireland (73%). The smallest percentages are observed in Albania (17%) and Lithuania (18%), and also Latvia (28%), Kosovo (29%) and Romania (29%).

In many cases, in countries where people say family is important, they say that friends are important too. Perhaps people value sociability more in some parts of Europe than in other parts where they are better able to occupy themselves alone? There are some interesting exceptions, for example countries where family is considered important but friends much less so.

MAP 2.009 – WHICH GEOGRAPHIC GROUP DO YOU FEEL YOU BELONG TO MOST?
Distribution of people who feel that they belong most to Europe
Source: European Values Survey, 2008

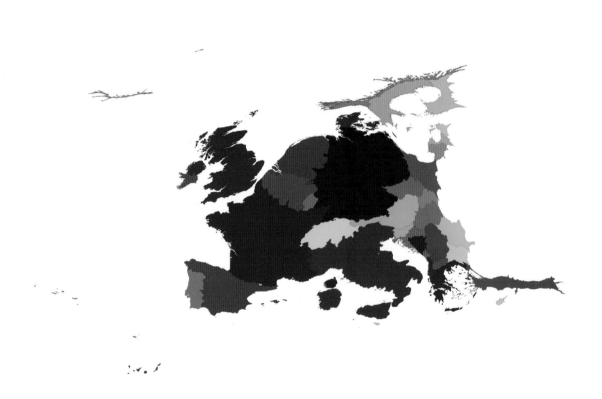

Europe is a thought that needs to become a feeling.

Bono, addressing delegates at the European People's Party Congress in Dublin, 7 March 2014 (RTE, 2014)

The European Values Survey includes the question: 'Which geographic group do you feel you belong to most?', with the following possible answers: 'locality or town', 'region/country', 'country as a whole', 'Europe', 'world as a whole'. This map shows the survey-based estimates of total numbers answering 'Europe', which comprise just 3% of the total population of Europe. However, it is a very interesting small group, comprising those who could be considered to be most European in terms of their identity. The largest percentage of people declaring that they are European above other identities is observed in Luxembourg (20%), followed by Switzerland (7%), Belgium (6%), Finland (6%) and Austria (6%). The smallest percentages are in Turkey (0.5%), Poland (1.0%), Romania (1.3%), Albania (1.6%) and Ireland (1.9%). In some of the countries with the highest percentages, many people are immigrants from other parts of Europe and so may identify more with Europe as a whole than with the country where they are currently living. In many of the countries with the lowest percentages of people who consider themselves to be European, there are very few people now living (or who have ever lived) in that country who were not born or brought up there.

WHICH GEOGRAPHIC GROUP DO YOU FEEL YOU BELONG TO MOST?
Note that twice as many people (6%) see themselves belonging to the world as a whole as those who see themselves as being primarily European in terms of geographic identity

44%	17%	30%	3%	6%
LOCALITY OR TOWN	REGION COUNTY	COUNTRY AS A WHOLE	EUROPE	WORLD AS A WHOLE

MAP 2.010 – ARE YOU AFRAID OF LOSING YOUR NATIONAL IDENTITY/CULTURE?
Distribution of people who feel 'very much afraid' of losing their national identity/culture
Source: European Values Survey, 2008

People learn how to appreciate peace. Croatian people know that the European Union is the guarantee for that peace.

Drazen Gregurevic, Deputy Mayor of Zadar, Croatia, the 28th member of the EU as of 1 July 2013 (BBC News, 2013a)

The European Values Survey asks a number of questions about 'fears' of people in the European Union. One of these questions, with a 10-point answer scale (1 = very much afraid to 10 = not afraid at all), explores such fears in relation to loss of national identity and culture. This map shows the spatial distribution of the 19% of Europeans who answered that they were 'very much afraid'.

In relative terms, the largest percentage of the population afraid of losing their national identity is found in Turkey (38%), followed by the United Kingdom (35%), Kosovo (28.5%), Ireland (26%) and FYR Macedonia (22%). The smallest percentages are in Slovakia (5.8%), the Netherlands (6.0%), Norway (6.6%), Lithuania (7.4%) and Estonia (10.0%).

Interestingly, countries located further towards the periphery of Europe appear to think they have the most to fear. Those located more centrally within the continent seem to be less fearful that their national identity is under threat. Perhaps people in these latter countries have already adjusted to their location?

ARE YOU AFRAID OF LOSING YOUR NATIONAL IDENTITY/CULTURE?
This question elicited one of the widest range of answers in the survey

| 19% | 10% | 11% | 9% | 13% | 6% | 6% | 8% | 5% | 13% |

VERY MUCH AFRAID (1)   NOT AFRAID AT ALL (10)

MAP 2.011 – TAKING ALL THINGS TOGETHER, HOW HAPPY ARE YOU?
Distribution of Europeans who consider themselves 'very happy'
Source: European Values Survey, 2008

TAKING ALL THINGS TOGETHER, HOW HAPPY ARE YOU?
Europe appears to be quite a happy place: 84% are at least 'quite happy'. (International comparisons often label South America as the happiest continent)

26%   58%   13%   3%

VERY HAPPY   NOT AT ALL HAPPY

When we look at the world's great thinkers ... [we] find them different in time, different in place, different in language and culture. Yet inevitable though these differences are, they cannot obscure the deep similarities in how we search for happiness.
Schoch, 2007, p 13

When asked the question 'Taking all things together, how happy are you?' and given four answers to choose from ('very happy', 'quite happy', 'not very happy', 'not at all happy'), 26% of respondents in the European Values Survey answered 'very happy'. This map shows the geographical distribution of these apparently 'very happy' Europeans.

The largest number of 'very happy' people as a percentage of a country's total population live in the Netherlands (56%), followed by Iceland (51%), Denmark (47%), Ireland (43.5%) and Belgium (43.5%). The smallest percentages are in Lithuania (6.3%), Latvia (9.9%), Estonia (11%), Albania (12%) and Germany (13%). However, caution is needed when looking at the geography of happiness (Ballas and Dorling, 2013), as there may be possible cultural (Tiberius, 2004; Lu and Gilmour, 2004; Uchida et al, 2004) as well as perhaps linguistic (Veenhoven, 1993) issues affecting the responses to happiness questions in surveys.

MAP 2.012 – HOW SATISFIED ARE YOU WITH YOUR LIFE?
Distribution of Europeans stating they are 'dissatisfied' with their life
Source: European Values Survey, 2008

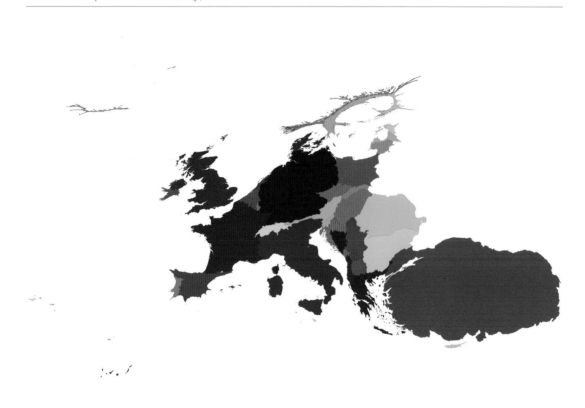

> Quality of life depends on people's objective conditions and capabilities. Steps should be taken to improve measures of people's health, education, personal activities and environmental conditions. In particular, substantial effort should be devoted to developing and implementing robust, reliable measures of social connections, political voice, and insecurity that can be shown to predict life satisfaction.
>
> *Stiglitz et al, 2009*

This map shows the geographical distribution of Europeans who said on a scale from 1 to 10 (1 = dissatisfied, 10 = satisfied) that they were 'dissatisfied' when rating their general life satisfaction. Most of the 3% who gave an answer of 1 (dissatisfied) are living in Turkey (8.9%), followed by Bulgaria (8.9%), FYR Macedonia (4.6%), Romania (4.5%) and Serbia (3.4%), all among the poorest countries in Europe. The smallest percentages of dissatisfaction are found in the Netherlands (0.1%), Portugal (0.5%), Finland (0.8%), Spain (0.8%) and Iceland (0.9%). At least three of these least unhappy countries were experiencing extreme austerity (Portugal and Spain) or a massive devaluation of their currency (Iceland). Therefore perhaps this result indicates how people in those countries have the imagination to see that their situation, although bad, could get even worse – so they reserve the 1 box for that eventuality. People in other countries may be more prepared to tick that 1 box.

HOW SATISFIED ARE YOU WITH YOUR LIFE?
Just half of all Europeans are satisfied with their life to a high degree (scoring 8 out of 10 or more)

DISSATISFIED (1)   VERY SATISFIED (10)

MAP 2.013 – IS COMPETITION GOOD FOR PEOPLE?
Distribution of Europeans who consider competition is 'good' for people
Source: European Values Survey, 2008

Europe needs to stand united and to act swiftly and with determination to overcome this difficult period. We must use all the tools we have crafted in six decades of integration to defend our common interests. And I am firmly convinced that competition policy has pride of place among these tools. Effective competition control in the Single Market is crucial to help our economy become more resilient and more competitive.

Joaquín Almunia, Vice President of the European Commission, 21 March 2013 at the IBA 9th Competition Mid-Year Conference, Sydney (Almunia, 2013)

When asked to rate on a scale from 1 to 10 whether competition is good or harmful for people (1 = good, 10 = harmful), 16% of respondents in the European Values Survey chose the lowest value of 1.

The largest number of strong supporters of competition as a percentage of the total population is found in Romania (40.3%), followed by Bulgaria (37%), Malta (36%), Serbia (34%) and FYR Macedonia (29.5%). In contrast, the smallest percentages are in the Netherlands (4.4%), Finland (7.6%), Belgium (7.7%), Spain (7.9%) and France (8.9%). Competition tends to be seen more favourably in former socialist countries and is less popular in those countries that were part of the original free trade area, which has experienced more open competition for the longest period of time.

IS COMPETITION GOOD FOR PEOPLE?
Europe is split on the issue of whether competition is good or harmful

16% 11% 16% 13% 19% 8% 6% 5% 2% 4%

COMPETITION GOOD (1)   COMPETITION HARMFUL (10)

MAP 2.014 – ROMA PEOPLE
Geographical distribution of Roma people
Source: Wikipedia

It can be argued that a key feature of European identity is demographic accountability and respect for social diversity. This European identity encompasses and requires the presence of, tolerance of, and support for numerous minorities across all European countries. This map shows the geographical distribution of the Roma people, who represent the largest and perhaps the most disadvantaged minority in the Union. As Ringold et al (2005, p xiii) put it:

The Roma are Europe's largest and [most] vulnerable minority. Unlike other groups, they have no historical homeland and live in nearly all the countries in Europe and Central Asia. The origins of Roma in Europe are widely debated. Historical records indicate that they migrated in waves from northern India into Europe between the ninth and fourteenth centuries. Roma are extremely diverse, with multiple subgroups based on [variations in] language, history, religion, and occupations. While Roma in some countries are nomadic, most in Central and Eastern Europe have settled over time, some under Ottoman rule and others more recently under socialism.

Although the Roma population is arguably the largest minority, it is very difficult to obtain reliable statistics on the exact size of the population by country. This map is based on estimates collated by Wikipedia using data from many different sources. Although the reliability of this data is questionable, it can be argued that the picture drawn is consistent with most relevant studies to date. The highest absolute numbers of Roma people are found in Turkey, Romania, Spain, Serbia and France. However, the highest estimated share as a percentage of total population is found in eastern Europe, especially in Bosnia and Herzegovina (11.7%), followed by Serbia (8.2%), Bulgaria (5.0%), FYR Macedonia (4.8%) and Romania (4.7%).

The Union is founded on the values of respect for human dignity, freedom, democracy, equality, the rule of law and respect for human rights, including the rights of persons belonging to minorities. These values are common to the Member States in a society in which pluralism, non-discrimination, tolerance, justice, solidarity and equality between women and men prevail.

Article 2, Treaty of the European Union, 2008

MAP 2.015 – TOTAL VOTES RECEIVED, EUROVISION SONG CONTEST 2013
Source: Eurovision

Voting patterns in the Eurovision Song Contest is a popular theme for the analysis of European identity and culture. It has long been argued that there are clear patterns based on geographical regions as well as cultural and linguistic bonds. There has typically been labelling of groups of countries that give their votes to each other as 'blocs', such as the 'Scandinavian bloc', the 'Mediterranean', 'Western', 'Eastern' and 'Balkan' blocs etc. Political considerations may also affect these voting patterns: in the 2013 Eurovision Song Contest, voting patterns were possibly influenced by the ongoing political and economic crisis in Europe.

Each country gives 12 points to its favourite song, 10 points to the second favourite, 8 to the third, and 7 to 1 points in descending order to the remaining seven ranked songs. These points are allocated via telephone voting and all countries taking part in the final and the two semi-finals are eligible to vote. It should be noted that not all countries took part in the final round of the contest or in the voting.

The map representing the total number of votes received is dominated by the winner Denmark, which received a total of 281 points – 90 more than the second-placed country, Norway. The remaining maps show the number of points given to selected individual countries. They highlight the patterns for the votes that were given to Denmark, Germany (18 points), Greece (152 points) and the United Kingdom (23 points).

MAP 2.016 – TOTAL VOTES GIVEN TO DENMARK, EUROVISION SONG CONTEST 2013
Source: Eurovision

MAP 2.017 – TOTAL VOTES GIVEN TO GERMANY, EUROVISION SONG CONTEST 2013
Source: Eurovision

MAP 2.018 – TOTAL VOTES GIVEN TO GREECE, EUROVISION SONG CONTEST 2013
Source: Eurovision

MAP 2.019 – TOTAL VOTES GIVEN TO THE UK, EUROVISION SONG CONTEST 2013
Source: Eurovision

The voting behaviour for Germany and the United Kingdom shows a polarised pattern which – putting aspects of the quality of the performance aside – also reflects some persisting affinities as well as contemporary hostilities or irrelevances in a European context. Germany mainly relies on its neighbours and places where there may be a larger number of German expats or tourists at the time of the contest; this point could also apply to the UK result. Currently Germany is widely seen as a political scapegoat, while the relevance of the UK within Europe is seen as less important, which could help to explain why these countries received so few votes.

The map of votes for Greece – which has also been at the centre of political and economic attention within Europe and internationally in the past three years – represents a total of 152 points. Greece also seems to rely on its neighbours or places with which it has strong actual or perceived cultural and linguistic bonds. It also depends on other places which have long had relatively large Greek or Greek-speaking populations or where there may be relatively large numbers of Greeks now living; over the last three years many Greeks have moved to other countries as a result of Greece's severe economic crisis. Greece received 12 points from Cyprus and San Marino, 10 from Albania, 8 points from Montenegro, Switzerland and the United Kingdom, 7 points from Austria, Bulgaria, Italy and Romania and 6 points from Denmark and Germany.

3

DEMOGRAPHICS

DISTRIBUTION OF THE EUROPEAN POPULATION BY AGE AND SEX

EUROPEAN UNION

BY AGE AND SEX (2012), SEX RATIO (M/F): 0.955
MALES: 245,969,224 | FEMALES: 257,694,286
TOTAL POPULATION: 503,663,510

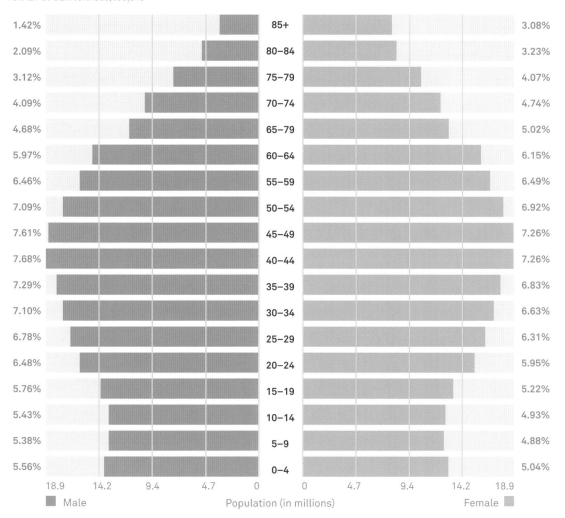

Male %	Age	Female %
1.42%	85+	3.08%
2.09%	80–84	3.23%
3.12%	75–79	4.07%
4.09%	70–74	4.74%
4.68%	65–79	5.02%
5.97%	60–64	6.15%
6.46%	55–59	6.49%
7.09%	50–54	6.92%
7.61%	45–49	7.26%
7.68%	40–44	7.26%
7.29%	35–39	6.83%
7.10%	30–34	6.63%
6.78%	25–29	6.31%
6.48%	20–24	5.95%
5.76%	15–19	5.22%
5.43%	10–14	4.93%
5.38%	5–9	4.88%
5.56%	0–4	5.04%

18.9   14.2   9.4   4.7   0   0   4.7   9.4   14.2   18.9

■ Male   Population (in millions)   Female ■

"In all EU member states, the proportion of older people has increased in recent decades, because of a combination of low fertility and longer life expectancy. However, there are some variations between countries and time periods in the contributions of these factors."

Rechel et al, 2013, p 1312

This diagram, known as a population pyramid, shows the distribution of the 503 million men and women in the European Union by different age groups. The shape of this diagram is often described as a 'constrictive pyramid', which is typical of developed societies with low fertility and mortality rates and with relatively older populations. The population aged 15–65 years is 335 million, whereas nearly one fifth of the total population is over 65 years old. There are only 78 million children aged 0–15. The male:female ratio in the EU is 0.95.

It is interesting to compare the population pyramid for the whole of the EU with similar diagrams for separate countries in Europe. Most member state pyramids look similar to that of the EU. However, the pyramids for Albania and to a lesser extent Turkey have a more 'pyramid-like' shape, suggesting either relatively higher outmigration rates in the recent past and/or a lower life expectancy. Fertility in these countries is not much higher than the EU average. On the other hand, Germany, the Netherlands and Andorra seem to have higher than average elderly populations.

Also of interest is the fact that Andorra has the highest male:female ratio, while Latvia, Lithuania and Estonia have the lowest ratios.

ALBANIA

BY AGE AND SEX (2012), SEX RATIO (M/F): 0.993
MALES: 1,568,611 | FEMALES: 1,580,358
TOTAL POPULATION: 3,148,969

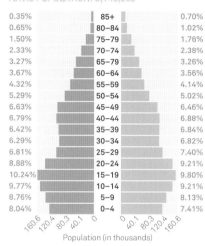

0.35%	85+	0.70%
0.65%	80–84	1.02%
1.50%	75–79	1.76%
2.33%	70–74	2.38%
3.27%	65–79	3.26%
3.67%	60–64	3.56%
4.32%	55–59	4.14%
5.29%	50–54	5.02%
6.63%	45–49	6.46%
6.79%	40–44	6.88%
6.42%	35–39	6.84%
6.29%	30–34	6.82%
6.81%	25–29	7.40%
8.88%	20–24	9.21%
10.24%	15–19	9.80%
9.77%	10–14	9.21%
8.76%	5–9	8.13%
8.04%	0–4	7.41%

160.6 120.4 80.3 40.1 0 40.1 80.3 120.4 160.6
Population (in thousands)

ANDORRA

BY AGE AND SEX (2012), SEX RATIO (M/F): 1.083
MALES: 44,197 | FEMALES: 40,818
TOTAL POPULATION: 85,015

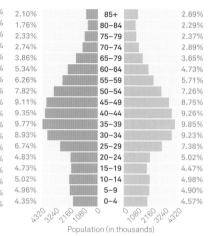

2.10%	85+	2.69%
1.76%	80–84	2.29%
2.33%	75–79	2.37%
2.74%	70–74	2.89%
3.86%	65–79	3.65%
5.34%	60–64	4.73%
6.26%	55–59	5.71%
7.82%	50–54	7.26%
9.11%	45–49	8.75%
9.35%	40–44	9.26%
9.77%	35–39	9.85%
8.93%	30–34	9.23%
6.74%	25–29	7.38%
4.83%	20–24	5.02%
4.73%	15–19	4.47%
5.02%	10–14	4.98%
4.96%	5–9	4.90%
4.35%	0–4	4.57%

4320 3240 2160 1080 0 1080 2160 3240 4320
Population (in thousands)

AUSTRIA

BY AGE AND SEX (2012), SEX RATIO (M/F): 0.952
MALES: 4,118,035 | FEMALES: 4,324,983
TOTAL POPULATION: 8,443,018

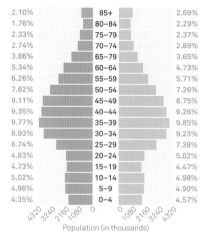

2.10%	85+	2.69%
1.76%	80–84	2.29%
2.33%	75–79	2.37%
2.74%	70–74	2.89%
3.86%	65–79	3.65%
5.34%	60–64	4.73%
6.26%	55–59	5.71%
7.82%	50–54	7.26%
9.11%	45–49	8.75%
9.35%	40–44	9.26%
9.77%	35–39	9.85%
8.93%	30–34	9.23%
6.74%	25–29	7.38%
4.83%	20–24	5.02%
4.73%	15–19	4.47%
5.02%	10–14	4.98%
4.96%	5–9	4.90%
4.35%	0–4	4.57%

4320 3240 2160 1080 0 1080 2160 3240 4320
Population (in thousands)

BELGIUM

BY AGE AND SEX (2012), SEX RATIO (M/F): 0.966
MALES: 5,451,780 | FEMALES: 6,643,070
TOTAL POPULATION: 11,094,850

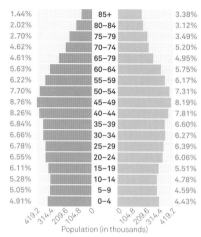

1.44%	85+	3.38%
2.02%	80–84	3.12%
2.70%	75–79	3.49%
4.62%	70–74	5.20%
4.61%	65–79	4.95%
5.63%	60–64	5.75%
6.22%	55–59	6.17%
7.70%	50–54	7.31%
8.76%	45–49	8.19%
8.26%	40–44	7.81%
6.84%	35–39	6.60%
6.66%	30–34	6.27%
6.78%	25–29	6.39%
6.55%	20–24	6.06%
6.11%	15–19	5.51%
5.28%	10–14	4.78%
5.05%	5–9	4.59%
4.91%	0–4	4.43%

419.2 314.4 209.6 104.8 0 104.8 209.6 314.4 419.2
Population (in thousands)

BULGARIA

BY AGE AND SEX (2012), SEX RATIO (M/F): 0.948
MALES: 3,566,767 | FEMALES: 3,760,457
TOTAL POPULATION: 7,327,224

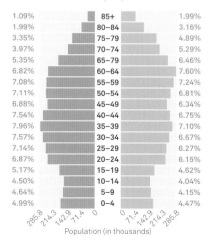

1.09%	85+	1.99%
1.99%	80–84	3.16%
3.35%	75–79	4.89%
3.97%	70–74	5.29%
5.35%	65–79	6.46%
6.82%	60–64	7.60%
7.08%	55–59	7.24%
7.11%	50–54	6.81%
6.88%	45–49	6.34%
7.54%	40–44	6.75%
7.96%	35–39	7.10%
7.57%	30–34	6.67%
7.14%	25–29	6.27%
6.87%	20–24	6.87%
5.17%	15–19	4.62%
4.50%	10–14	4.04%
4.64%	5–9	4.15%
4.99%	0–4	4.47%

285.8 214.3 142.9 71.4 0 71.4 142.9 214.3 285.8
Population (in thousands)

CROATIA

BY AGE AND SEX (2012), SEX RATIO (M/F): 0.934
MALES: 2,114,500 | FEMALES: 2,264,472
TOTAL POPULATION: 4,378,972

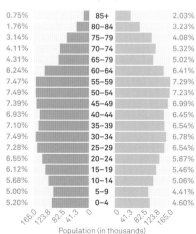

0.75%	85+	2.03%
1.76%	80–84	3.23%
3.14%	75–79	4.08%
4.11%	70–74	5.32%
4.31%	65–79	5.02%
6.24%	60–64	6.41%
7.47%	55–59	7.29%
7.49%	50–54	7.23%
7.39%	45–49	6.99%
6.93%	40–44	6.45%
7.10%	35–39	6.54%
7.49%	30–34	6.78%
7.28%	25–29	6.54%
6.55%	20–24	5.87%
6.12%	15–19	5.46%
5.68%	10–14	5.06%
5.00%	5–9	4.41%
5.20%	0–4	4.60%

165.0 123.8 82.5 41.3 0 41.3 82.5 123.8 165.0
Population (in thousands)

CYPRUS

BY AGE AND SEX (2012), SEX RATIO (M/F): 0.946
MALES: 418,993 | FEMALES: 443,018
TOTAL POPULATION: 862,011

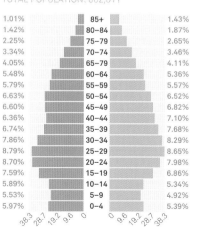

1.01%	85+	1.43%
1.42%	80–84	1.87%
2.25%	75–79	2.65%
3.34%	70–74	3.46%
4.05%	65–79	4.11%
5.48%	60–64	5.36%
5.79%	55–59	5.57%
6.63%	50–54	6.52%
6.60%	45–49	6.82%
6.36%	40–44	7.10%
6.74%	35–39	7.68%
7.86%	30–34	8.29%
8.79%	25–29	8.65%
8.70%	20–24	7.98%
7.59%	15–19	6.86%
5.89%	10–14	5.34%
5.53%	5–9	4.92%
5.97%	0–4	5.39%

38.3 28.7 19.2 9.6 0 9.6 19.2 28.7 38.3
Population (in thousands)

CZECH REPUBLIC

BY AGE AND SEX (2012), SEX RATIO (M/F): 0.965
MALES: 5,158,210 | FEMALES: 5,347,235
TOTAL POPULATION: 10,505,445

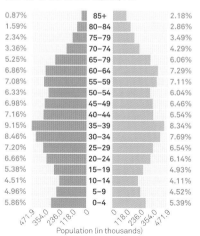

0.87%	85+	2.18%
1.59%	80–84	2.86%
2.34%	75–79	3.49%
3.36%	70–74	4.29%
5.25%	65–79	6.06%
6.86%	60–64	7.29%
7.08%	55–59	7.11%
6.33%	50–54	6.04%
6.98%	45–49	6.46%
7.16%	40–44	6.54%
9.15%	35–39	8.34%
8.46%	30–34	7.69%
7.20%	25–29	6.54%
6.66%	20–24	6.14%
5.38%	15–19	4.93%
4.51%	10–14	4.11%
4.96%	5–9	4.52%
5.86%	0–4	5.39%

471.9 354.0 236.0 118.0 0 118.0 236.0 354.0 471.9
Population (in thousands)

DENMARK

BY AGE AND SEX (2012), SEX RATIO (M/F): 0.983
MALES: 2,766,7676 | FEMALES: 2,813,740
TOTAL POPULATION: 5,580,516

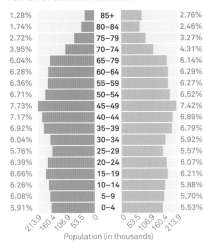

	Age	
1.28%	85+	2.76%
1.74%	80–84	2.46%
2.72%	75–79	3.27%
3.95%	70–74	4.31%
6.04%	65–79	6.14%
6.28%	60–64	6.29%
6.36%	55–59	6.27%
6.71%	50–54	6.52%
7.73%	45–49	7.42%
7.17%	40–44	6.89%
6.92%	35–39	6.79%
6.04%	30–34	5.92%
5.76%	25–29	5.57%
6.39%	20–24	6.07%
6.66%	15–19	6.21%
6.26%	10–14	5.88%
6.08%	5–9	5.70%
5.91%	0–4	5.53%

Population (in thousands)

ESTONIA

BY AGE AND SEX (2012), SEX RATIO (M/F): 0.856
MALES: 617,822 | FEMALES: 721,749
TOTAL POPULATION: 1,339,571

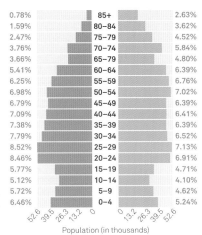

	Age	
0.78%	85+	2.63%
1.59%	80–84	3.62%
2.47%	75–79	4.52%
3.76%	70–74	5.84%
3.66%	65–79	4.80%
5.41%	60–64	6.39%
6.25%	55–59	6.76%
6.98%	50–54	7.02%
6.79%	45–49	6.39%
7.09%	40–44	6.41%
7.38%	35–39	6.39%
7.79%	30–34	6.52%
8.52%	25–29	7.13%
8.46%	20–24	6.91%
5.77%	15–19	4.71%
5.12%	10–14	4.10%
5.72%	5–9	4.62%
6.46%	0–4	5.24%

Population (in thousands)

FINLAND

BY AGE AND SEX (2012), SEX RATIO (M/F): 0.965
MALES: 2,652,534 | FEMALES: 2,748,733
TOTAL POPULATION: 5,401,267

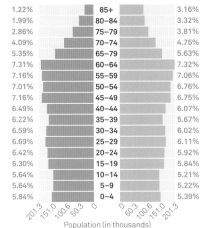

	Age	
1.22%	85+	3.16%
1.99%	80–84	3.32%
2.86%	75–79	3.81%
4.09%	70–74	4.75%
5.35%	65–79	5.63%
7.31%	60–64	7.32%
7.16%	55–59	7.06%
7.01%	50–54	6.76%
7.16%	45–49	6.75%
6.49%	40–44	6.07%
6.22%	35–39	5.67%
6.59%	30–34	6.02%
6.69%	25–29	6.11%
6.42%	20–24	5.92%
6.30%	15–19	5.84%
5.64%	10–14	5.21%
5.64%	5–9	5.22%
5.84%	0–4	5.39%

Population (in thousands)

FRANCE

BY AGE AND SEX (2012), SEX RATIO (M/F): 0.939
MALES: 31,635,128 | FEMALES: 33,692,596
TOTAL POPULATION: 65,327,724

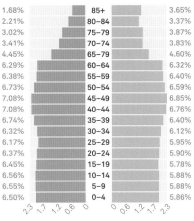

	Age	
1.68%	85+	3.65%
2.21%	80–84	3.37%
3.02%	75–79	3.87%
3.41%	70–74	3.83%
4.45%	65–79	4.60%
6.29%	60–64	6.32%
6.38%	55–59	6.40%
6.73%	50–54	6.59%
7.08%	45–49	6.85%
7.08%	40–44	6.76%
6.74%	35–39	6.40%
6.32%	30–34	6.12%
6.17%	25–29	5.95%
6.37%	20–24	5.90%
6.45%	15–19	5.78%
6.56%	10–14	5.88%
6.55%	5–9	5.88%
6.50%	0–4	5.86%

Population (in millions)

FYR OF MACEDONIA

BY AGE AND SEX (2012), SEX RATIO (M/F): 1.004
MALES: 1,031,831 | FEMALES: 1,027,530
TOTAL POPULATION: 2,059,361

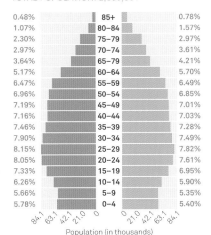

	Age	
0.48%	85+	0.78%
1.07%	80–84	1.57%
2.30%	75–79	2.97%
2.97%	70–74	3.61%
3.64%	65–79	4.21%
5.17%	60–64	5.70%
6.47%	55–59	6.49%
6.96%	50–54	6.85%
7.19%	45–49	7.01%
7.16%	40–44	7.03%
7.46%	35–39	7.28%
7.90%	30–34	7.49%
8.15%	25–29	7.82%
8.05%	20–24	7.61%
7.33%	15–19	6.95%
6.26%	10–14	5.90%
5.66%	5–9	5.35%
5.78%	0–4	5.40%

Population (in thousands)

GERMANY

BY AGE AND SEX (2012), SEX RATIO (M/F): 0.966
MALES: 40,206,663 | FEMALES: 41,637,080
TOTAL POPULATION: 81,843,743

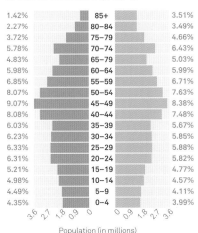

	Age	
1.42%	85+	3.51%
2.27%	80–84	3.49%
3.72%	75–79	4.66%
5.78%	70–74	6.43%
4.83%	65–79	5.03%
5.98%	60–64	5.99%
6.85%	55–59	6.71%
8.07%	50–54	7.63%
9.07%	45–49	8.38%
8.08%	40–44	7.48%
6.03%	35–39	5.67%
6.23%	30–34	5.85%
6.33%	25–29	5.88%
6.31%	20–24	5.82%
5.21%	15–19	4.77%
4.98%	10–14	4.57%
4.49%	5–9	4.11%
4.35%	0–4	3.99%

Population (in millions)

GREECE

BY AGE AND SEX (2012), SEX RATIO (M/F): 0.981
MALES: 5,590,131 | FEMALES: 5,699,936
TOTAL POPULATION: 11,290,067

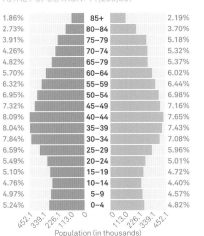

	Age	
1.86%	85+	2.19%
2.73%	80–84	3.70%
3.91%	75–79	5.18%
4.26%	70–74	5.32%
4.82%	65–79	5.37%
5.70%	60–64	6.02%
6.32%	55–59	6.44%
6.95%	50–54	6.98%
7.32%	45–49	7.16%
8.09%	40–44	7.65%
8.04%	35–39	7.43%
7.84%	30–34	7.08%
6.59%	25–29	5.96%
5.49%	20–24	5.01%
5.10%	15–19	4.72%
4.76%	10–14	4.40%
4.97%	5–9	4.57%
5.24%	0–4	4.82%

Population (in thousands)

HUNGARY

BY AGE AND SEX (2012), SEX RATIO (M/F): 0.905
MALES: 4,731,724 | FEMALES: 5,226,007
TOTAL POPULATION: 9,957,731

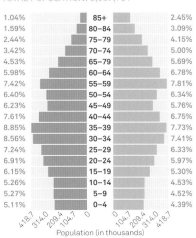

	Age	
1.04%	85+	2.45%
1.59%	80–84	3.09%
2.44%	75–79	4.15%
3.42%	70–74	5.00%
4.53%	65–79	5.69%
5.98%	60–64	6.78%
7.42%	55–59	7.81%
6.40%	50–54	6.34%
6.23%	45–49	5.76%
7.61%	40–44	6.75%
8.85%	35–39	7.73%
8.56%	30–34	7.41%
7.24%	25–29	6.33%
6.91%	20–24	5.97%
6.15%	15–19	5.30%
5.26%	10–14	4.53%
5.27%	5–9	4.52%
5.11%	0–4	4.39%

Population (in thousands)

ICELAND

BY AGE AND SEX (2012), SEX RATIO (M/F): 1.007
MALES: 160,364 | FEMALES: 15 9,211
TOTAL POPULATION: 319,575

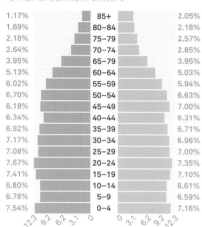

1.17%	85+	2.05%
1.69%	80–84	2.18%
2.18%	75–79	2.57%
2.64%	70–74	2.85%
3.95%	65–79	3.95%
5.13%	60–64	5.03%
6.02%	55–59	5.94%
6.70%	50–54	6.63%
6.18%	45–49	7.00%
6.34%	40–44	6.31%
6.92%	35–39	6.71%
7.17%	30–34	6.96%
7.08%	25–29	7.00%
7.67%	20–24	7.35%
7.41%	15–19	7.10%
6.80%	10–14	6.61%
6.78%	5–9	6.59%
7.54%	0–4	7.16%

Population (in thousands)

IRELAND

BY AGE AND SEX (2012), SEX RATIO (M/F): 0.981
MALES: 2,269,831 | FEMALES: 2,312,938
TOTAL POPULATION: 4,582,769

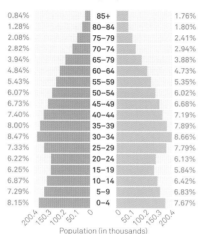

0.84%	85+	1.76%
1.28%	80–84	1.80%
2.08%	75–79	2.41%
2.82%	70–74	2.94%
3.94%	65–79	3.88%
4.84%	60–64	4.73%
5.43%	55–59	5.35%
6.07%	50–54	6.02%
6.73%	45–49	6.68%
7.40%	40–44	7.19%
8.00%	35–39	7.89%
8.47%	30–34	8.66%
7.33%	25–29	7.79%
6.22%	20–24	6.13%
6.25%	15–19	5.84%
6.87%	10–14	6.42%
7.29%	5–9	6.83%
8.15%	0–4	7.67%

Population (in thousands)

ITALY

BY AGE AND SEX (2012), SEX RATIO (M/F): 0.943
MALES: 29,512,404 | FEMALES: 31,308,292
TOTAL POPULATION: 60,820,696

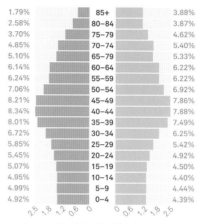

1.79%	85+	3.88%
2.58%	80–84	3.87%
3.70%	75–79	4.62%
4.85%	70–74	5.40%
5.10%	65–79	5.33%
6.14%	60–64	6.22%
6.24%	55–59	6.22%
7.06%	50–54	6.92%
8.21%	45–49	7.86%
8.34%	40–44	7.88%
8.01%	35–39	7.49%
6.72%	30–34	6.25%
5.85%	25–29	5.42%
5.45%	20–24	4.92%
5.07%	15–19	4.50%
4.95%	10–14	4.40%
4.99%	5–9	4.44%
4.92%	0–4	4.39%

Population (in millions)

LATVIA

BY AGE AND SEX (2012), SEX RATIO (M/F): 0.842
MALES: 933,114 | FEMALES: 1,108,649
TOTAL POPULATION: 2,041,763

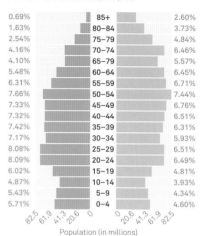

0.69%	85+	2.60%
1.63%	80–84	3.73%
2.54%	75–79	4.84%
4.16%	70–74	6.46%
4.10%	65–79	5.57%
5.48%	60–64	6.45%
6.31%	55–59	6.71%
7.66%	50–54	7.44%
7.33%	45–49	6.76%
7.32%	40–44	6.51%
7.42%	35–39	6.31%
7.17%	30–34	5.93%
8.08%	25–29	6.51%
8.09%	20–24	6.49%
6.02%	15–19	4.81%
4.87%	10–14	3.93%
5.43%	5–9	4.34%
5.71%	0–4	4.60%

Population (in millions)

LIECHTENSTEIN

BY AGE AND SEX (2012), SEX RATIO (M/F): 0.979
MALES: 18,042 | FEMALES: 18,433
TOTAL POPULATION: 36,475

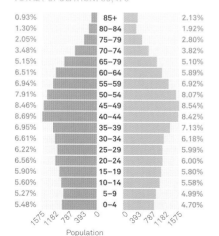

0.93%	85+	2.13%
1.30%	80–84	1.92%
2.05%	75–79	2.80%
3.48%	70–74	3.82%
5.15%	65–79	5.10%
6.51%	60–64	5.89%
6.94%	55–59	6.92%
7.91%	50–54	8.07%
8.46%	45–49	8.54%
8.69%	40–44	8.42%
6.95%	35–39	7.13%
6.61%	30–34	6.18%
6.22%	25–29	5.99%
6.56%	20–24	6.00%
5.90%	15–19	5.80%
5.60%	10–14	5.58%
5.27%	5–9	4.99%
5.48%	0–4	4.70%

Population

LITHUANIA

BY AGE AND SEX (2012), SEX RATIO (M/F): 0.854
MALES: 1,385,671 | FEMALES: 1,622,087
TOTAL POPULATION: 3,007,758

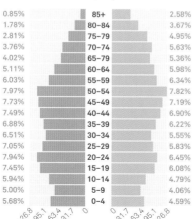

0.85%	85+	2.58%
1.78%	80–84	3.67%
2.81%	75–79	4.95%
3.76%	70–74	5.63%
4.02%	65–79	5.36%
5.11%	60–64	5.98%
6.03%	55–59	6.34%
7.97%	50–54	7.82%
7.73%	45–49	7.19%
7.49%	40–44	6.90%
6.88%	35–39	6.22%
6.51%	30–34	5.55%
7.05%	25–29	5.83%
7.94%	20–24	6.45%
7.45%	15–19	6.08%
5.94%	10–14	4.79%
5.00%	5–9	4.06%
5.68%	0–4	4.59%

Population (in thousands)

LUXEMBOURG

BY AGE AND SEX (2012), SEX RATIO (M/F): 0.995
MALES: 261,820 | FEMALES: 263,033
TOTAL POPULATION: 524,853

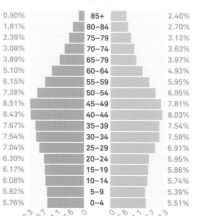

0.90%	85+	2.40%
1.81%	80–84	2.70%
2.39%	75–79	3.13%
3.08%	70–74	3.63%
3.89%	65–79	3.97%
5.10%	60–64	4.93%
6.15%	55–59	5.95%
7.38%	50–54	6.95%
8.51%	45–49	7.81%
8.43%	40–44	8.03%
7.67%	35–39	7.54%
7.54%	30–34	7.59%
7.04%	25–29	6.91%
6.30%	20–24	5.95%
6.17%	15–19	5.86%
6.08%	10–14	5.74%
5.82%	5–9	5.39%
5.76%	0–4	5.51%

Population (in thousands)

MALTA

BY AGE AND SEX (2012), SEX RATIO (M/F): 0.990
MALES: 207,677 | FEMALES: 209,843
TOTAL POPULATION: 417,520

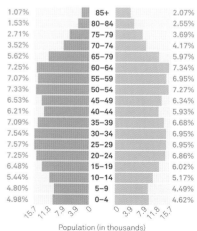

1.07%	85+	2.07%
1.53%	80–84	2.55%
2.71%	75–79	3.69%
3.52%	70–74	4.17%
5.62%	65–79	5.97%
7.25%	60–64	7.34%
7.07%	55–59	6.95%
7.33%	50–54	7.27%
6.53%	45–49	6.34%
6.21%	40–44	5.93%
7.09%	35–39	6.68%
7.54%	30–34	6.95%
7.57%	25–29	6.95%
7.25%	20–24	6.86%
6.48%	15–19	6.02%
5.44%	10–14	5.17%
4.80%	5–9	4.49%
4.98%	0–4	4.62%

Population (in thousands)

MONTENEGRO

BY AGE AND SEX (2012), SEX RATIO (M/F): 0.976
MALES: 306,804 | FEMALES: 314,436
TOTAL POPULATION: 621,240

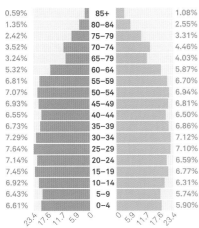

0.59%	85+	1.08%
1.35%	80–84	2.55%
2.42%	75–79	3.31%
3.52%	70–74	4.46%
3.24%	65–79	4.03%
5.32%	60–64	5.87%
6.81%	55–59	6.70%
7.07%	50–54	6.94%
6.93%	45–49	6.81%
6.55%	40–44	6.50%
6.73%	35–39	6.86%
7.29%	30–34	7.12%
7.64%	25–29	7.10%
7.14%	20–24	6.59%
7.45%	15–19	6.77%
6.92%	10–14	6.31%
6.43%	5–9	5.74%
6.61%	0–4	5.90%

23.4 17.6 11.7 5.9 0 0 5.9 11.7 17.6 23.4
Population (in thousands)

NETHERLANDS

BY AGE AND SEX (2012), SEX RATIO (M/F): 0.981
MALES: 8,282,871 | FEMALES: 8,447,477
TOTAL POPULATION: 16,730,348

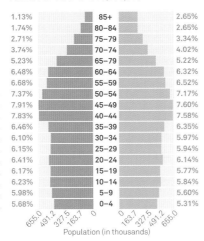

1.13%	85+	2.65%
1.74%	80–84	2.65%
2.71%	75–79	3.34%
3.74%	70–74	4.02%
5.23%	65–79	5.22%
6.48%	60–64	6.32%
6.68%	55–59	6.52%
7.37%	50–54	7.17%
7.91%	45–49	7.60%
7.83%	40–44	7.58%
6.46%	35–39	6.35%
6.10%	30–34	5.97%
6.15%	25–29	5.94%
6.41%	20–24	6.14%
6.17%	15–19	5.77%
6.23%	10–14	5.84%
5.98%	5–9	5.60%
5.68%	0–4	5.31%

655.0 491.2 327.5 163.7 0 163.7 327.5 491.2 655.0
Population (in thousands)

NORWAY

BY AGE AND SEX (2012), SEX RATIO (M/F): 1.005
MALES: 2,498,871 | FEMALES: 2,486,999
TOTAL POPULATION: 4,985,870

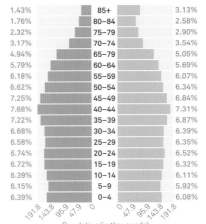

1.43%	85+	3.13%
1.76%	80–84	2.58%
2.32%	75–79	2.90%
3.17%	70–74	3.54%
4.94%	65–79	5.05%
5.79%	60–64	5.69%
6.18%	55–59	6.07%
6.62%	50–54	6.34%
7.25%	45–49	6.84%
7.68%	40–44	7.31%
7.22%	35–39	6.87%
6.68%	30–34	6.39%
6.58%	25–29	6.35%
6.74%	20–24	6.52%
6.72%	15–19	6.32%
6.39%	10–14	6.11%
6.15%	5–9	5.92%
6.39%	0–4	6.08%

191.8 143.8 95.9 47.9 0 47.9 95.9 143.8 191.8
Population (in thousands)

POLAND

BY AGE AND SEX (2012), SEX RATIO (M/F): 0.938
MALES: 18,654,577 | FEMALES: 19,883,870
TOTAL POPULATION: 38,538,447

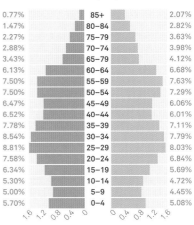

0.77%	85+	2.07%
1.47%	80–84	2.82%
2.27%	75–79	3.63%
2.88%	70–74	3.98%
3.43%	65–79	4.12%
6.13%	60–64	6.68%
7.50%	55–59	7.63%
7.50%	50–54	7.29%
6.47%	45–49	6.06%
6.52%	40–44	6.01%
7.78%	35–39	7.11%
8.54%	30–34	7.79%
8.81%	25–29	8.03%
7.58%	20–24	6.84%
6.34%	15–19	5.69%
5.30%	10–14	4.72%
5.00%	5–9	4.45%
5.70%	0–4	5.08%

1.6 1.2 0.8 0.4 0 0 0.4 0.8 1.2 1.6
Population (in thousands)

PORTUGAL

BY AGE AND SEX (2012), SEX RATIO (M/F): 0.913
MALES: 5,031,231 | FEMALES: 5,510,609
TOTAL POPULATION: 10,541,840

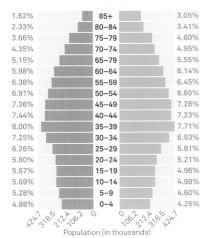

1.62%	85+	3.05%
2.33%	80–84	3.41%
3.66%	75–79	4.60%
4.35%	70–74	4.95%
5.15%	65–79	5.55%
5.98%	60–64	6.14%
6.38%	55–59	6.45%
6.91%	50–54	6.89%
7.36%	45–49	7.28%
7.44%	40–44	7.23%
8.00%	35–39	7.71%
7.25%	30–34	6.93%
6.26%	25–29	5.81%
5.80%	20–24	5.21%
5.67%	15–19	4.96%
5.69%	10–14	4.98%
5.28%	5–9	4.60%
4.88%	0–4	4.26%

424.7 318.5 212.4 106.2 0 106.2 212.4 318.5 424.7
Population (in thousands)

ROMANIA

BY AGE AND SEX (2012), SEX RATIO (M/F): 0.948
MALES: 10,394,402 | FEMALES: 10,961,447
TOTAL POPULATION: 21,355,849

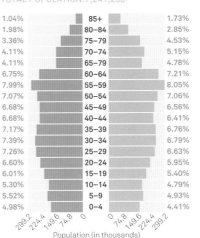

0.85%	85+	1.54%
1.63%	80–84	2.62%
2.73%	75–79	4.04%
3.50%	70–74	4.77%
3.71%	65–79	4.50%
5.49%	60–64	6.13%
6.66%	55–59	7.06%
6.45%	50–54	6.47%
5.53%	45–49	5.29%
9.19%	40–44	8.57%
8.31%	35–39	7.52%
8.65%	30–34	7.80%
8.01%	25–29	7.22%
7.77%	20–24	7.08%
5.67%	15–19	5.13%
5.41%	10–14	4.87%
5.24%	5–9	4.70%
5.22%	0–4	4.68%

955.0 716.3 477.5 238.8 0 238.8 477.5 716.3 955.0
Population (in thousands)

SERBIA

BY AGE AND SEX (2012), SEX RATIO (M/F): 0.947
MALES: 3,522,675 | FEMALES: 3,718,620
TOTAL POPULATION:7,241,295

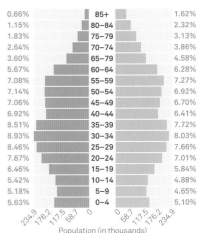

1.04%	85+	1.73%
1.98%	80–84	2.85%
3.36%	75–79	4.53%
4.11%	70–74	5.15%
4.11%	65–79	4.78%
6.75%	60–64	7.21%
7.99%	55–59	8.05%
7.07%	50–54	7.06%
6.68%	45–49	6.56%
6.68%	40–44	6.41%
7.17%	35–39	6.76%
7.39%	30–34	6.79%
7.26%	25–29	6.63%
6.60%	20–24	5.95%
6.01%	15–19	5.40%
5.30%	10–14	4.79%
5.52%	5–9	4.93%
4.98%	0–4	4.41%

299.2 224.4 149.6 74.8 0 74.8 149.6 224.4 299.2
Population (in thousands)

SLOVAKIA

BY AGE AND SEX (2012), SEX RATIO (M/F): 0.949
MALES: 2,631,752 | FEMALES: 2,772,570
TOTAL POPULATION: 5,404,322

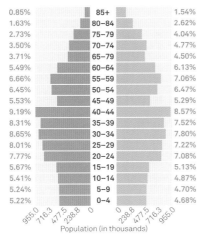

0.66%	85+	1.62%
1.15%	80–84	2.32%
1.83%	75–79	3.13%
2.64%	70–74	3.86%
3.60%	65–79	4.58%
5.67%	60–64	6.28%
7.08%	55–59	7.27%
7.14%	50–54	6.92%
7.06%	45–49	6.70%
6.92%	40–44	6.41%
8.51%	35–39	7.72%
8.93%	30–34	8.03%
8.46%	25–29	7.66%
7.67%	20–24	7.01%
5.42%	15–19	5.84%
5.18%	10–14	4.88%
5.18%	5–9	4.65%
5.63%	0–4	5.10%

234.9 176.2 117.5 58.7 0 58.7 117.5 176.2 234.9
Population (in thousands)

SLOVENIA

BY AGE AND SEX (2012), SEX RATIO (M/F): 0.979
MALES: 1,016,731 | FEMALES: 1,038,765
TOTAL POPULATION: 2,055,496

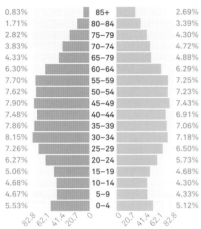

Male	Age	Female
0.83%	85+	2.69%
1.71%	80–84	3.39%
2.82%	75–79	4.30%
3.83%	70–74	4.72%
4.33%	65–79	4.88%
6.30%	60–64	6.29%
7.70%	55–59	7.25%
7.62%	50–54	7.23%
7.90%	45–49	7.43%
7.48%	40–44	6.91%
7.86%	35–39	7.06%
8.15%	30–34	7.18%
7.26%	25–29	6.50%
6.27%	20–24	5.73%
5.06%	15–19	4.68%
4.68%	10–14	4.30%
4.67%	5–9	4.33%
5.53%	0–4	5.12%

Population (in thousands)

SPAIN

BY AGE AND SEX (2012), SEX RATIO (M/F): 0.967
MALES: 22,705,443 | FEMALES: 23,490,833
TOTAL POPULATION: 46,196,276

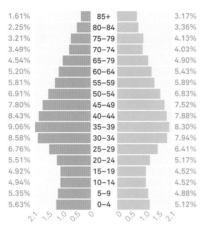

Male	Age	Female
1.61%	85+	3.17%
2.25%	80–84	3.36%
3.21%	75–79	4.13%
3.49%	70–74	4.03%
4.54%	65–79	4.90%
5.20%	60–64	5.43%
5.81%	55–59	5.89%
6.91%	50–54	6.83%
7.80%	45–49	7.52%
8.43%	40–44	7.88%
9.06%	35–39	8.30%
8.58%	30–34	7.94%
6.76%	25–29	6.41%
5.51%	20–24	5.17%
4.92%	15–19	4.52%
4.94%	10–14	4.52%
5.35%	5–9	4.88%
5.63%	0–4	5.12%

Population (in thousands)

SWEDEN

BY AGE AND SEX (2012), SEX RATIO (M/F): 0.994
MALES: 4,726,834 | FEMALES: 4,756,021
TOTAL POPULATION: 69,482,855

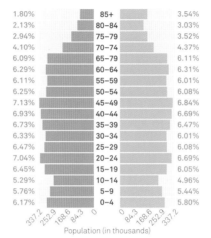

Male	Age	Female
1.80%	85+	3.54%
2.13%	80–84	3.03%
2.94%	75–79	3.52%
4.10%	70–74	4.37%
6.09%	65–79	6.11%
6.29%	60–64	6.31%
6.11%	55–59	6.01%
6.25%	50–54	6.08%
7.13%	45–49	6.84%
6.93%	40–44	6.69%
6.73%	35–39	6.47%
6.33%	30–34	6.01%
6.47%	25–29	6.08%
7.04%	20–24	6.69%
6.45%	15–19	6.05%
5.29%	10–14	4.96%
5.76%	5–9	5.44%
6.17%	0–4	5.80%

Population (in thousands)

SWITZERLAND

BY AGE AND SEX (2012), SEX RATIO (M/F): 0.973
MALES: 3,922,253 | FEMALES: 4,032,409
TOTAL POPULATION: 7,954,662

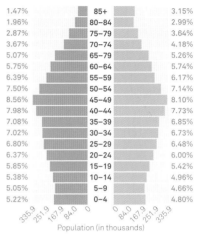

Male	Age	Female
1.47%	85+	3.15%
1.96%	80–84	2.99%
2.87%	75–79	3.64%
3.67%	70–74	4.18%
5.07%	65–79	5.26%
5.75%	60–64	5.74%
6.39%	55–59	6.17%
7.50%	50–54	7.14%
8.56%	45–49	8.10%
7.98%	40–44	7.73%
7.08%	35–39	6.85%
7.02%	30–34	6.73%
6.80%	25–29	6.48%
6.37%	20–24	6.00%
5.85%	15–19	5.42%
5.38%	10–14	4.96%
5.05%	5–9	4.66%
5.22%	0–4	4.80%

Population (in thousands)

TURKEY

BY AGE AND SEX (2012), SEX RATIO (M/F): 1.009
MALES: 37,532,954 | FEMALES: 37,191,315
TOTAL POPULATION: 74,724,269

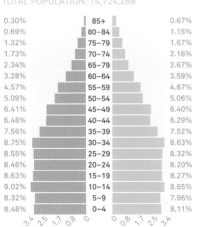

Male	Age	Female
0.30%	85+	0.67%
0.69%	80–84	1.15%
1.32%	75–79	1.67%
1.73%	70–74	2.16%
2.34%	65–79	2.67%
3.28%	60–64	3.59%
4.57%	55–59	4.67%
5.09%	50–54	5.06%
6.41%	45–49	6.40%
6.48%	40–44	6.29%
7.56%	35–39	7.52%
8.75%	30–34	8.63%
8.55%	25–29	8.32%
8.46%	20–24	8.20%
8.63%	15–19	8.27%
9.02%	10–14	8.65%
8.32%	5–9	7.96%
8.48%	0–4	8.11%

Population (in thousands)

UNITED KINGDOM

BY AGE AND SEX (2012), SEX RATIO (M/F): 0.972
MALES: 31,040,303 | FEMALES: 31,949,248
TOTAL POPULATION: 62,989,551

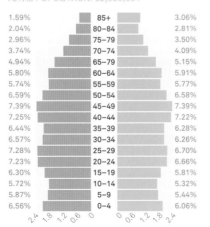

Male	Age	Female
1.59%	85+	3.06%
2.04%	80–84	2.81%
2.96%	75–79	3.50%
3.74%	70–74	4.09%
4.94%	65–79	5.15%
5.80%	60–64	5.91%
5.74%	55–59	5.77%
6.59%	50–54	6.58%
7.39%	45–49	7.39%
7.25%	40–44	7.22%
6.44%	35–39	6.28%
6.57%	30–34	6.26%
7.28%	25–29	6.70%
7.23%	20–24	6.66%
6.30%	15–19	5.81%
5.72%	10–14	5.32%
5.87%	5–9	5.44%
6.56%	0–4	6.06%

Population (in thousands)

MAP 3.020 – POPULATION AGED 15–65 AS A PERCENTAGE OF TOTAL POPULATION, BY REGION
Source: Eurostat | Basemap: Hennig Projection Gridded Population Cartogram

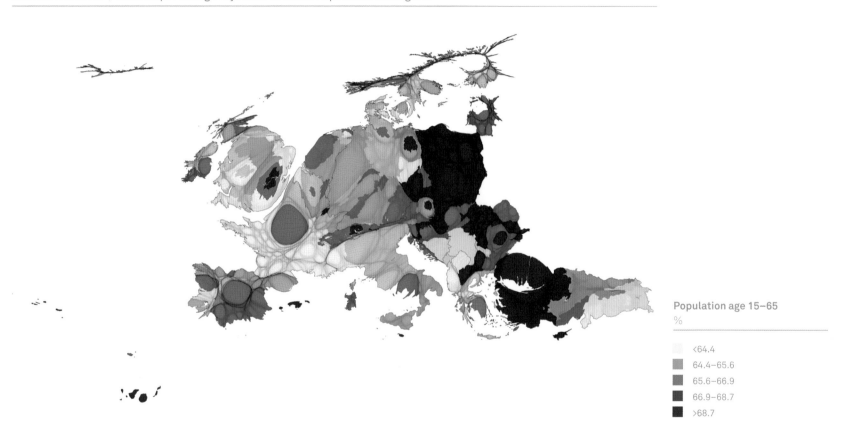

Population age 15–65
%

	<64.4
	64.4–65.6
	65.6–66.9
	66.9–68.7
	>68.7

It is possible to explore the geographical dimension of the data presented in the population pyramids above, by examining them at the regional level. This map is a cartogram highlighting areas with the greatest geographical concentrations of populations of traditional working age (15–65 years) across European regions.

The lowest percentage of working age population (as a proportion of the total population in the region) is 55%, and it is observed in the region of *Mardin*, one of the oldest settled areas in the world, in southeast Turkey. The highest percentage is 74%, in *Inner London*. There are also very high rates in Poland, the Slovak

Republic and Croatia. Here there are fewer elderly people and fewer children. Within Turkey, rates are high where people have migrated westwards.

It is interesting to note that the percentage of working-age population is higher in the cities and regions of Europe that are also major employment centres, whereas it tends to be lower in the periphery where there are typically fewer jobs.

MAP 3.021 – POPULATION AGED 0–15 AS A PERCENTAGE OF TOTAL POPULATION, BY REGION

Source: Eurostat | Basemap: Hennig Projection Gridded Population Cartogram

Population under age 15
%

	<13.8
	13.8–14.9
	14.9–16.4
	16.4–17.9
	>17.9

The region with the lowest proportion of children as a share of its total population is *Principado de Asturias* in northwest Spain, where 10.8% of the population is aged 0–15. Other areas with very small percentages (all below 12%) include the German regions of *Schleswig-Holstein*, *Saarland* and *Thüringen*, and the Italian region of *Liguria*. The region with the highest proportion (40.9%) of its population aged 0–15 is *Mardin* in Turkey – which is also the region with the lowest percentage of working-age population. Here a number of children – more than elsewhere – are left by parents to be cared for by grandparents.

Many of the regions with high child populations are in Turkey. The top 15 regions (including *Mardin*) are all in Turkey, all with over 25% of their populations being children. The next largest area that is not located in Turkey is the region of *Border, Midlands and Western* in the Republic of Ireland, where 22.4% of the population is aged 0–15.

There is also an interesting contrast between Paris and London. A high proportion of families with children live within Paris, while around London there is a ring where there are more children, but fewer families with children can afford to live actually within the city.

MAP 3.022 – POPULATION AGED 65 AND OVER AS A PERCENTAGE OF TOTAL POPULATION, BY REGION

Source: Eurostat | Basemap: Hennig Projection Gridded Population Cartogram

Population aged 65 and older

%

	<14.4
	14.4–16.8
	16.8–18.8
	18.8–20.5
	>20.5

The region with the smallest share of its population aged 65 and over as a percentage of its total population is *Van* in eastern Turkey – just 3.3%. In Europe, 34 regions have percentages of less than 10% and of those, 33 are in Turkey. This may be due to the fact that the demographic transition from high births and high death rates typical in less developed countries to low births and low death rates, typical in industrialised countries, was observed in Turkey later than the rest of Europe. The only region outside Turkey with such a low share of elderly people is *Inner London* where only 8.9% of the population is aged 65 or over. This may be due to retirement migration to other parts of the UK and the rest of Europe. The region with the largest percentage (27%) is *Liguria* in Italy. The elderly of Europe are also found in greater than normal proportions in northern Germany, and also along the Mediterranean coast and in the interior of France, in northern Spain and southwest England. A lot of these regions are typically attractive for retired people and may also be characterised by low fertility rates.

MAP 3.023 – MALE:FEMALE RATIO, BY REGION

Source: Eurostat | Basemap: Hennig Projection Gridded Population Cartogram

**Male:female ratio
in population**

- <0.944
- 0.944–0.959
- 0.959–0.974
- 0.974–0.991
- >0.991

The area with the lowest male:female ratio (0.84) – that is, far fewer men than women – is Latvia, followed closely by Lithuania (0.85) and Estonia (0.86). Areas within these three Baltic states, all considered to be entire European NUTS 2 regions, have even lower ratios. This may be the consequence of a higher mortality rate due to high levels of alcohol consumption by men in the Baltic states (see McKee et al, 2000). Other regions with low male:female ratios of less than 0.90 are *Közép-Magyarország* in central Hungary (which also includes the capital, Budapest), the Bucharest capital region *Bucureşti-Ilfov* in Romania, and the Madeira Islands region (*Região Autónoma da Madeira*) in Portugal. The ratio is lowest where more men than women have died or left, and/or where more women have moved into an area.

The highest male:female ratio (1.07) is in the northern Aegean island region of *Voreio Aigaio* in Greece, closely followed by the southern Aegean island region – also in Greece – of *Notio Aigaio* (1.06), the region of *Ağrı* (1.06) in eastern Turkey, and the Mediterranean coastal region of *Antalya* in southwest Turkey (1.05). Ratios tend to be highest in areas where there is high emigration of women.

MAP 3.024 – POPULATION BORN OUTSIDE THE COUNTRY OF RESIDENCE, 2010
Source: World Bank

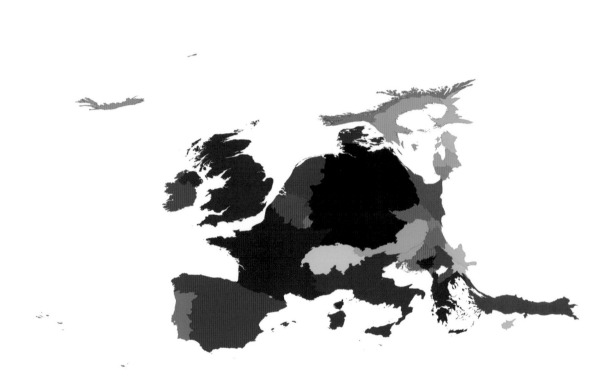

For a century from around the middle of the 19th century, Europe's dominant experience was mainly to send people to other continents, not to receive migrants. Only in the last half century has the net movement reversed, and since the 1980s another radical change has occurred: Greece, southern Italy, Spain and Portugal, which through most of the 20th century were regions of rural depopulation and emigration to northern Europe, the Americas and Australia, have become regions of return migration and of immigration from eastern Europe and other continents.

Warnes et al. 2004, p 311

This map is based on the most recent data from the World Bank[5] giving estimates of the numbers of people born in a country that is different from the one where they are now living. According to this data, the number of such people in Europe in 2010 was – to be a little too precise! – 52,225,829, which is 8.5% of the total population of all European states that are included in this atlas. As with all the entries here, these are estimates, but they are judged to be fair estimates.

In absolute terms the largest numbers are in Germany, followed by France and the United Kingdom. However, in relative terms, the state with the highest share of lifetime immigrants as a proportion of its total population (after the Vatican City where the percentage is 100%) is Monaco (71.2%), followed by Andorra. The state with the lowest number in relative terms is Romania, where just 0.6% of its resident population in 2010 were born outside the country, followed by Bosnia and Herzegovina (0.7%), Bulgaria (1.5%) and Turkey (1.9%).

5 There was no data on Kosovo.

MAP 3.025 – POPULATION BORN OUTSIDE THE COUNTRY OF RESIDENCE, INCREASE 2000–10
Source: World Bank

Is it not the case that without immigrants, the women in your country would grow moustaches, because you would have ended up marrying your first cousins?

Bulgarian TV interview question to Nigel Farage, leader of the UK Independence Party, broadcast by Channel 4 (YouTube, 2013)

This map shows the absolute increases in the number of residents who were 'born abroad' during the first decade of the 21st century. The largest absolute increase is observed in Spain, followed by Italy, the United Kingdom and Germany. Spain also experienced the greatest relative increase over that period: the number of residents born outside the country rose from 1,752,869 in 2000 to 6,377,524 in 2010, which represents an increase of 263% (but note that this is only as a share of the original immigrant population, not of the population as a whole). The second largest rate of change, measured as a share of the original immigrant population, was recorded in Iceland (134%), followed by Ireland (133%) and Italy (110%). Since the year 2010 it is very likely that in at least two, if not all three of these countries, the share of those born overseas will have fallen, as all were hit badly by the financial crisis.

MAP 3.026 – POPULATION BORN OUTSIDE THE COUNTRY OF RESIDENCE, DECLINE 2000–10
Source: World Bank

But 'send your daughters to sweep our floors while we destroy your way of life with agribusiness' never sounds great anywhere. Here, on the new faultline of Europe, they will have to come up with something better.

Paul Mason's report from Transnistria in The Guardian *(Mason, 2014)*

This map shows the total absolute decline in the number of residents born abroad but living in each country, as measured between 2000 and 2010. Nine countries experienced a decline in numbers of lifetime immigrants over this period. The country with the highest decrease is Serbia, followed by Latvia, Lithuania, Bosnia and Herzegovina, Estonia, Montenegro, Slovenia, Romania and the Czech Republic. However, the country that experienced the highest rate of decline of all was Bosnia and Herzegovina (–71%), followed by Lithuania (–39%) and Serbia (–38%). This may be due to geopolitical upheavals like war in former Yugoslavia, or the emigration of some Russians returning to Russia after the fall of the USSR and the independence of the Baltic states. Commentators rarely consider that rates of immigration fall as well as rise.

As rates of mobility tend to increase over time, in general there will be higher and higher proportions of people born in one nation state living in another. Occasionally, when there is economic disaster, war, or a similar calamity, rates of immigration decline.

4

EDUCATION

MAP 4.027 – POPULATION THAT HAS NEVER HAD ANY FORMAL SCHOOL EDUCATION
Source: Eurostat, Barro-Lee educational attainment dataset

NO FORMAL EDUCATION

This map is based on Eurostat population data and a dataset created by Barro and Lee (2013) to analyse educational attainment across the world between 1950 and 2010. The dataset uses UNESCO's International Standard Classification of Education (ISCED), which is one of the most suitable for comparisons of '*education statistics and indicators across countries on the basis of uniform and internationally-agreed definition*' (Barro and Lee, 2013, p 185). Educational comparisons are never ideal, but some are better than others. The meaning of 'no school' can range from *arrived from outside Europe having never been to school*, to *hardly ever attended school*, which will be the case for many older people, through to *attended school but achieved so little that in terms of educational benefit it is as if the person never went*.[6]

Using the data for the latest year (2010), the map shows the distribution of the estimated numbers of people aged 15 years and over in Europe who have had no formal schooling. The total number is nearly 19 million, representing 3.7% of all Europe's population aged 15 and over living in the countries mapped in this atlas. The highest numbers of people who have had no schooling are in Turkey, followed by Italy, Germany and the United Kingdom. However, it is interesting, and surprising, to see that the highest percentage is observed in Switzerland (11.7%). This is followed by Turkey (10.5%), Portugal (10.1%), Cyprus (10.0%) and Luxembourg (6.2%). On the other hand, the lowest percentages are observed in the Czech Republic (0.1%), Denmark (0.14%), Estonia (0.2%) and Norway (0.2%).

---

6 In some countries 'no formal schooling' may include the category 'being entirely home educated'.

MAP 4.028 – POPULATION WITH, AT MOST, PRIMARY EDUCATIONAL ATTAINMENT

Source: Eurostat, Barro-Lee educational attainment dataset

PRIMARY EDUCATIONAL ATTAINMENT

3.69 20.77 58.46 17.08

Around one in seven children leave school or training early and this has an impact on individuals, society and economies ... Early leavers from education and training and tertiary educational attainment are headline indicators for the Europe 2020 strategy.

European Commission, 2013c

This map uses data from the same study conducted by Barro and Lee (2013) as was used for the map on the previous page. The total estimated number of people across Europe who have, at most, primary education is 106 million people, representing about 21% of all residents aged 15 and over. The highest number is in Turkey, the second highest in the United Kingdom and third highest in Italy. The largest proportion of people in this category is observed in Portugal (44.0%), followed by Turkey (41.1%), Denmark (40.8%), Iceland (34.5%) and Serbia (33.7%). The lowest percentages are in Norway (2.8%), Slovenia (3.8%), Latvia (5.1%), Hungary (5.1%) and Estonia (6%). Where rates are low, secondary education was introduced earlier in these countries, and attendance was better secured.

MAP 4.029 – POPULATION WITH, AT MOST, SECONDARY EDUCATIONAL ATTAINMENT
Source: Eurostat, Barro-Lee educational attainment dataset

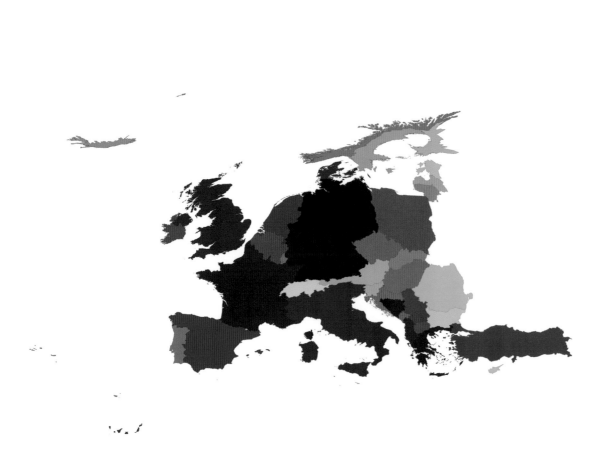

SECONDARY EDUCATIONAL ATTAINMENT

3.69   20.77   58.46   17.08

All European citizens should benefit from high quality education and training – irrespective of where they live. It is time to deliver on the commitments which have been made. Tackling geographic inequality in education is a pre-requisite for balanced regional development and social cohesion. The European Structural Funds can and should be used to help address inequalities.

Androulla Vassiliou, European Commissioner for Education, Culture, Multilingualism and Youth, cited in a press release (European Commission, 2012c)

Using data from Eurostat and Barro and Lee (2013), it is estimated that there are nearly 300 million people in Europe aged 15 years and over with, at most, secondary educational attainment, representing 58% of all people in this age category. Completion of secondary education is the most common situation across Europe (however, 42% of all adult Europeans have either had less education or more education than this norm). The map shows the spatial distribution across Europe of those who attained secondary education, at most. Germany has the highest absolute number, followed by Italy and France. In relative terms, the highest rate is seen in Albania and Hungary (both 80.0%), followed by Slovenia (79.0%), Latvia (76.6%) and the Czech Republic (75.3%). The lowest rates are in Iceland (34.3%), Portugal (34.8%), Turkey (37.0%) and Denmark (40.0%).

MAP 4.030 – POPULATION WITH TERTIARY EDUCATIONAL ATTAINMENT
Source: Eurostat, Barro-Lee educational attainment dataset

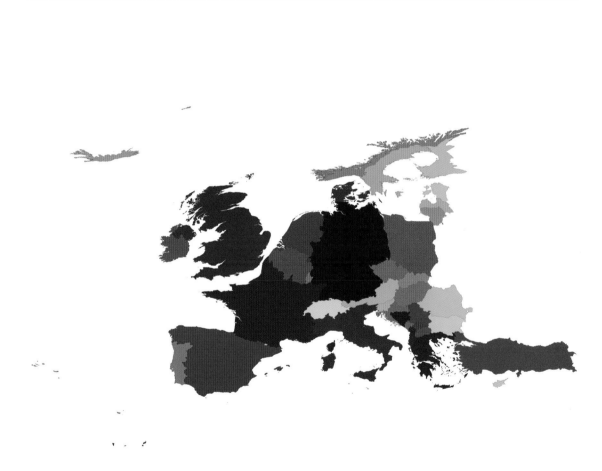

TERTIARY EDUCATIONAL ATTAINMENT

3.69 20.77 58.46 17.08

Given the overwhelming evidence about the importance of human capital and knowledge for regional development and economic performance, there should be renewed emphasis on efforts to expand and widen participation in tertiary education across the EU.

Ballas et al, 2012, p 162

This map shows the spatial distribution of people who have a university degree or equivalent. Using data from Eurostat and Barro and Lee (2013), it is estimated that there are 87 million Europeans who had attained tertiary education by the first decade of the 21st century. The number is rising rapidly. Currently this group represents 17% of all Europeans aged 15 and over. The highest number is in Germany, closely followed by the United Kingdom and France. University graduates are most numerous as a proportion of all the population aged 15 and over in the Republic of Ireland (30.5%), followed by Iceland (29.7%) and Estonia (25.9%). It is also worth noting that France, Sweden, the United Kingdom, the Netherlands, Cyprus, Greece, Lithuania, Finland, Belgium, Spain and Norway all have percentages between 20% and 25%. At the other end of the distribution are three countries with percentages of less than ten: Albania (9.2%) Italy (9.3%) and Croatia (9.6%). One factor that may have a bearing on these rates is how easy it is for school leavers to get a job without a university degree (for example, it may be much easier to do so in Germany, particularly in the industrial sector, than it is in France).

MAP 4.031 – STUDENT MOBILITY: NUMBERS OF INCOMING STUDENTS
Source: Eurostat

Student mobility is understood as the short-term stay abroad, usually one academic year of nine to twelve months duration. This experience posited as an instrument of European construction, represents an ambiguous venture in university education. The stay abroad induces direct contact with a language and culture, qualitatively different from institutional learning, transcending it in a way. Its impact and outcomes are still perplexing and difficult to assess. As a small minority, mobile students are indeed undefined, little known. Who are these young people who take up the challenge of mobility when the vast majority of their peers disregard it?"

Murphy-Lejeune, 2002, p 2

According to Eurostat data, in 2010 there was an estimated total of 670,000 European students enrolled in tertiary education at a university in a different country from their own. Over a quarter of all these students are in the United Kingdom. Germany, Austria and France also host large numbers of incoming students. This is not surprising given that the official languages spoken in these countries are also the most common languages taught and learnt as a foreign language across Europe. It is also interesting to note the relatively very high number in Austria. This may be due to its attractiveness for students coming from countries with strong linguistic and cultural links, possibly related to the imperial legacy of the Austrian-Hungarian empire.

MAP 4.032 – STUDENT MOBILITY: NUMBERS OF OUTGOING STUDENTS
Source: Eurostat

Until recently, a UK student on a European campus could bank on modest celebrity status. They were a rare breed, and sightings at the library, lecture hall or bar caused quite a stir. But that's all changing. Although full-time UK students are still fairly unusual at universities throughout Europe, more and more are heading beyond the Channel for their degree.

Moore, 2014

This map shows the university students studying abroad by country of origin in 2010, according to Eurostat data. Germany has the highest number of outgoing students (92,000), followed by France and Turkey. Cyprus, Greece and Portugal also seem to have relatively large numbers of outgoing students, especially in relation to their total population. There is a relatively small number of outgoing students from the United Kingdom, given its total population and the fact that it is the most popular destination of students from abroad (see map on previous page).

The small number of outgoing students from the UK is especially interesting because currently the cost of higher education in the UK is much higher than in almost any other European country. That cost varies within the UK. Students travelling from the rest of the EU to Scotland still benefit from normal education costs, but English, Welsh and Northern Irish students do not. This last group would have to travel outside of the UK, elsewhere in Europe, to benefit from average fees or, in some cases, almost free university education.

MAP 4.033 – TOTAL NUMBER OF STUDENTS IN TERTIARY EDUCATION (ISCED LEVELS 5 AND 6), AS A PERCENTAGE OF THE POPULATION AGED 20–24 YEARS, BY NUTS 2 REGIONS, 2010

Source: Eurostat | Basemap: Hennig Projection Gridded Population Cartogram

Total number of students in tertiary education (ISCED levels 5 and 6)

% of the population aged 20–24

	< 39.3
	39.3–47.4
	47.4–54.7
	54.7–69.3
	> 69.3

There is a relatively limited amount of information available for all European regions, but it is well worth examining what there is. This map shows a gridded-population cartogram highlighting areas with the greatest total numbers of students as a percentage of all the population aged 20–24 years. Nearly all of these areas are located around Europe's large cities and city regions. The share of students can often be higher than 100%, because more students live in a city than the numbers of 20–24-year-olds that the city itself generates. Also, many students are outside the stated age group (that is, aged 18, 19 or over 24).

The highest percentage (202%) is in the Romanian capital city region of *Bucuresti-Ilfov* where there seem to be very large numbers of students outside the 20–24 age group. The second largest percentage is in the Czech capital city region of *Praha* (197%), followed by Slovakia's *Bratislavský kraj* (186%) and the nearby Austrian capital city region of *Wien* (149%).

The lowest percentages are in *Mardin*, southeast Turkey (3.5%), *Severozapaden* in northwest Bulgaria (4.3%), *Strední Cechy* in the Czech Republic (5.2%), *Sanliurfa*, southeast Turkey (9.0%) and in the Italian border region (bordering Austria) of *Provincia Autonoma Bolzano/Boxen* (9.6%).

MAP 4.034 – PEOPLE AGED 25–64 YEARS WITH TERTIARY EDUCATIONAL (ISCED LEVELS 5 AND 6) ATTAINMENT, BY NUTS 2 REGIONS, 2010

Source: Eurostat | Basemap: Hennig Projection Gridded Population Cartogram

Persons aged 25–64 with tertiary educational (ISCED levels 5 and 6) attainment
% of 25–64 year-olds

- <15.3
- 15.3–21.8
- 21.8–27.7
- 27.7–33.1
- >33.1

This map highlights areas with the greatest geographical concentration of populations aged 25–64 years with tertiary educational attainment, across European regions. Here the effect of student migration is removed, as most people in this age group will have completed their studies and moved on from where they studied.

The highest percentage of these individuals is in *Inner London*, which is also the only region in Europe where more than half (53.1%) of the population belonging to this age group hold a tertiary education degree. Other regions with very high percentages include *Prov. Brabant Wallon* (49.5%) in Belgium and the Norwegian capital city region *Oslo Og Akershus* (47.9%), and also several economically successful city regions mostly found in northern and western Europe.

On the other hand, there are 15 regions where less than 10% of the population aged 25–64 years have tertiary educational attainment. Of these 13 are in Turkey, including the region with the lowest percentage – *Ağrı* in eastern Turkey (6.4%). The other two regions are *Severozápad* in the Czech Republic and the island region *Região Autónoma dos Açores* in Portugal.

MAP 4.035 – PARTICIPATION RATES OF 4-YEAR-OLDS IN PRE-PRIMARY AND PRIMARY EDUCATION (ISCED LEVELS 0 AND 1), BY NUTS 2 REGIONS, 2010

Source: Eurostat | Basemap: Hennig Projection Gridded Population Cartogram

Participation of four year-olds in pre-primary and primary education (ISCED levels 0 and 1)

% of four year-olds

- <57.9
- 57.9–91.3
- 91.3–96.5
- 96.5–99.4
- >99.4

This map highlights areas with the highest participation rates of 4-year-olds in pre-primary and primary education across European regions. There are 35 regions where the participation rate is virtually 100%. Five of these are in Belgium, 11 in Spain, 12 in France, 4 in Italy and 1 each in Austria, the Netherlands and the United Kingdom. Most of the regions with the lowest participation rates are in Turkey and other parts of southeast Europe. The lowest rate (8%) is observed in *Hatay*, a region in southern Turkey on the Mediterranean coast, bordering Syria.

These differences can be explained by different national education policy approaches. For example, in countries like France pre-primary schooling is considered to be very important whereas this is not the case in countries like Finland, where children do not have to attend school until they are 6 years old, so the rate there is relatively low. There is an ongoing debate about how beneficial formal primary and pre-primary education is for young children, and whether they are not better served by having more opportunities to play rather than learn (Lev and Dorling, 1983).

MAP 4.036 – EARLY LEAVERS FROM EDUCATION AND TRAINING, BY NUTS 2 REGIONS, 2010

Source: Eurostat | Basemap: Hennig Projection Gridded Population Cartogram

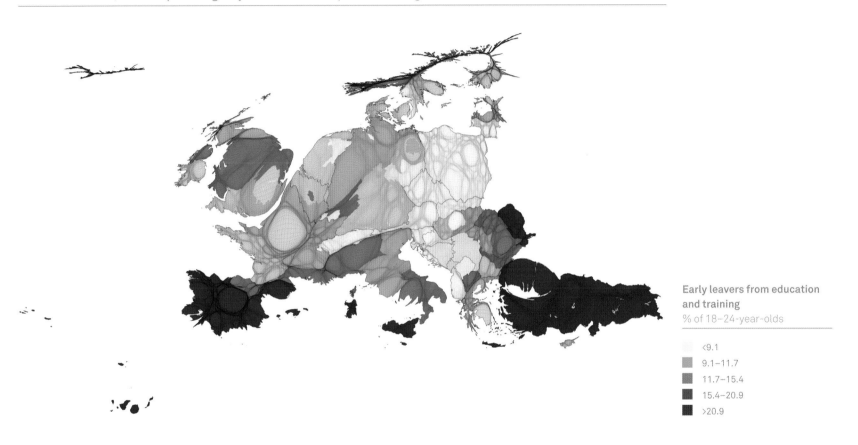

Early leavers from education and training

% of 18–24-year-olds

- <9.1
- 9.1–11.7
- 11.7–15.4
- 15.4–20.9
- >20.9

This map shows areas with the greatest geographical concentration of proportions of people aged 18–24 years having attained at most a lower secondary education and not being involved in further education or training. There are three regions where more than half of the population in this age group are classified as 'early leavers', all in east Turkey: *Güneydogu Anadolu* (60.0%), *Kuzeydogu Anadolu* (58.1%) and *Ortadogu Anadolu* (57.9%). Overall, out of the top ten regions with the highest rates (all over 37%), eight are in Turkey. These are also amongst the poorest regions compared to the rest of Europe.

The other two are the Portuguese island regions of *Região Autónoma dos Açores* (45.2%) and *Região Autónoma da Madeira* (37.3%). It is interesting to consider how education might be developed in such places to encourage more children to remain in education.

The lowest rates (all below 5%) are observed in *Croatia*, *Slovakia*, the *Czech Republic* and the Polish regions *Poludniowy*, *Centralny* and *Wschodni*. These regions are in post-communist countries and to some extent these low rates may be explained by the importance placed on completing compulsory education under communism.

5

EMPLOYMENT

MAP 5.037 – ECONOMICALLY ACTIVE FEMALE POPULATION
Source: International Labour Organisation

The participation of women in the labour market in the European Union has been growing steadily in recent years, and their increasing participation is seen as a key factor in achieving the goals of the European Employment Strategy and the Europe 2020 Strategy. At policy level, it is recognised that the economic success of Member States depends on women being able to reach their full potential. The Commission's focus in this area is on ensuring that women have the opportunity to work when they want and that they can balance work with other family responsibilities.

Eurofound, 2012

This map shows the spatial distribution of the economically active female population – that is, women who are in work or who are looking for work – across Europe in 2010. The highest absolute number is in Germany, followed by the United Kingdom, France, Italy and Spain. However, in relative terms Estonia and Lithuania have the largest proportions of economically active females as a share of the total economically active population (49.4% and 49.3% respectively), followed by Latvia (48.8%), Finland (47.8%) and France (47.5%). It is interesting to note that in the former USSR, the active female population was typically very high. In contrast, the lowest percentages are observed in Turkey (26.6%) and Malta (33.5%).

MAP 5.038 – NUMBERS OF UNEMPLOYED PEOPLE
Source: Eurostat, The World Bank, International Labour Organisation

29,817,744

This map is based on the most recent data from Eurostat and the World Bank. It shows the total numbers of unemployed people as they were distributed across Europe in 2012. The estimated total number for the whole of Europe at that time was 29,817,744, and it has risen since then. Nearly one fifth of this number live in Spain, which is the country with the highest absolute number of unemployed residents in Europe. In relative terms, the highest percentage is observed in Kosovo, a very poor country, where an estimated 45% of the economically active population are unemployed. The second highest estimated unemployment rate is in FYR Macedonia (31%), followed by Bosnia and Herzegovina (27%), Spain (25%) and Greece (24%). The countries with the lowest unemployment rates (all below 5%) are Austria, Switzerland, Norway, San Marino, Monaco, Liechtenstein and Andorra, which are among the richest countries in Europe. It is interesting to note that most of Europe's people are not as free to move and settle in some of these high employment countries as they are to move to other parts of Europe.

MAP 5.039 – YOUTH UNEMPLOYMENT
Source: Eurostat, International Labour Organisation, The World Bank

The UK's young unemployed could form a dole queue stretching from London to Edinburgh, research by MPs and the Commons library has calculated. As MPs prepare to launch a new cross-party group dealing with youth unemployment, the figures suggest that out-of-work 16- to 24-year-olds could stand in a line that extends for 434 miles. This is equivalent to an area the size of Leeds, assuming each young person has 0.75 metres (2.5 feet) square to stand in.

Rowena Mason, political correspondent for The Guardian (Mason, R., 2014)

This map shows the spatial distribution across Europe of the 7 million people aged 15–24 who are estimated to be unemployed. The map uses the latest data (2012) from Eurostat (including the European Labour Force survey), the International Labour Organisation and the World Bank. About one seventh of this group (964,000) are in the United Kingdom, with a similar number in Spain (945,000). France, Turkey and Italy also have very large absolute numbers of young unemployed people (all above 500,000). In relative terms, the highest estimated youth unemployment rate is observed in Bosnia and Herzegovina (63%), followed by Kosovo (55%), Greece (55%), FYR Macedonia (54%), Spain (53%) and Serbia (51%).

MAP 5.040 – NUMBERS OF UNEMPLOYED PEOPLE: INCREASE BETWEEN 2007 AND 2012

Source: Eurostat, The World Bank, International Labour Organisation

There is growing 'austerity fatigue' in Europe, and this might provoke a crisis ... the overwhelming result from U.S. political studies is that the level of unemployment matters hardly at all for elections; all that matters is the rate of change in the months leading up to the election. In other words, high unemployment could become accepted as the new normal, politically as well as in economic analysis.

Krugman, 2013

It is shocking to explore the statistics on the geography of total unemployment increases in Europe since the economic crisis started in 2008, and to see how much a few areas have suffered while others have seen very little rise in unemployment at all. This map shows the total increases between 2007 and 2012 in the numbers of people out of work and looking for work across Europe. The largest absolute increase is observed in Spain, which had nearly 4 million more unemployed people in 2012 than it had in 2007 and which is a country very badly hit by the real estate crisis. Italy, the United Kingdom, Greece and France also experienced very large absolute increases. In contrast, Germany recorded one of its lowest rates of unemployment for two decades during this period. It only appears in the map above at all because of the size of some of its neighbours – if it did not matter to keep them separated it would not appear at all!

MAP 5.041 – NUMBERS OF UNEMPLOYED PEOPLE: DECLINE BETWEEN 2007 AND 2012

Source: Eurostat, The World Bank, International Labour Organisation

Very few countries in Europe experienced a decline in the total number of unemployed people between 2007 and 2012. The country with by far the largest decline was Germany, which had 1,285,000 fewer unemployed people in 2012 than it had in 2007. FYR Macedonia, Bosnia and Herzegovina and Kosovo also experienced absolute declines in the number of unemployed people during this period. However, note that in many of these countries unemployment remained very high – just not as high as it had been.

Often in Europe today there is talk of Germany having 'exported unemployment' as its people benefited from being in the eurozone. As Germany exported more goods to other countries, the cost of those goods did not rise, because they were being bought in euros. Because the cost did not rise, Germany was able to carry on selling as much as before. Its small initial advantage became a much greater later advantage, and as the export earnings flowed into Germany, more jobs were created. Southern European countries might have fared better had their currencies been able to fall.

MAP 5.042 – YOUTH UNEMPLOYMENT: INCREASE BETWEEN 2007 AND 2012
Source: Eurostat, The World Bank, International Labour Organisation

This map shows the total increase between 2007 and 2012 in the numbers of unemployed aged 15–24. The largest increase is observed in Spain where there were half a million more young unemployed people in 2012 than in 2007. The United Kingdom, Italy, France, Greece and Portugal also experienced very high absolute increases in youth unemployment.

This is the generation that will remember the crash of 2008 most acutely. These young people would not have started off their working lives being unemployed, had it not been for the economic crash and the way it was dealt with. If there had been a 'new deal' across Europe, millions of young people might have been employed in state-funded work, ensuring that the long recession ended early. In fact, extreme austerity was imposed, very few young people were hired into new jobs, and so they had less money to spend, especially on local services, and more jobs were lost in turn. Things might have been very different if countries near the centre of Europe had been as much affected as those around the periphery.

MAP 5.043 – YOUTH UNEMPLOYMENT: DECLINE BETWEEN 2007 AND 2012
Source: Eurostat, The World Bank, International Labour Organisation

Without work, educated young people lose their skills. Unable to enter training programs because of public expenditure cuts, they cannot obtain the skills which would underpin recovery should it occur. Out of work and out of school, they face lives of idle desperation in which criminality beckons as a false exit from destitution.

Weeks, 2013

Six countries experienced a decline in the number of young unemployed (aged 15–24 years) between 2007 and 2012. Germany had the largest decline with 216,000 fewer young unemployed in 2012 compared with 2007. This may be due to a strong decline in births in Germany between 1990 and 1995. It is also interesting to see a considerable decline in youth unemployment in Turkey, and in FYR Macedonia, Bosnia and Herzegovina, Romania and Kosovo. In many cases this observed decline in number may be due to an outmigration of young economically active people from some of these countries. It is also important to remember that the numbers of all young people fluctuate due to changing numbers of births in each area 15 to 24 years ago, and a little earlier too. Nevertheless the map does suggest that Germany and a few countries to its southeast have done well in a very difficult period.

MAP 5.044 – ECONOMICALLY ACTIVE FEMALE POPULATION BY REGION

Source: Eurostat | Basemap: Hennig Projection Gridded Population Cartogram

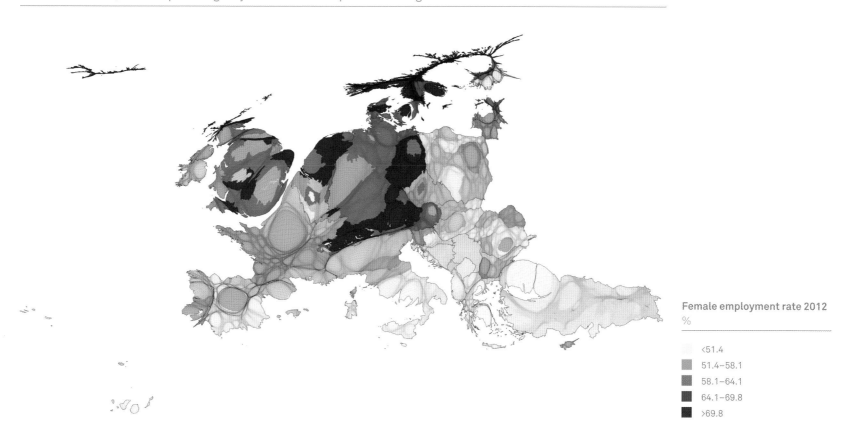

Female employment rate 2012

%

	<51.4
	51.4–58.1
	58.1–64.1
	64.1–69.8
	>69.8

This cartogram shows economically active females as a proportion of the whole economically active population by region for the countries where Eurostat data was available. The area of each region is drawn in proportion to the size of its population, and that area is then shaded by the proportion of workers

(and people looking for work) who are women. The largest proportion of female workers is a remarkable 80.5%, observed in the Finnish *Åland* islands. Other regions with very high female representation among the workforce (all above 75%) are in parts of Iceland, Switzerland, Sweden, Norway and

Germany. It may be that more women have moved to the areas shaded blue on the map, rather than that more men have moved away.

The region where women are least often found in the workforce (27.6%) is *Campania* in southern Italy. Most regions with relatively low rates are in southern

Europe – exceptions include Cyprus, the metropolitan regions of Madrid and Lisbon, and most regions in central and northern France (all above 55% for female participation). Women now make up the majority of workers in much of Europe although more women are employed in part-time work than men.

MAP 5.045 – UNEMPLOYMENT BY REGION
Source: Eurostat | Basemap: Hennig Projection Gridded Population Cartogram

Unemployment rate 2012
%

- <4.9
- 4.9–7.1
- 7.1–9.3
- 9.3–13.8
- >38.5

This map shows the regional distribution of unemployment rates in Europe in 2012 for the countries where Eurostat data was available. The region with the highest unemployment rate (38.5%) is *Ciudad Autónoma de Ceuta*, the Spanish autonomous city in the north of Africa, bordering Morocco. Its population is so low that it is not possible to see it on the cartogram. The second highest rate (34.6%) is observed in Andalucía in southern Spain. Three more regions with unemployment rates of 30% and above are the Canary Islands and the region *Extremadura* in southwest Spain, bordering Portugal, and the *Dytiki Makedonia* region in northern Greece. Most regions in Portugal, Italy, Spain, Greece and the Republic of Ireland have very high rates of unemployment (above 15%). The lowest unemployment rate (1.7%) is observed in the *Åland* islands in Finland. Several regions in Austria, Germany, Norway, Switzerland, the Netherlands and Belgium have unemployment rates below 4%. It is also worth noting that unemployment is now often highest in areas where more women have moved away compared with the number of men who have emigrated.

MAP 5.046 – UNEMPLOYMENT RATES BY REGION: CHANGE BETWEEN 2007 AND 2012
Source: Eurostat | Basemap: Hennig Projection Gridded Population Cartogram

Difference between unemployment rate in 2012 and unemployment rate in 2007

% point change

- <0.7
- 0.7 to +1
- +1 to +2.4
- +2.4 to +5.1
- >+5.1

This map shows the differences between unemployment rates in 2012 and 2007 across European regions in countries and regions where such data was available from Eurostat. The highest increase is observed in the Canary Islands in Spain, where the unemployment rate in 2007 was 22.6% – it went up to 33.0%

in 2012. This rate is a proportion of everyone who is available for work, including those who are working. Several regions experienced increases almost as high as that in the Canaries, mostly in Spain, Greece, Portugal and Italy, all countries very badly hit by the economic crisis. On the other hand, there were

80 regions across Europe where the unemployment rate in 2012 was lower than that of 2007. The region with the highest negative difference (–6.9%) is *Şanlıurfa* in Turkey. Most of the other regions with negative differences in the unemployment rates between 2007 and 2012 are in Germany and Turkey,

due to strong economic growth in these countries, contrary to the rest of Europe but these more successful areas also include some regions in Poland, Romania, Finland, Belgium, France and Switzerland.

MAP 5.047 – EMPLOYMENT IN HIGH-TECHNOLOGY SECTORS (% OF TOTAL EMPLOYMENT), 2008
Source: European Commission | Basemap: Hennig Projection Gridded Population Cartogram

Employment in high-technology sectors, 2008
% of total employment

- <1.14
- 1.14–2.89
- 2.89–4.11
- 4.11–5.13
- >5.13

This cartogram shows the geographical distribution of employment in high-technology sectors across European regions. The rate of employment in each place is shown as a proportion of total employment. Data is missing for a few countries but what is there shows a remarkably interesting pattern. Within almost every country there is at least one area that is 'hi-tech' where there appear to be clusters of opportunities. But there are many clusters: Europe does not appear to have developed an agglomeration as large as the US Silicon Valley; Europe has dozens of small 'silicon valleys'.

The highest percentage (11.3%) is observed in *Berkshire*, *Buckinghamshire* and *Oxfordshire* in the United Kingdom, followed by the Swedish capital city region *Stockholm* (9.3%), and the German regions *Karlsruhe* (9.1%), *Oberbayern* (8.7%) and *Mittelfranken* (8.4%). At the other end of the range, there are a total of 30 regions with percentages under 2%. These regions are mostly found in Bulgaria, Greece, Poland, Portugal, Spain, Romania, Germany and the United Kingdom. The lowest value of 1% is observed in three regions: Romania's *Sud-Vest Oltenia* and the Greek regions *Peloponnisos* and *Anatoliki Makedonia*, *Thraki*.

6

INDUSTRY AND OCCUPATION

MAP 6.048 – PEOPLE WORKING IN AGRICULTURE

Source: The World Bank, CIA World Factbook, International Labour Organisation

Agriculture represents 10% of the European Union total GDP, and it plays an essential role in the European culture and environmental protection. Indeed, agriculture occupies a great part of the territory and helps maintain the lifestyle and economy of many rural areas.

Food and Water Watch Europe, 2014

By making the area of countries proportional to their agricultural workforce, this map shows the spatial distribution of the total estimated economically active population across Europe who are working in agriculture. Turkey has by far the largest number, followed by Romania, Poland, France and Italy. In relative terms, the largest share of workers in agriculture in any one nation state as a proportion of each country's total economically active population is in Albania (48.0%), followed by Romania (31.6%), Turkey (25.5%) and Kosovo (23.6%). The smallest percentages are in Sweden, the United Kingdom, Malta and Germany (all below 2%).

WORKING IN AGRICULTURE

7.54 24.71 67.75

MAP 6.049 – PEOPLE WORKING IN INDUSTRY
Source: The World Bank, CIA World Factbook, International Labour Organisation

WORKING IN INDUSTRY

Europe needs its real economy now more than ever to underpin the recovery of economic growth and jobs and it needs to reindustrialise for the 21st century. Immediate action should contribute to revert the current downward trend and to promote the re-industrialisation of Europe. Currently industry accounts for about 16% of EU GDP. Therefore, the European Commission has set its goal that industry's share of GDP should be around 20% by 2020.

European Commission, 2014a

There are an estimated 69 million people in Europe working in industry. This category is mainly made up of people involved in manufacturing. About 15% of the industrial workforce of Europe are in Germany, Europe's leading industrial power. About 10% are in Italy and another 10% in France. In relative terms, the country with the largest number working in industry as a proportion of its total economically active population is the Czech Republic (38.6%), followed by Bulgaria (35.2%) and Slovenia (35.0%), all former communist countries. The smallest percentage of a country's workers employed in industry is in Andorra (4.7%).

At first glance this map looks very similar to the next map showing people working in service occupations. However, there are differences: for example, the number of workers in the industrial sector is larger in Turkey and smaller in the UK compared with those in services.

MAP 6.050 – PEOPLE WORKING IN SERVICES
Source: The World Bank, CIA World Factbook, International Labour Organisation

WORKING IN SERVICES

7.54 24.71 67.75

There are an estimated 188 million people working in services across Europe. This number represents 67% of the total economically active population living in the countries mapped here. The largest absolute number of service workers is in Germany, followed by the United Kingdom, France and Italy. In relative terms, the largest share of people working in services as a proportion of the total economically active population is found in Andorra (94.9%), Luxembourg (80.4%), the United Kingdom (80.4%), the Netherlands (80.0%) and Denmark (77.0%) countries where the financial and trade sectors are very important in the economy. In contrast, the smallest percentage is in Albania (29.0%), which together with Bosnia and Herzegovina (47.0%), Romania (47.3%) and Turkey (48.3%) are the only countries with percentages less than 50%. These are amongst the least developed countries in Europe.

The European workforce is now overwhelmingly employed in service industries, not growing food or making goods. For every worker who makes or grows something, between two and three people are employed in services. Often service jobs involve selling goods made by others, and the goods are often made outside of Europe. Catering, restaurants, hotels and cafés are also service jobs, as is work in finance and insurance, education, health, housing, government and social care.

MAP 6.051 – MANAGERS
Source: European Union Statistics on Income and Living Conditions | Basemap: Population Cartogram

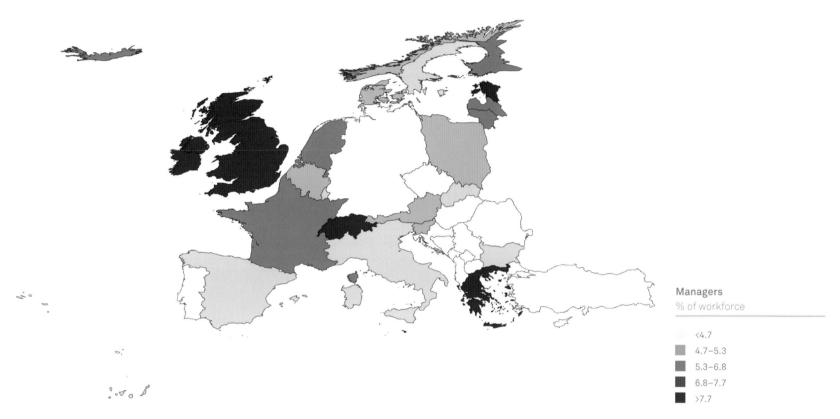

Managers
% of workforce

- <4.7
- 4.7–5.3
- 5.3–6.8
- 6.8–7.7
- >7.7

This and the following eight maps are population cartograms of Europe (each country is drawn in proportion to the size of its total population) but shaded accordingly to show the geographical variation of people working in different occupations as a proportion of the total economically active population in each country, classified using the International

Standard Classification of Occupations. In these cartograms area is always proportional to population, while the shading shows how common it is for people to be employed in a particular sector of the economy in each part of Europe for which data is available. These maps are based on data from the European Union Statistics on Income

and Living Conditions (EU-SILC) for the years 2011 and 2009, and include information on all current EU member states except Croatia, as well as for Switzerland, Iceland and Norway.

This map shows areas according to the distribution of 'managers'. The highest percentage is in Ireland (16.3%), followed by Switzerland (9.4%) and the United

Kingdom (9.2%), Estonia (8.2%), Greece (8.1%) and Malta (7.9%). The lowest percentage is in Cyprus (2.0%), and Romania, Hungary, the Czech Republic, Germany and Portugal all have relatively low numbers of managers as a proportion of their workforce. Note that the word 'manager' may suggest different degrees of management in different countries.

MAP 6.052 – PROFESSIONALS
Source: European Union Statistics on Income and Living Conditions | Basemap: Population Cartogram

Synonyms for 'professional' tend to be highly complimentary such as: 'expert, accomplished, skilful, adept, masterly, masterful, excellent, fine, polished, finished, skilled, proficient, competent, capable, able, efficient, experienced, practised, trained, seasoned, slick, businesslike, deft, dexterous; *informal* ace, crack, stellar, top-notch'.

Google, 2014a

Professionals
% of workforce

- <12.2
- 12.2–13.8
- 13.8–16.0
- 16.0–20.5
- >20.5

The highest percentages of professionals are found in Norway, Sweden, the Netherlands and Denmark, where nearly a quarter of the total economically active population have this classification. In contrast, the smallest percentage is in Portugal (10.8%) and there are also relatively small percentages in Italy, Romania, Slovakia, Hungary and the Czech Republic.

Again, what is meant by the term 'professional' may differ between countries, but a job can be made more professional if a greater degree of autonomy is given to the individuals undertaking that work, if higher qualifications and more training are required to undertake it, and if a more competent outcome is expected. So, for instance, a nurse in Norway may be regarded and trained as a 'professional' whereas in Slovakia he or she might be regarded, trained, treated and listed as being in a less professional category of work.

MAP 6.053 – TECHNICIANS AND ASSOCIATE PROFESSIONALS

Source: European Union Statistics on Income and Living Conditions | Basemap: Population Cartogram

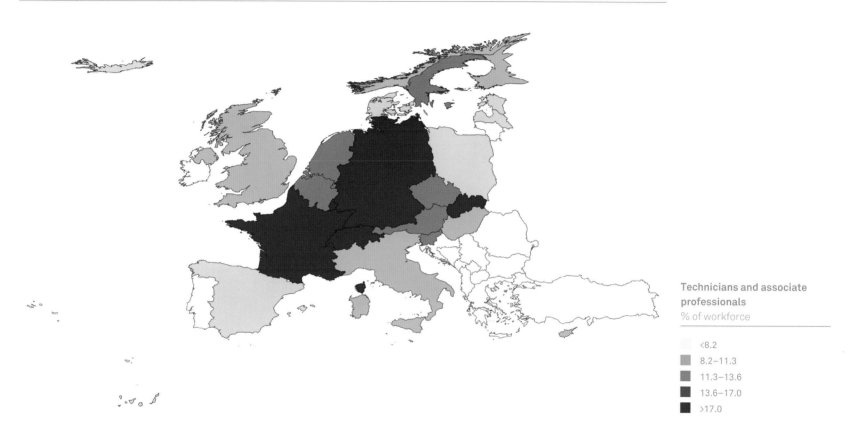

Technicians and associate professionals
% of workforce

- <8.2
- 8.2–11.3
- 11.3–13.6
- 13.6–17.0
- >17.0

The highest percentage of 'technicians and associate professionals' is observed in Germany (22.4% of the workforce) and there are also relatively high shares of the workforce in Slovakia, Switzerland and France. On the other hand, the smallest percentage is found in Ireland (5.3%). Romania, Bulgaria, Greece and Portugal also have relatively small numbers in this category.

It was noted on Map 6.051 that Ireland has by far the highest proportion of managers to be found anywhere in Europe. It is possible that all the managers in Ireland really are managing other people, perhaps arranged in a chain where each manages another manager. Or, more likely, many jobs and forms of work that would be labelled as 'technical or associate professional' elsewhere in Europe might be called 'management' in Ireland (and to a lesser extent in the United Kingdom). Different words carry different levels of stigma, rank and honour at different times and places in Europe.

MAP 6.054 – CLERICAL SUPPORT WORKERS

Source: European Union Statistics on Income and Living Conditions | Basemap: Population Cartogram

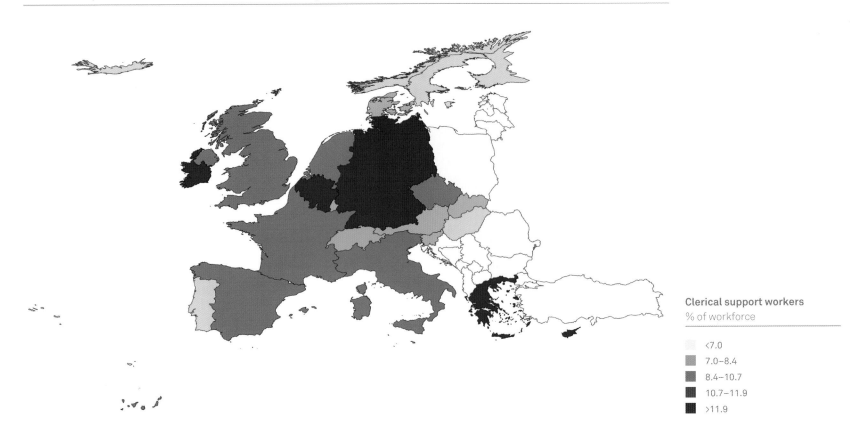

Clerical support workers
% of workforce

	<7.0
	7.0–8.4
	8.4–10.7
	10.7–11.9
	>11.9

The highest percentage of 'clerical support workers' is found in Germany (15.8%). The next highest are found in Belgium and Ireland. Greece and Cyprus also have relatively high numbers in this occupational group as a proportion of their total workforce. The smallest percentages are observed in eastern Europe, with Lithuania having the lowest figure (4.1%). Romania, Estonia, Bulgaria, Latvia and Poland all have rates below or equal to 7%. These are all former communist countries where industry has traditionally been dominant in the economy and therefore these types of jobs may have been less important.

Clerical jobs were once ranked among some of the highest paid occupations, at a time when bank clerks were very rare, few people could perform the arithmetic required well, and when mostly middle-class men did this work. The work then became more automated, and in many parts of Europe more women were employed in this sector. Clerical work became a lower ranking occupation which included secretaries – another activity that began as a very high-ranking occupation (as in 'secretary to the board'). Over time clerical work has changed in meaning, and it now has different meanings in different countries. The term can also be translated in various ways.

MAP 6.055 – SERVICE AND SALES WORKERS

Source: European Union Statistics on Income and Living Conditions | Basemap: Population Cartogram

Service and sales workers
% of workforce

	<13.9
	13.9–14.7
	14.7–17.5
	17.5–19.7
	>19.7

The highest percentages of 'service and sales workers' are observed in Norway, Sweden, Denmark, Iceland and Ireland where about a fifth of the workforce belong to this group. The smallest percentage is in Romania (11.5%), and Lithuania, Belgium and Estonia also have relatively small numbers as a proportion of their total economically active population. It is interesting to note that these are all former communist countries where service workers were not very numerous before the 1990s.

As the proportion of people working in sales has increased, this group is now often separated out from the general area of services. For example, in the United Kingdom about a tenth of the workforce are employed in retail sales out of the roughly 80% who are service workers. The majority of service workers in any country are not working in sales but are employed as child-minders, teaching support staff, carers, cleaners, social workers, dental health workers, hairdressers, academic support staff, researchers, housing managers, banking staff, insurance agents and the countless other service jobs that now employ the great majority of Europeans – who are now mostly paid to look after one another.

MAP 6.056 – SKILLED AGRICULTURAL, FORESTRY AND FISHERY WORKERS
Source: European Union Statistics on Income and Living Conditions | Basemap: Population Cartogram

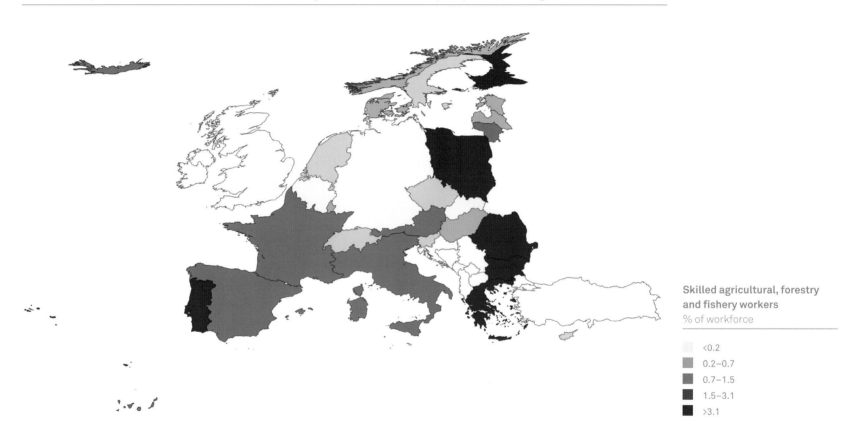

Skilled agricultural, forestry and fishery workers
% of workforce

- <0.2
- 0.2–0.7
- 0.7–1.5
- 1.5–3.1
- >3.1

Romania has the highest number of 'skilled agricultural, forestry and fishery workers' as a proportion of its total workforce (19.3%). There are also relatively high percentages in Greece (14.2%) and Poland (12.0%). In contrast, the smallest percentages are observed in the Republic of Ireland, the United Kingdom, Slovakia, Germany, Belgium, Malta and Slovenia (all below 2%).

Apart from the UK and Ireland, the map does show the influence of being located near the sea, with landlocked countries tending to have lower rates of employment in this sector – perhaps partly because fishing here is less common. Perhaps the larger size of farms and the higher degree of mechanisation in the north of Europe is also indicated. Alternatively, another possible explanation for the geographical variation may relate to the different rates of urbanisation across Europe. Again language plays a part: for centuries the most common occupation in Europe was 'peasant', and this may explain why the term 'skilled' is now applied to these occupational groups.

MAP 6.057 – CRAFT AND RELATED TRADES WORKERS

Source: European Union Statistics on Income and Living Conditions | Basemap: Population Cartogram

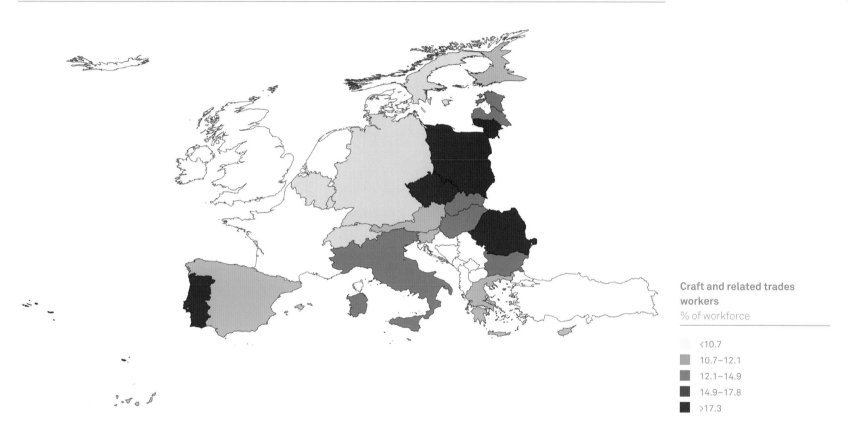

Craft and related trades
workers
% of workforce

<10.7
10.7–12.1
12.1–14.9
14.9–17.8
>17.3

The highest number of 'craft and related trades workers' as a proportion of the total economically active population is observed in Romania (20.2%), closely followed by Portugal (19.6%). The Czech Republic, Lithuania, Poland, Italy, Slovakia and Hungary all have relatively high percentages (all above 17%). On the

other hand, the smallest percentages (below 10%) are observed in the United Kingdom (8.9%) and Norway (9.9%).

Again there is a clear geographic pattern to be seen. Rates of employment in these occupations are higher the further east and south you travel in Europe. It is very likely that this

partly reflects nuances of language and tradition: occupations may be regarded as craft in one country and as manufacturing in another. For example, producing luxury goods may be considered as craft in Italy but as manufacturing in France. It is therefore hard to tell how much of this pattern

reflects differences in actual work performed, or how different types of work are described in different places.

MAP 6.058 – PLANT AND MACHINE OPERATORS AND ASSEMBLERS

Source: European Union Statistics on Income and Living Conditions | Basemap: Population Cartogram

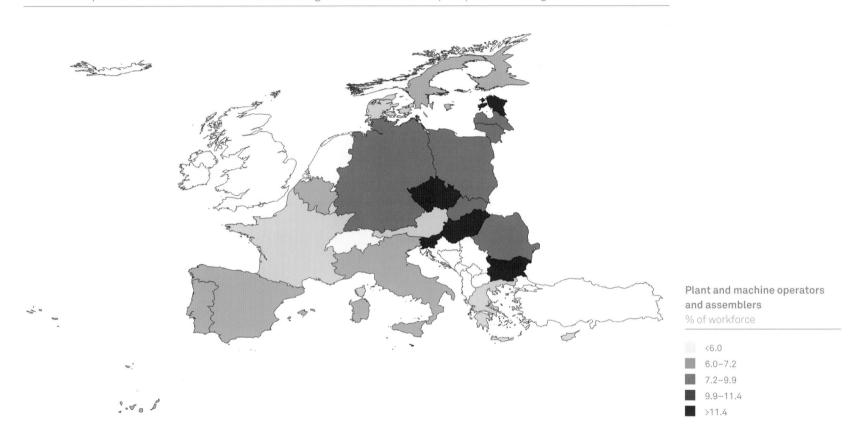

Plant and machine operators
and assemblers
% of workforce

<6.0
6.0–7.2
7.2–9.9
9.9–11.4
>11.4

The highest numbers of 'plant and machine operators and assemblers' as a proportion of the total economically active population are observed in Malta (13.8%), Hungary (13.4%), the Czech Republic (13.3%), Estonia (13.3%), Bulgaria (12.8%) and Slovenia (12.5%). In contrast, the lowest percentages

are seen in the Netherlands, Ireland and Switzerland, where 4.3% of the total workforce is in this category. The Republic of Ireland, Norway, the United Kingdom and Austria also have relatively low percentages.

Here the split is more East–West than North–South, a possible heritage from

the Cold War with Eastern European economies relying more on these kinds of jobs. This may better reflect actual work done rather than the same work being named differently in different places, as assembly-line work is harder to mistake. However, if the same amount of goods were produced by a series of

workers, each working alone, that might be described as craft work; while the very same goods made by people working each on a separate part of the manufacture would be called assembly work.

MAP 6.059 – ELEMENTARY OCCUPATIONS
Source: European Union Statistics on Income and Living Conditions | Basemap: Population Cartogram

Synonyms for 'elementary' tend to be highly derogatory, such as: 'easy, simple, straightforward, uncomplicated, undemanding, unexacting, effortless, painless, uninvolved, child's play, plain sailing; rudimentary, facile, simplistic; *informal* easy-peasy, no sweat, kids' stuff'.

Google, 2014b

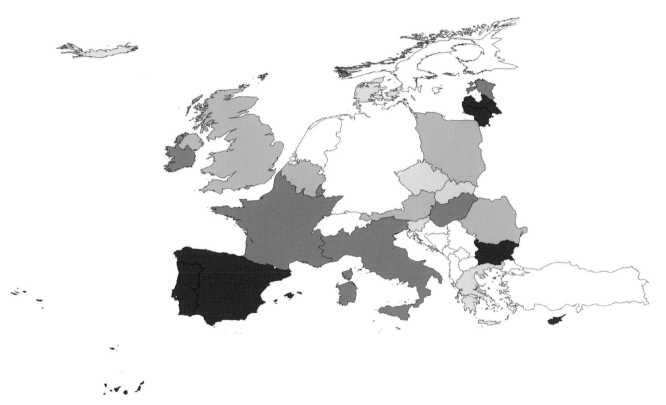

Elementary occupations
% of workforce

- <7.0
- 7.0–9.5
- 9.5–11.5
- 11.5–14.8
- >14.8

Cyprus has the largest number of individuals with occupations classified as 'elementary' as a proportion of its total economically active population (18.5%). Latvia, Bulgaria, Spain and Portugal also have relatively high percentages. In contrast, Norway has the lowest number as a proportion of its workforce

(3.9%), with the other Scandinavian countries, and the Netherlands and Germany, also all having relatively low percentages.

Often work that is quite skilled is labelled as 'elementary'. Caring for elderly people is a very difficult job which often requires tact but because

it is usually very poorly paid it is often characterised as 'elementary'. Again, however, there are clear patterns, with central northern Europe and the Scandinavian countries being least likely to label jobs in this way and/or to have people working in such jobs.

MAP 6.060 – SHARE OF AGRICULTURE IN THE ECONOMY, BY NUTS 2 REGIONS, 2010
Gross value added at basic prices (% of total value added)

Source: Eurostat Regional Yearbook | Basemap: Hennig Projection Gridded Population Cartogram

... value added generated by agriculture 2010 was EUR 145.3 billion [in the EU27], and this was 2.3 % lower than it had been in 2005 (down from EUR 148.7 billion); during this period value added was volatile, peaking at EUR 156.5 billion in 2007 and falling as low as EUR 131.3 billion in 2009. Agriculture's contribution to the value added of the whole economy fell from 1.5% in 2005 to 1.2% in 2009 before picking up to 1.3% in 2010.

European Commission, 2013d, p 150

Share of agriculture in the economy, gross value added at basic prices

% of total value added

	<0.2
	0.2–0.7
	0.7–1.5
	1.5–3.1
	>3.1

The darker shaded areas on this map had the greatest share of agriculture in their regional economy in 2010 when measured in terms of 'gross value added at basic prices'. This term is defined as the total value received by the producer plus any subsidy on the product and minus any tax on the product; it also includes the total value of goods and services consumed as inputs in the process of production (European Commission, 2013d). The region with the highest share of agriculture in the local economy is *Severen Tsentralen* (14.1%) in Bulgaria, closely followed by *Severozapaden* (12.2%, also in Bulgaria) and FYR Macedonia (10.8%), all located in countries that are amongst the least economically developed in Europe. On the other hand there are ten regions where the share of agriculture in the economy in terms of value added is 0%. Two of these urban regions are in Germany (*Berlin* and *Bremen*), four in the United Kingdom (*Greater Manchester*, *West Midlands*, *Inner London* and *Outer London*), three in Spain (*Comunidad de Madrid*, *Ciudad Autónoma de Ceuta* and *Ciudad Autónoma de Melilla*) and one in Austria (the capital city region of *Wien*). It is worth noting that agriculture is especially clustered around some capital cities, such as Madrid, Paris and Athens.

MAP 6.061 – EMPLOYMENT IN THE INDUSTRIAL ECONOMY, BY NUTS 2 REGIONS, 2010

% share of non-financial business economy

Source: Eurostat Regional Yearbook | Basemap: Hennig Projection Gridded Population Cartogram

According to estimates made using annual structural business statistics, there were approximately 21.8 million enterprises active in the EU-27's non-financial business economy in 2010. Together, they generated EUR 5,934 billion of gross value added and employed some 132.5 million persons.

European Commission, 2013d, p 106

Industrial economy
% share of the non-financial business economy

	<11.1
	11.1–20.2
	20.2–26.9
	26.9–34.3
	>34.3

This map, like the following three maps, is based on Eurostat's structural business statistics – measurements of the economy covering industry, construction and non-financial services, which together are known as the non-financial business economy. Other activities that are not included here (in addition to financial services) are agriculture, forestry and fishing; public administration; and public services (such as defence, education and health).

This map shows the geographical distribution of the relative importance of industry in terms of employment as a share of the total non-financial business economy. Most of the regions with relatively high shares of industrial employment are concentrated in central and eastern Europe. The top five regions are *Severovýchod* (47.0%) and *Střední Morava* (46.7%) in the Czech Republic (47.0%), *Vest* (46.7%) and *Sud-Muntenia* (45.2%) in Romania (46.7%), and *Severozapaden* (44.8%) in Bulgaria. The lowest regional shares are observed in *Ciudad Autónoma de Melilla* (1.7%), which is that part of northwest Africa that is assigned to Spain; *Inner London* (3.0%) in the United Kingdome; the Greek island regions of *Notio Aigaio* (4.1%) and *Ionia Nisia* (4.3%); and in Portugal's *Algarve* (7.3%). It is also interesting to note that the EU-27 average is 24.6%. Thus industry accounts for just a little under a quarter of all jobs, and a little under a fifth of all economic output when measured in terms of monetary value.

MAP 6.062 – EMPLOYMENT IN CONSTRUCTION, BY NUTS 2 REGIONS, 2010
% share of non-financial business economy
Source: Eurostat Regional Yearbook | Basemap: Hennig Projection Gridded Population Cartogram

Construction
% share of the non-financial
business economy

- <6.1
- 6.1–9.5
- 9.5–11.2
- 11.2–13.7
- >13.7

This map shows the relative importance of construction in terms of employment as a share of all employment in the non-financial business economy. It is useful to compare it with the previous map. The average percentage for the EU is 10.1%. The regions with the largest shares are mostly found in Spain, Portugal, France, southern Italy and Cyprus. The region with the highest share (24.5%) is *Corse* (Corsica) in France, followed by *Extremadura* (21.0%) in southeast Spain, the Portuguese island region *Região Autónoma dos Açores* (20.7%), and *Languedoc-Roussillon* (20.4%) in southeast France. In contrast, the lowest shares are observed in the German regions *Hamburg* (3.7%), *Bremen* (3.9%) and *Köln* (4%), in *Inner London* (3.8%) in the United Kingdom, and in the Republic of Ireland region *Border, Midland and Western* (4%).

Note that the date given for the collection of this data is 2010. Some of the activity indicated here may have begun before that date, so the map could be showing the pattern of employment in construction in the immediate aftermath of the 2008 financial crash. In other words, what is shown here may reflect the work being done on building projects that were still ongoing, having been financed before the crash but completed after it. The map for this category is likely to look quite different in a few years' time.

MAP 6.063 – EMPLOYMENT IN THE NON-FINANCIAL SERVICES ECONOMY, BY NUTS 2 REGIONS, 2010

% share of non-financial business economy

Source: Eurostat Regional Yearbook | Basemap: Hennig Projection Gridded Population Cartogram

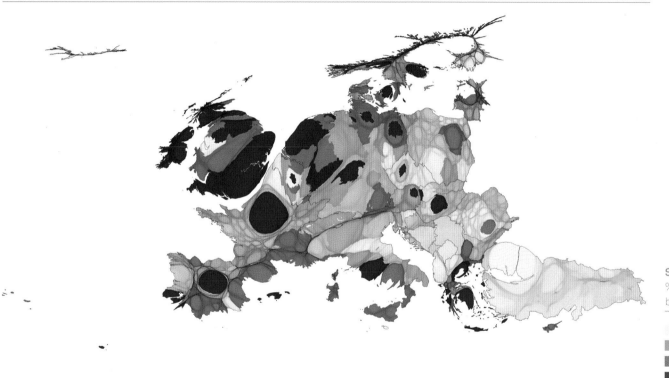

Services in non-financial sector
% share of the non-financial
business economy

	<47.1
	47.1–56.6
	56.6–62.5
	62.5–71.5
	>71.5

This map shows the share of employment in the non-financial services economy as a percentage of all employment in the non-financial business economy (see the two previous maps). The largest percentages are generally observed in larger city regions all across Europe, but with higher concentrations of activity towards the north and west.

The highest percentage is observed in *Inner London* in the United Kingdom (a massive 93.2%), followed by the Greek island regions *Notio Aigaio* (85.8%) and *Ionia Nisia* (85.2%), by *Outer London* (84.5%) and then by the Belgian capital city region *Région de Bruxelles-Capitale/Brussels Hoofdstedelijk Gewest* (83.8%). The smallest percentage is observed in the

Czech Republic region *Střední Morava*. The EU average is 65.2%.

It should be noted that this sector may represent an even higher proportion of economic output because of the way in which standard accounting is carried out. Because the salaries of workers in service industries tend to be higher on average than those of people working in agriculture

or in industry, services are, it is claimed, more productive. It is also worth noting that there is an extremely wide level of variation in salaries within the service sector, but the highest-paid people are not necessarily really the most productive when compared with the lowest-paid (who may empty their bins).

MAP 6.064 – REGIONAL BUSINESS CONCENTRATION, BY NUTS 2 REGIONS, 2010
Source: Eurostat Regional Yearbook | Basemap: Hennig Projection Gridded Population Cartogram

Business concentration
%, cumulative share of the five
largest activities in regional
non-financial business
economy employment

	<34.3
	34.3–40.1
	40.1–42.9
	42.9–46.2
	>46.2

This map depicts the geographical distribution of a measure of concentration of business activity across the EU. The indicator mapped here is the cumulative share of the five largest activities in the non-financial business economy workforce. According to the *Eurostat Regional Yearbook 2013* (European Commission, 2013d), it provides an indication of '*the extent to which a region is dependent on a small number of large activities, or, alternatively, whether it displays the characteristics of being more diversified*'. It is noted that:

High levels of employment concentration tend to be recorded in those regions where construction, distributive trades or other services dominate the non-financial business economy, as the distribution of industrial activities tends to be more fragmented. The most concentrated regions were generally those traditionally associated with tourism, in particular specific regions in Greece, Spain, France, Italy and Portugal, underlining the importance of construction, trade, transport, and accommodation and food service activities in tourism-oriented regions ...
By contrast, the lowest concentrations were mainly recorded in regions with a relatively small services sector and a relatively large manufacturing activity; this was often the case in Eastern Europe, in particular in the Czech Republic, Estonia, Hungary, Slovenia and Romania, but also in several regions in Germany, Italy, Finland and Sweden.

7

HEALTH

MAP 7.065 – FEMALE LIFE EXPECTANCY AT BIRTH, 2007
Source: European Commission | Basemap: Hennig Projection Gridded Population Cartogram

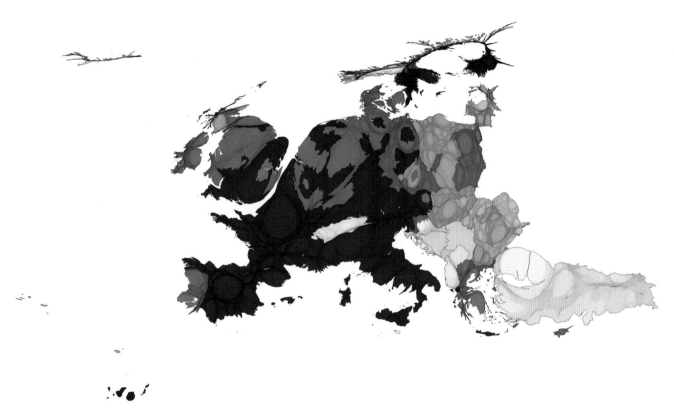

The EU has an enviably high life expectancy. In 2007, life expectancy at birth stood at 79 years in the EU compared to an average global expectancy of only 67 (UN). Outside Europe, only 6 countries in the world (Japan, Australia, Israel, Canada, New Zealand and Singapore) have a higher life expectancy.

European Commission, 2010, p 73

Female life expectancy at birth, 2007

	<75
	75–77
	77–80
	80–82.5
	>82.5

It is worth noting that the United States of America does not feature in the list in the quote above. This map and the next show the life expectancy at birth for females and males by region. The northeast Spanish region *Comunidad Foral de Navarra* has the highest female life expectancy at birth (86 years), followed by the French regions *Rhône-Alpes* (85.9),

Poitou-Charentes (85.8) and *Île de France* (85.8), and the Italian region *Marche* (85.7). On the other hand, the Bulgarian region *Yugoiztochen* has the lowest female life expectancy at birth (75.8). Other regions at the bottom end of the range include Bulgaria's *Severozapaden* (76.1) and *Severoiztochen* (76.3), and Romanian regions *Nord-Vest* (76.1) and *Vest* (76.3).

Women appear to live longer in southern Europe than women in the north. However, this pattern will be influenced by the migration of many elderly people across international borders and towards the sunshine of the south.

The highest male life expectancy at birth is found in the Italian regions *Marche* (80.1) and *Provincia Autonoma*

Bolzano/Bozen (79.8), followed by the UK regions *Dorset and Somerset* (79.7) and *Berkshire, Buckinghamshire and Oxfordshire* (79.7), and Italy's *Umbria* (79.6) and *Toscana* (79.6). The lowest life expectancy values are observed in the Baltic countries (mapped here as single NUTS 2 regions) *Lithuania* (64.8), *Latvia* (65.8) and *Estonia* (67.2), and also in the Hungarian regions ▶

MAP 7.066 – MALE LIFE EXPECTANCY AT BIRTH, 2007

Source: European Commission | Basemap: Hennig Projection Gridded Population Cartogram

Male life expectancy at birth, 2007

- <75
- 75–77
- 77–80
- 80–82.5
- >82.5

Észak-Magyarország (67.4) and *Észak-Alföld* (68.4). Men appear to live longer in Western Europe than those in the East. Again migration since birth clearly plays a part – not just the migration of men who tend to do better in life further West, but also possibly the much higher migration rates of young women from the East, leaving more men behind.

The health of men without female partners tends to be worse (but the reverse does not, in general, apply).

MAP 7.067 – MATERNAL MORTALITY RATIO

Source: Global Health Observatory, World Health Organisation | Basemap: Population Cartogram

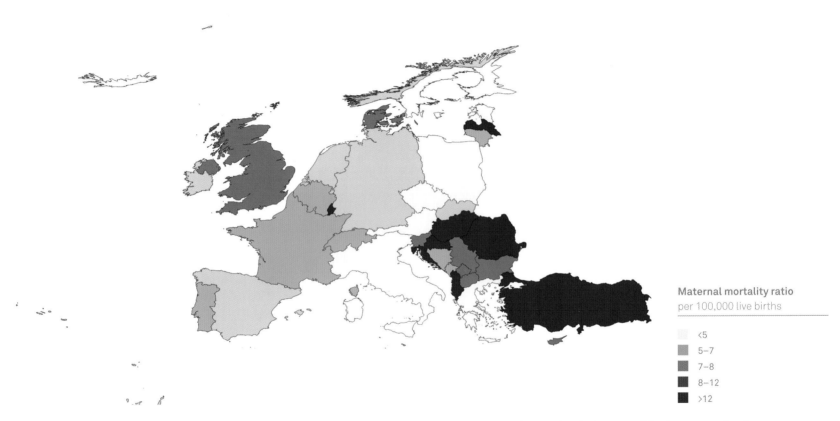

Maternal mortality ratio
per 100,000 live births

- <5
- 5–7
- 7–8
- 8–12
- >12

Latvia has the highest maternal mortality ratio (34 per 100,000 live births) in Europe, followed by Albania and Romania (27), Hungary (21), Luxembourg and Turkey (20). The lowest ratios are in Estonia (2), Greece (3), Austria (4), Sweden (4) and Italy (4). All these rates are still far too high, as almost all maternal mortality – the death of a woman while pregnant (especially when giving birth) – is preventable. Worldwide maternal mortality is one of the most significant premature killers of women. In Europe it used to be the most common cause of death in young adulthood for women but it is now extremely rare. Variations in the map almost entirely reflect variations in treatment and health services. Interestingly, it is a band of countries in the southeast and middle of Europe, reaching up from Greece and Italy through to Finland and including many countries of the former Eastern bloc, that have the lowest rates. The rates of childbirth in some of these countries are very low, so as fewer women tend to be pregnant, that will reduce the number of deaths associated with pregnancy and childbirth. There is also a tradition of providing good health services for women in Eastern Europe, where women's health was prioritised earlier than in the West.

MAP 7.068 – AGE-STANDARDISED MORTALITY RATE (AGES 30–70) – ALL CAUSES

Source: Global Health Observatory, World Health Organisation | Basemap: Population Cartogram

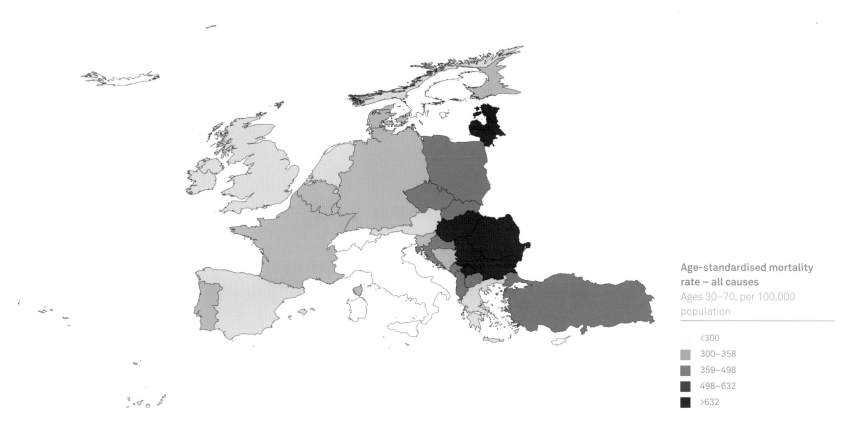

Age-standardised mortality rate – all causes

Ages 30–70, per 100,000 population

	<300
	300–358
	359–498
	498–632
	>632

This map shows a population cartogram of Europe (each country is drawn in proportion to the size of its total population) but shaded accordingly to show the geographical variation of the age-standardised mortality rate for all causes of death.

The age-standardised mortality rate is the ratio of the number of observed deaths in a study group to the number of expected deaths in a population. Lithuania has the highest rate (908 per 100,000, almost 1% dying a year before age 70) while Latvia, Hungary, Estonia, Romania, Bulgaria and Serbia all have rates over 650. In contrast, the lowest mortality rate is in San Marino (223), and the following countries have rates below 300: Cyprus, Iceland, Switzerland, Liechtenstein, Italy and Sweden.

The map partly reveals the old underlying East–West division within the continent. Mortality rates often reflect conditions of the past, and poverty rates rose rapidly in much of Eastern Europe after 1989. Mortality rates in Russia rose in absolute terms in the 1990s, and also in the countries of the former Yugoslavia during the same decade. The data shown here relates to deaths that occurred in 2008, less than a decade after the end of the conflict in the latter region. War, the disintegration of society and economic turmoil continue to have effects on overall population health outcomes for many years and decades after the initial events.

MAP 7.069 – CARDIOVASCULAR DISEASE AND DIABETES
Age-standardised mortality rate by cause (ages 30–70)
Source: Global Health Observatory, World Health Organisation | Basemap: Population Cartogram

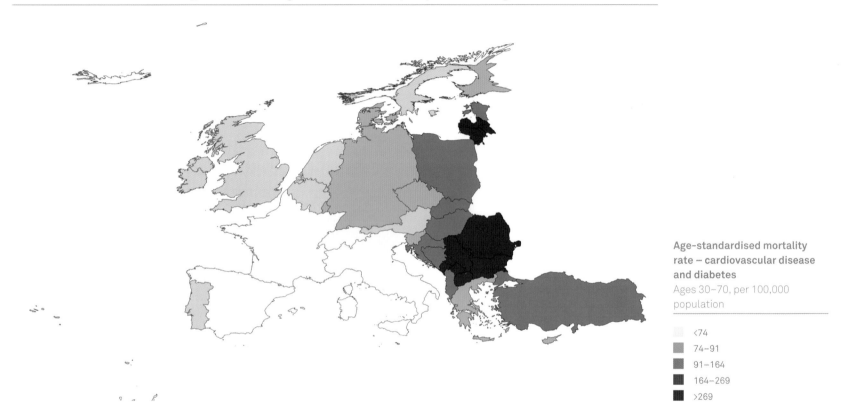

Age-standardised mortality rate – cardiovascular disease and diabetes
Ages 30–70, per 100,000 population

- <74
- 74–91
- 91–164
- 164–269
- >269

The highest age-standardised mortality rate (ages 30–70) for deaths from cardiovascular disease and diabetes is in Latvia (359), followed by Bulgaria (339), Lithuania (312), Montenegro (296), FYR Macedonia (284), Romania (280), Serbia (274) and Estonia (269). Switzerland has the lowest rate (59),

while Italy, France and Spain also have relatively low rates.

Again there is a clear East–West distinction in mortality from these causes. And again factors such as higher rates of smoking and air pollution towards the East, and also war and the turmoil that followed the fall of the Berlin Wall in 1989 have an effect.

However, other geographical patterns are also evident here. Rates of mortality are much lower in southwestern Europe, other than in Portugal. Iceland and Norway also report very low rates. Issues such as diet and exercise influence the patterns seen here, as well as the quality and availability of health services and an overall understanding of what most

damages human health. Rates of obesity are higher in some countries, such as the United Kingdom, which also influences the overall shading of this map.

MAP 7.070 – CHRONIC RESPIRATORY CONDITIONS
Age-standardised mortality rate by cause (ages 30–70)
Source: Global Health Observatory, World Health Organisation | Basemap: Population Cartogram

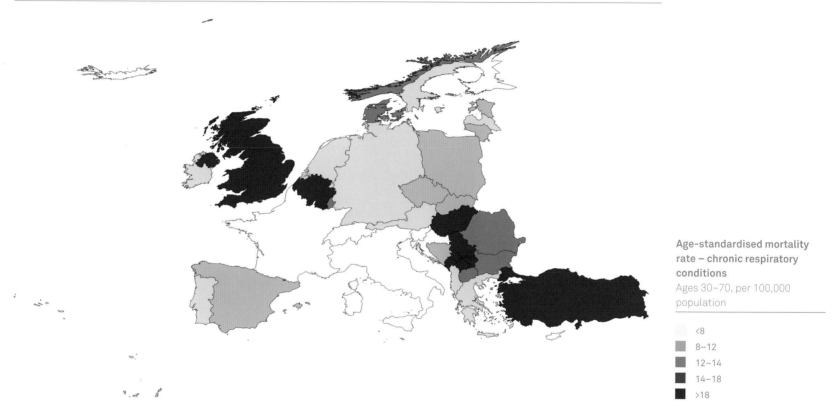

Age-standardised mortality
rate – chronic respiratory
conditions
Ages 30–70, per 100,000
population

- <8
- 8–12
- 12–14
- 14–18
- >18

Turkey has the highest age-standardised mortality rate for deaths from chronic respiratory conditions (30 per 100,000), closely followed by Hungary (29), while Montenegro, the United Kingdom, Serbia and Belgium also have relatively high rates. The lowest rates are in San Marino, Italy, France, Monaco, Finland and Cyprus.

This map shows a more complex pattern to a cause of mortality compared with the maps of more common diseases (eg see Map 7.069). There are differences in diagnosis and death certification between countries, and this factor can have an effect on some of the patterns seen here. For example, if doctors are taught to state the cause of death as

'chronic respiratory condition' whenever a respiratory disease is evident, then the reported death rate from this cause will be elevated – and consequently reduced for other possible causes that might have been suggested as the cause of the premature mortality. Aside from this potential variation in diagnosis, it is worth noting that susceptibility to this

disease is thought to be higher in areas where there is heavy air pollution caused by vehicles, which may explain part of the pattern seen in this map.

MAP 7.071 – CANCER
Age-standardised mortality rate by cause (ages 30–70)
Source: Global Health Observatory, World Health Organisation | Basemap: Population Cartogram

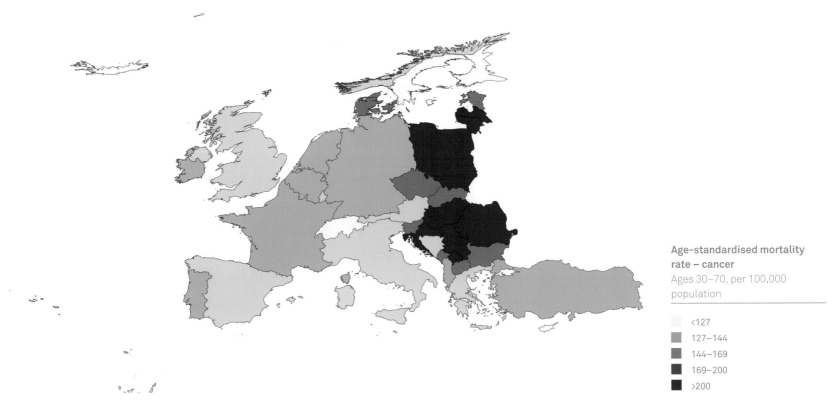

Age-standardised mortality rate – cancer
Ages 30–70, per 100,000 population

- <127
- 127–144
- 144–169
- 169–200
- >200

Hungary has the highest age-standardised mortality rate per 100,000 for deaths from cancer (262). Serbia, Poland, Lithuania, Croatia, Latvia, Romania and Slovakia also have relatively high rates (all above 200). At the other end of the scale, Cyprus has the smallest rate (75). Factors such as smoking rates in the past are important in predicting current rates of some cancer deaths, but there are many other environmental precursors to cancer, including overall air pollution and the presence of other toxins. Also important are factors related to how cancers are diagnosed and treated. Those areas with the worst rates of mortality from cancer recorded in 2008 will also have had some of the worst rates of early diagnosis and treatment in the 20 years prior to deaths attributable to cancers. Health services in the former Yugoslavian countries were clearly disrupted by war. In general terms, economic and social events in Eastern Europe over the two decades prior to 2008 will have had damaging effects; for example, many skilled medical staff migrated westwards. High rates of air pollution from industry in the East will also have elevated mortality from cancers, although pollution has diminished considerably as industries have closed down.

MAP 7.072 – DEATHS DUE TO CANCER
Age-standardised mortality rate per 100,000 inhabitants, three years average (2008–10)
Source: Eurostat | Basemap: Hennig Projection Gridded Population Cartogram

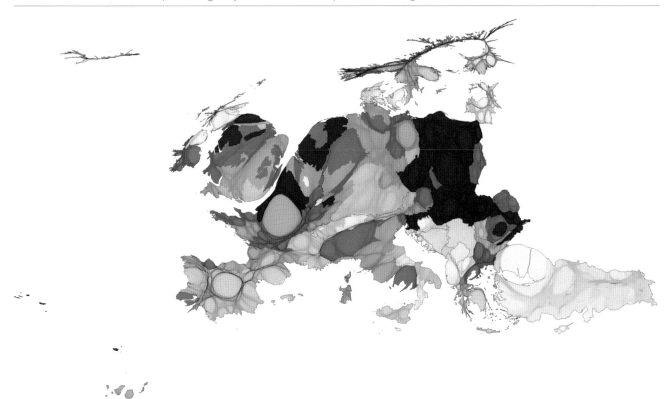

Deaths from cancer 2008–10
Age-standardised death rate
per 100,000

<137.2
137.2–155.2
155.2–164.3
164.3–181.7
>181.7

This and the next two maps shown here highlight the regional patterns of age-standardised mortality rates from cancer. The first map shows the geographical distribution of mortality from all cancers across Europe. The highest rates are observed in Hungary, in particular in the regions *Észak-Alföld* (253.6 deaths per 100,000 people),

Dél-Dunántúl (249.8), *Közép-Dunántúl* (243.8), *Észak-Magyarország* (243.4) and *Dél-Alföld* (235.5). At the other end of the range, the lowest rate is observed in the Belgian capital city region *Région de Bruxelles-Capitale / Brussels Hoofdstedelijk Gewest* (114.8), followed by Spain's *Ciudad Autónoma de Ceuta* (120.3), the Greek island region *Ionia Nisia* (125), *Itä-Suomi* in

eastern Finland (126.2), and *Ipeiros* (130.3) in western Greece. Different regional and historical patterns of smoking and industrial pollution will have played a part in creating the patterns seen here.

MAP 7.073 – DEATHS DUE TO BREAST CANCER
Age-standardised death rate per 100,000 inhabitants, three years average (2008–10)
Source: European Commission | Basemap: Hennig Projection Gridded Population Cartogram

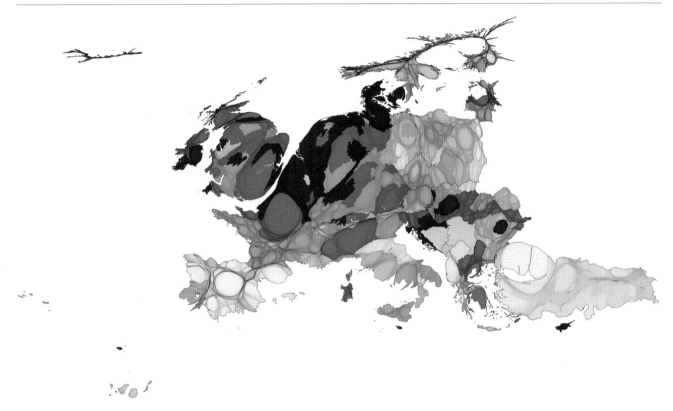

**Deaths from breast cancer
2008–10**
Age-standardised death rate
per 100,000 women

- <18.4
- 18.4–21.5
- 21.5–24.2
- 24.2–26.1
- >26.1

The highest female breast cancer death rate is observed in the Romanian capital city region of *Bucureşti-Ilfov* (33.2 deaths per 100,000 women), followed by Cyprus (32.6), the Portuguese island region *Região Autónoma da Madeira* (31.8), the Dutch region *Friesland* (31) and the Belgian region *Prov. Oost-Vlaanderen* (30.8). The lowest rates are observed in the Italian regions *Marche* (13.3) and *Emilia-Romagna* (13.6), the Spanish regions *Comunidad Foral de Navarra* (14.2) and *Castilla-La Mancha* (15.8), and in the region *Ipeiros* (14.8) in northwest Greece. Breast cancer mortality has become increasingly susceptible to improved medical interventions over recent years and so part of the pattern shown here may be the result of treatment being better in some areas than others. However, the patterns will also reflect a greater incidence of the disease in particular regions of Europe than in others.

MAP 7.074 – DEATHS DUE TO PROSTATE CANCER
Age-standardised mortality rate per 100,000 inhabitants, three years average (2008–10)
Source: European Commission | Basemap: Hennig Projection Gridded Population Cartogram

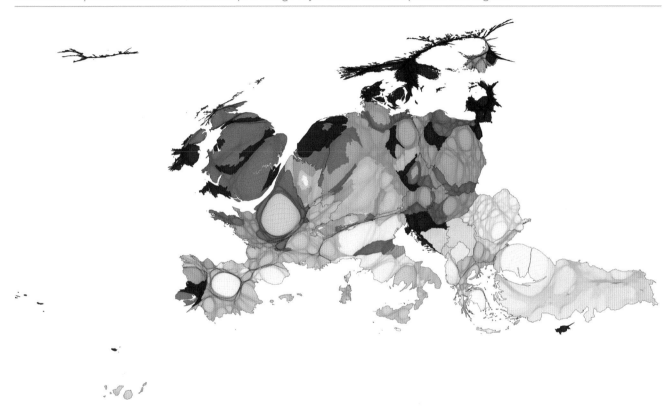

**Deaths from prostate cancer
2008–10**
Age-standardised death rate per
100,000 men

	<15.6
	15.6–19.4
	19.4–21.6
	21.6–24.7
	>24.7

The highest male prostate cancer death rate is observed in the Finnish island region of *Åland* (47.6 deaths per 100,000 men), followed by *Agder og Rogaland* (37.9) in Norway, *Estonia* (37.6), *Mellersta Norrland* (37.3) in Sweden, and the Portuguese island region *Região Autónoma dos Açores* (35.9). The lowest rates are observed in the Romanian regions *Sud-Vest Oltenia* (9.3) and *Sud-Muntenia* (10.6), the Greek regions *Ipeiros* (11.2) and *Ionia Nisia* (12.1), and Spain's *Ciudad Autónoma de Melilla* (12). Death rates from prostate cancer are often higher in areas where people tend to live longer. Very many men develop prostate cancer in old age. To die of that condition requires not dying of something else first. Prostate cancer is also often treatable, especially if it is detected early enough, so again this map may partly represent variations in both treatment and surveillance programmes.

MAP 7.075 – NUMBER OF DOCTORS
Source: The Guardian Data Blog (Rogers, 2012), citing the World Health Organisation, 2010

How can we prioritize the health needs of those that need health care the most? The answer is by going beyond needs and ensuring the *right to health* to everyone on this planet.

Beracochea et al, 2011, p 4 (emphasis in original)

This map shows the spatial distribution of doctors across Europe by making the area of each country proportional to the number of doctors working in that country. There is an estimated total of 1,872,959 doctors in Europe. About 300,000 of them work and live in Germany, which has the highest absolute number, followed by France, Italy, Spain and the United Kingdom. However, in relative terms the highest number is observed in San Marino (473 per 10,000 population) followed by Greece (61.67 per 10,000) and Monaco (58.1). Albania has the lowest number in relative terms (11.53 per 10,000 people).

Within any one country, access to doctors will vary. In some countries doctors are relatively evenly spread across the population, available roughly equally to all potential patients; or doctors may be more concentrated in places where more people tend to be ill. In other countries doctors are concentrated in the more affluent areas, so more wealthy people will have easier access to a doctor. Mortality rates would be expected to be higher in countries where access to health services is harder to secure and where there are fewer services – that is, where there are fewer doctors to access in the first place.

MAP 7.076 – NUMBER OF PRACTISING PHYSICIANS (PER 100,000 INHABITANTS) BY NUTS 2 REGIONS

Source: Eurostat Regional Yearbook 2013 | Basemap: Hennig Projection Gridded Population Cartogram

Healthcare personnel
– number of practising
physicians
per 100,000 inhabitants

	<229
	229–292
	292–345
	345–395
	>395

This map shows the number of practising physicians measured as a proportion of all the people in each region. The five regions best served by physicians are the Spanish territory *Ciudad Autónoma de Ceuta* in north Africa (941 physicians per 100,000 inhabitants), followed by the capital city regions of Greece (*Attiki* 829),

Austria (*Wien* 664), the Czech Republic (*Praha* 657) and the Slovak Republic (*Bratislavský Kraj* 643). In contrast, the five regions least well served are all in Turkey: *Ağrı, Kars, Iğdır, Ardahan* (100 physicians per 100,000 inhabitants), *Mardin, Batman, Şırnak, Siirt* (103), *Hatay, Kahramanmaraş, Osmaniye* (115) and *Gaziantep, Adıyaman, Kilis* (119).

It is worth noting that the number of physicians working in the United Kingdom – a richer country than many other parts of Europe – is very low when measured per person, especially in England outside of London. While not as low as in Turkey, or in other parts of Eastern Europe, the low numbers in the UK contrast with better provision in

neighbouring countries. However, one reason for a low number of physicians in a country or region may be that more nurses and (in particular) midwives are employed in some countries to take on more specialised aspects of the work, so freeing up the time of physicians (see also the next map, 7.077).

MAP 7.077 – NURSING AND MIDWIFERY PERSONNEL
Source: World Health Organisation

Constant attention by a good nurse may be just as important as a major operation by a surgeon.

Dag Hammarskjöld, Swedish diplomat, the second UN Secretary-General (1953–61) and Nobel Peace Prize recipient (Wikiquote, 2014)

There is an estimated total of 3,497,399 nurses and midwives working across Europe. Germany has the largest number (nearly a third of the total), followed by the United Kingdom and Spain. In relative terms, Norway has the highest ratio of nurses and midwives per 10,000 population (319.32), followed by Finland (239.56) and Switzerland (164.56). Some smaller countries have a large number of doctors and fewer nurses, and in some countries doctors are employed more often than midwives to help deliver babies. However, these factors alone do not explain the huge variation shown in this map.

Other factors that may explain why there are more nurses and midwives in some northern European countries than in many southern European countries include: income and wealth; the presence of an older population in need of more care; the traditional model of providing care, whether that is in hospitals or more community-based, and how that is changing; and how primary health care is provided (for example the extent to which nurses are based in local health centres). All these factors can change over time and also vary dramatically across Europe.

MAP 7.078 – DENTISTRY PERSONNEL
Source: World Health Organisation

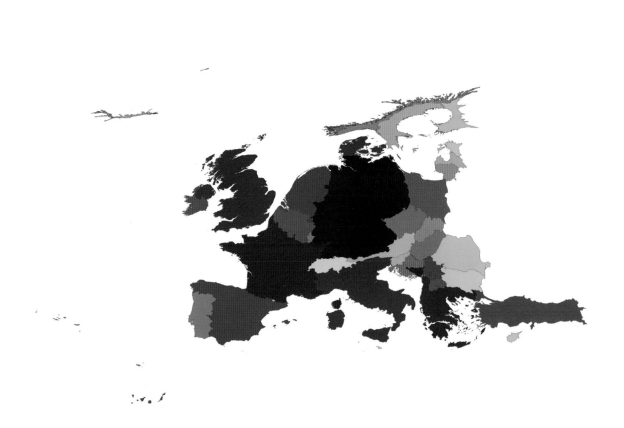

According to data from the World Health Organisation, there is a total of 351,545 dentistry personnel working in Europe, most of them dentists. This map shows how they are geographically distributed across the continent. Dentists are distributed in a pattern that is more evenly arranged across the distribution of their potential patients than for nurses and midwives, but the spread is less even across the continent than for doctors. The highest absolute number of dentists is found in Germany, followed by France, the United Kingdom, Italy and Spain. In relative terms, however, the highest number is in Greece, with 13.2 dentistry personnel per 10,000 population, followed by Iceland (10.2) and Cyprus (9.18). On the other hand, the lowest ratio per 10,000 population is in Montenegro (0.58).

Different countries have different traditions for prioritising different aspects of health care, and this map largely reflects those historical factors. Again, within any country provision may not be even: some people, especially more wealthy people, may find it easier to gain access to dentists than others. In such countries many dentists may be working more on cosmetic treatments than to relieve pain. However, where there is a saturation of dentists, such as in Greece, one would hope that the generally very high level of availability means that fewer people suffer from a lack of access. In Montenegro, on the other hand, one would expect the few dentists there to concentrate mostly on emergency cases.

MAP 7.079 – PHARMACEUTICAL PERSONNEL
Source: World Health Organisation

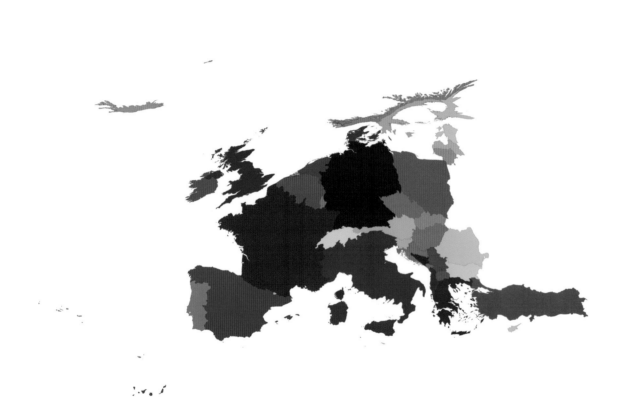

Among at least the longer standing
EU Member States, there is a common
model or approach to health care
provision based on social solidarity
and universal coverage.
Mossialos et al. 2010, p 12

There are an estimated 374,477 people working
as pharmaceutical personnel across Europe.
The country with the largest number is France,
followed by Italy and Germany. In relative
terms, Iceland has the highest number in
relation to its population (19.38 per 10,000
population), followed by France (11.91), Belgium
(11.88), Andorra (11.47) and Ireland (10.33).
In contrast, Bosnia and Herzegovina has the
lowest ratio (0.93).

It is useful to compare this map showing
the distribution of pharmacists with Map
7.077 showing the distribution of nurses, and
considering whether in countries such as
France and Italy, where the number of nurses is
very low, pharmacists might not partly replace
them. Pharmacists can help families to access
medicines to treat themselves rather than be
treated by a nurse. For the larger European
countries (other than France and Spain) the
number of pharmacists per head is very low.
As with most other ways of categorising people
in this atlas, different definitions may apply in
different countries. The qualifications required
to be a pharmacist are not standardised across
Europe, especially among older practitioners.

MAP 7.080 – HOSPITAL BEDS, BY NUTS 2 REGIONS, 2010 (PER 100,000 INHABITANTS)
Source: Eurostat Regional Yearbook 2013 | Basemap: Hennig Projection Gridded Population Cartogram

Hospital beds
per 100,000 inhabitants

- <315
- 315–459
- 459–603
- 603–745
- >754

This map uses data available for the most recent year (mostly 2010, but in some cases going as far back as 2002) and at more general levels. England is mapped here as a single region because detailed statistical data was unavailable.

Most regions in central Europe (and all regions in Germany) have more than 600 beds per 100,000 inhabitants – well above the average figure for the whole of the EU, which is 538 hospital beds per 100,000 inhabitants. Also, there is a general urban/rural divide which could be explained to some extent by the presence of specialised hospitals in the big cities. The region with the largest number of hospital beds in relation to population size is *Mecklenburg-Vorpommern* in Germany (1,265 per 100,000 people), followed by the Polish region of *Zachodniopomorskie* (1,194), the Romanian capital city region of *Bucureşti-Ilfov* (990) and the German regions *Thüringen* (985) and *Schleswig-Holstein* (945). The bottom five regions comprise *Ağrı, Kars, Iğdır, Ardahan* (131 hospital beds per 100,000 people) and *Mardin, Batman,* *Şırnak, Siirt* (132), all in Turkey; *Flevoland* in the Netherlands (164 beds, but note that this is using data from 2002); and *Hatay, Kahramanmaraş, Osmaniye* (172) and *Şanlıurfa, Diyarbakır* (182), again all in Turkey.

MAP 7.081 – PREVALENCE OF HIV AMONG ADULTS AGED 15–49
Source: World Health Organisation

The vision for the European Region is zero new HIV infections, zero AIDS-related deaths and zero discrimination in a world in which people living with HIV are able to live long, healthy lives.

WHO Regional Office for Europe, 2014a

Using the latest data (2011) from the World Health Organisation on HIV prevalence and applying it to the respective total population figures, the number of adults aged 15–49 in Europe with HIV is estimated to be around 374,973 (with a wide margin of error). The map shows how this number is distributed geographically. France has the largest number, followed by Italy and the United Kingdom. In relative terms, however, the largest percentage of adults aged 15–49 with HIV is in Estonia (1.3%), followed by Portugal and Latvia (0.7%).

This is not just a map of the number of people with HIV; it also shows how good medical services have become at keeping people alive who contract this virus. In the 1980s and early 1990s most people who acquired HIV in Europe died. Now most survive past age 49, and where services became better earlier, the number of younger survivors, included in this map, will be higher. Thus this is a map not just of people contracting the virus but also of people being treated for it and surviving to be counted.

MAP 7.082 – ALCOHOL CONSUMPTION AMONG ADULTS AGED OVER 15 YEARS
Source: World Health Organisation

Alcohol intake in the WHO European Region is the highest in the world. Harmful use of alcohol is related to premature death and avoidable disease and is a major avoidable risk factor for neuropsychiatric disorders, cardiovascular diseases, cirrhosis of the liver and cancer.

WHO Regional Office for Europe, 2014b

This map shows the distribution of alcohol consumption across Europe. Germany has the highest absolute consumption, followed by France, the United Kingdom and Italy. In relative terms the country with the highest consumption is Estonia, with 16.24 litres of pure alcohol per person aged 15 and over consumed per year. Estonia is followed by the Czech Republic (14.82), Ireland (13.35) and France (13.24). In contrast, Turkey has the smallest consumption in relative terms (1.35 litres per person aged 15 and over).

Alcohol consumption is becoming a more important precursor of illness in later life as other causes of premature mortality are diminishing in importance across Europe. As people smoke less and as the old infectious diseases are reduced, the harm that alcohol causes to people in Europe, especially to young people, becomes more evident. This is an issue across the whole of the continent, although currently it is least problematic in the south and east and a much greater problem in northern Europe.

8

POLITICS

MAP 8.083 – DEMOCRACY: IS IT THE BEST POLITICAL SYSTEM?
Distribution of Europeans 'disagreeing strongly' that democracy is the best political system
Source: European Values Survey, 2008

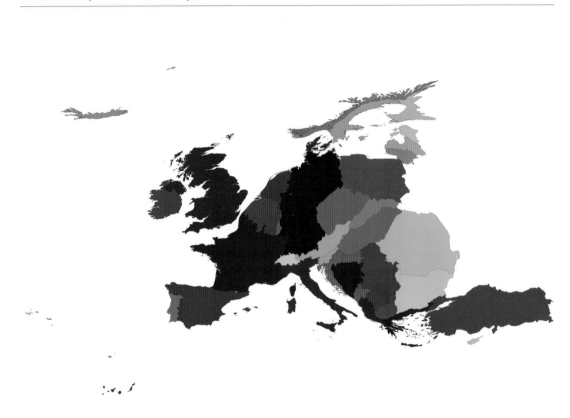

> The spirit of democracy is not a mechanical thing to be adjusted by abolition of forms. It requires change of the heart.

Mahatma Gandhi (Bombay Sarvodaya Mandal/Gandhi Book Centre, 2014)

Preserving democratic governance and human rights is considered to be one of the key contemporary values of Europe. It is also one of the key 'Copenhagen criteria' that needs to be met before any country can be considered as a potential member of the European Union.

According to the 2008 European Values Survey, only a very small fraction of Europeans said they 'disagreed strongly' when asked if democracy is the best political system. This map shows their geographical distribution. Kosovo has the largest percentage of population strongly disagreeing with this statement. However, the value for Kosovo is only 4.5%, followed by Bulgaria (3.1%).

People disagreeing strongly with the statement that democracy is the best political system may, of course, believe that there is a better system that no one has invented yet, and that what many countries currently have is not the best there could ever be. Alternatively they may think that what is called a democratic system is, in fact, easily manipulated by a few 'special interests' with access to money, the media and politicians. This group may also include people who can remember, or have been told stories about, less democratic times in their own country when they thought the area was better run than it is today. It is notable that in Italy and Greece in 2008, very few people were strongly opposed to democracy.

DEMOCRACY: IS IT THE BEST POLITICAL SYSTEM?

1%

43%   49%   7%

STRONGLY AGREE   STRONGLY DISAGREE

MAP 8.084 – ARMY RULE: IS IT A GOOD POLITICAL SYSTEM?
Distribution of Europeans agreeing that army rule is a very good political system
Source: European Values Survey, 2008

ARMY RULE: IS IT A GOOD POLITICAL SYSTEM?

2%
8%
25%
65%

VERY GOOD

VERY BAD

At 57, the thrice-married mother-of-three has long been a ubiquitous presence on the political landscape of Greece, a defining figure who began as the iconic 'voice of the Polytechnic' during the 1973 students' revolt against the military dictatorship ... Damanaki, who would spend seven months in prison after the regime crushed the rebellion, still bears the scars of that time. Memories of days spent in solitary confinement in a darkened cell at Athens's notorious military police headquarters return to haunt her.

Smith, 2010, on Maria Damanaki, European Commissioner for Maritime Affairs and Fisheries

According to the 2008 European Values Survey, an estimated 2% of all respondents believe that the army ruling the country would be a very good political system. This map shows their geographical distribution. Nearly half of these are in Turkey, where 10.5% of the respondents agreed with this statement. Turkey also has the highest figure in relative terms, closely followed by Kosovo (10.2%) and Serbia (9.7%).

Again it is worth thinking about what people might be thinking when they express such attitudes. They may be saying that given all the other alternatives they can think of working practically where they live, they believe that having the army in charge is the safest option, and for them safest means a 'very good' political system. In various parts of Europe in recent decades the army has been in charge, either officially or unofficially. These include areas that have had a recent war or war-like situation, as in Northern Ireland and Turkey.

MAP 8.085 – HOW INTERESTED ARE YOU IN POLITICS?
Distribution of Europeans who are 'not at all interested' in politics
Source: European Values Survey, 2008

You don't have to listen to my political point of view. But it's not that I'm not voting out of apathy. I'm not voting out of absolute indifference and weariness and exhaustion from the lies, treachery, deceit of the political class that has been going on for generations now and which has now reached fever pitch where you have a disenfranchised, disillusioned, despondent underclass that are not being represented by that political system, so voting for it is tacit complicity with that system and that's not something I'm offering up.

Russell Brand, interviewed by Jeremy Paxman, 27 October 2013 (Corrente, 2013)

According to the latest data (2008) from the European Values Survey, some 23% of all Europeans said they were 'not at all interested' when asked how interested they were in politics. This map shows how these apparently politically disaffected Europeans are geographically distributed. The country with the highest absolute number is Turkey, followed by the United Kingdom, Spain and Italy. However, in relative terms the highest estimated share of the population who are 'not at all interested in politics' as a proportion of all people aged 15 and over is found in Albania (36.9%), closely followed by Montenegro (36.6%).

In contrast, the smallest percentage is observed in Denmark (6.7%), while Norway, Iceland and Germany all have percentages of less than 10% saying they have no interest in politics. People not interested in politics are found everywhere, but some are even less interested than others.

HOW INTERESTED ARE YOU IN POLITICS?

12% 35% 30% 23%

VERY INTERESTED

NOT AT ALL INTERESTED

MAP 8.086 – WHICH POLITICAL PARTY WOULD YOU VOTE FOR, ON A SCALE OF 1 (LEFT) TO 10 (RIGHT)?

Distribution of Europeans supporting left-wing parties (responses 1–3 on the scale)

Source: European Values Survey, 2008

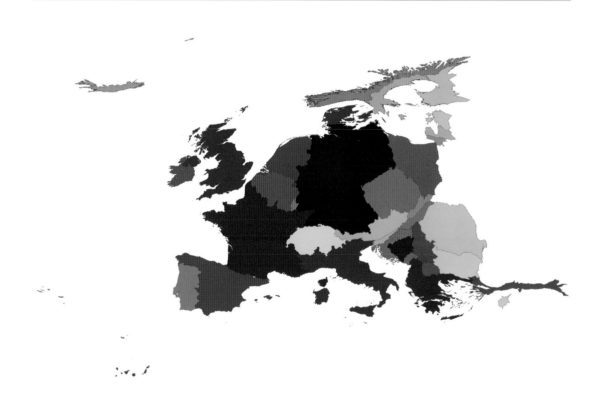

WHICH POLITICAL PARTY WOULD YOU VOTE FOR? (SCALE OF 1 (LEFT) TO 10 (RIGHT))

LEFT (1)   RIGHT (10)

... a party of order or stability and a party of progress or reform are both necessary elements of a healthy state of political life ...

John Stuart Mill (1806–73), 1974, p 110

The European Values Survey asks a number of questions regarding political affiliation. One of these explores the party respondents would vote for 'if there was a general election tomorrow', and the responses were then recoded according to the placement of parties on the political spectrum on a scale of 1 (Left) to 10 (Right). According to the latest survey (2008), 2% of all Europeans specified a party associated with the 1st point of the scale ('Left') and another 2% with the 10th point ('Right'). This map shows the geographical distribution of Europeans who said they would vote for a party classified as 1, 2 or 3 on the Left–Right scale.

Germany has the largest absolute number, followed by France, Italy and the United Kingdom. In relative terms, Albania has the largest number of estimated supporters of a party classified as 'Left' (48%), followed by Cyprus (46.4%), the Czech Republic (43.1%), Norway (38.7%), Switzerland (35.4%) and Croatia (30.8%). On the other hand, Kosovo, Slovenia, Turkey, Lithuania, Slovakia, Malta, Luxembourg and Hungary report very small percentages (less than 5%).

MAP 8.087 – HAVE YOU EVER JOINED IN A BOYCOTT?
Distribution of Europeans who have taken part in a boycott
Source: European Values Survey, 2008

HAVE YOU EVER JOINED IN A BOYCOTT?

9%	36%	55%
HAVE DONE	MIGHT DO	WOULD NEVER DO

Individuals resist or protest what they dislike in many ways. They distance themselves from their organizational roles; they ignore rules they dislike; they criticize and complain; they sabotage their bosses' project in various degrees; they pilfer supplies. Quiet resistance can grow more public, as when individuals write letters to their legislators or newspapers.

Jasper, 1997, p 5

This map shows the geographical distribution of Europeans who said, on a scale from 1 to 3 (1 = have done, 2 = might do, 3 = would never do so), that they have taken part in some kind of boycott. France has the highest absolute number, followed by the United Kingdom, then Italy and Germany. In relative terms, the largest percentages of people who have joined a boycott are found in Iceland (30.2%), followed by Finland and Sweden (23.7%), while the smallest rates are in Romania (1.8%), Lithuania (1.8%), Hungary (2%) and Slovakia (2.5%). Boycotts can vary in intensity, but it is unlikely, for example, that many people would include 'not buying a newspaper they don't like' as a boycott (which is a very easy thing to do)!

MAP 8.088 – HAVE YOU EVER ATTENDED A LAWFUL DEMONSTRATION?
Distribution of Europeans who have taken part in a lawful demonstration
Source: European Values Survey, 2008

HAVE YOU EVER ATTENDED A LAWFUL DEMONSTRATION?

23% | 36% | 41%

HAVE DONE | MIGHT DO | WOULD NEVER DO

Protestors are a diverse lot; everyone of us cares about something deeply enough so that, under the right circumstances, we might join a protest movement.
Jasper, 1997, p 15

According to latest data (2008) from the European Values Survey, 23% of all survey respondents have attended lawful demonstrations. This map shows how they are geographically distributed across Europe. The largest number of protestors are found in France, followed by Germany, Italy and Spain. France is also at the top of the list in relative terms, with an estimated 45.6% of its population aged 15 and over having taken part in a demonstration at some time, followed by Spain (38.6%) and Italy (37.8%). In contrast, the smallest percentages are found in Hungary (3.9%), while the Slovak Republic, Estonia, Turkey, Bosnia and Herzegovina, Romania, Lithuania, Poland, Bulgaria and Croatia all have percentages of less than 10%. It was, of course, famously in Hungary where Soviet tanks invaded in 1956 to suppress demonstrations.

MAP 8.089 – HAVE YOU EVER JOINED AN UNOFFICIAL STRIKE?
Distribution of Europeans who have taken part in an unofficial strike
Source: European Values Survey, 2008

HAVE YOU EVER JOINED AN UNOFFICIAL STRIKE?

5%	21%	74%
HAVE DONE	MIGHT DO	WOULD NEVER DO

Agitators are a set of interfering, meddling people, who come down to some perfectly contented class of the community, and sow the seeds of discontent amongst them. That is the reason why agitators are so absolutely necessary. Without them, in our incomplete state, there would be no advance towards civilisation.

Oscar Wilde, 1891

This map shows the geographical distribution of an estimated 5% who said in the 2008 European Values Survey that they had joined an unofficial strike at some time. The country with the largest absolute number is France, followed by Italy, Spain and the United Kingdom. In relative terms, however, the country with the largest percentage of respondents is Denmark (18.4%), with France in second place (11.5%) and Spain third (9.3%). Hungary, Cyprus, Estonia and the Slovak Republic have the lowest percentages (all below 1%). Unofficial strikes appear much more common towards the western side of Europe.

MAP 8.090 – HAVE YOU EVER OCCUPIED BUILDINGS/FACTORIES?
Distribution of Europeans who have taken part in an occupation of buildings/factories
Source: European Values Survey, 2008

In the fall of 2011, the Occupy movement occupied the western media headlines for weeks. Photos showed activists – so-called Occupiers – and their tents on squares in major cities like New York, London, Tel Aviv and Amsterdam. Occupy was hot. What makes this movement so newsworthy?

Van Stekelenburg, 2012, p 224

According to the 2008 European Values Survey, 4% of all Europeans aged 16 years and over have taken part in the occupation of buildings or factories. The largest number of these are found in Italy, followed by France and Germany. Italy and France are also at the top of the list in relative terms, with percentages of 9.4% and 8.6% respectively, followed by Greece (7.5%). These occupations could include school buildings or university buildings being occupied by protesting students. According to this particular statistic there is no time limit on how long someone has to have been occupying a building to count as an occupier. It is also interesting to note how many people cannot envisage any circumstances in which they might ever believe they needed to occupy a building in protest.

HAVE YOU EVER OCCUPIED BUILDINGS/FACTORIES?

HAVE DONE   MIGHT DO

WOULD NEVER DO

MAP 8.091 – DO YOU BELONG TO A WELFARE ORGANISATION?
Distribution of Europeans who belong to a welfare organisation
Source: European Values Survey, 2008

DO YOU BELONG TO A WELFARE ORGANISATION?

5%   95%

MENTIONED   NOT MENTIONED

In the European Year of Citizenship we are recognising that to volunteer is to be a citizen.

Volonteurope 'tweet', 31 May 2013 (Twitter, 2013)

The 2008 European Values Survey asked a number of questions regarding membership in voluntary organisations and groups. Five per cent of all respondents said that they do belong to a 'welfare organisation'. France had the largest number in absolute terms, followed by Germany, the Netherlands and the United Kingdom. In relative terms, the Netherlands has the largest percentage (21.0%), closely followed by Iceland (20.3%). Hungary, Poland, Bosnia and Herzegovina, Greece, Bulgaria, Turkey, Spain, Malta and Lithuania all have very small percentages (less than 2%).

What is considered to be a welfare organisation varies from place to place but does not appear to include trade unions. Voluntary societies where members pledge to look after or insure each other in case of trouble may well make up the majority of the organisations included here. They will also include organisations where work is done in any organised context – that is, the work is carried out without obligation but is done in order to promote the welfare of its members or of others.

MAP 8.092 – DO YOU BELONG TO ANY RELIGIOUS ORGANISATION?
Distribution of Europeans who belong to a religious organisation
Source: European Values Servey, 2008

DO YOU BELONG TO A RELIGIOUS ORGANISATION?

8%

92%

MENTIONED   NOT MENTIONED

The religious issue has been used to seek a place in the overall framework of 'governance' by way of partnership in the civil society recognized by Brussels. Religious bodies have claimed a specific place as an actor in the domain of public policies. The EU's organizational logic and discourse have reshaped the particularism of religious actors. In practical terms, 'Europeanization' entails accepting pluralistic politics and the Brussels rules of the game.

Schlesinger and Foret, 2006, p 76

According to the 2008 European Values Survey, 8% of all respondents across Europe mentioned that they belong to a religious organisation. This map shows how these respondents are distributed geographically. The United Kingdom, Germany and Italy have the largest absolute numbers. In relative terms the highest percentages are found in Iceland (63.5%) and Denmark (61.6%), followed by the Netherlands (31.1%) and the Republic of Ireland (28.4%). Note that this category is not about people being members of a church or having a particular religious belief or affiliation. If it was, the percentages would be far higher in many countries.

MAP 8.093 – DO YOU BELONG TO ANY PEACE MOVEMENT?
Distribution of Europeans who belong to a peace movement
Source: European Values Survey, 2008

DO YOU BELONG TO A PEACE MOVEMENT?

1%

99%

MENTIONED   NOT MENTIONED

Protest movements have important benefits for modern societies in the way they develop and disseminate new perspectives, especially but not exclusively moral visions.

Jasper, 1997, p 6

According to the 2008 European Values Survey, 1% of all respondents across Europe mentioned that they belong to some form of a peace movement. Italy has the largest number, followed by the United Kingdom and the Netherlands. In relative terms, the largest percentage is observed in Kosovo (6.2%), followed by Albania (4.8%) and the Netherlands (3.1%).

Peace movements in Europe began to grow in number following the First World War. They saw a revival after the Second World War, and then grew in number during the Cold War when Europe was divided in two and with the partition of Germany. As war within the continent becomes a more distant memory for most Europeans, peace movements also diminish in their membership. New wars, declared supposedly as being 'on terror' or other abstract concepts, may lead more young people to take part in organisations that protect liberty and promote peace.

9

ECONOMICS

MAP 9.094 – GROSS DOMESTIC PRODUCT, 2012
Source: The World Bank

According to data from the World Bank, the total gross domestic product (GDP) of all the countries mapped in this atlas in 2012 was 18 trillion and 673 billion US dollars, which is approximately one quarter of the estimated total GDP of the world. The total GDP of a country is equal to the market value of the goods and services produced by all sectors of that country's economy in a year. To allow comparison outside of Europe, GDP per person (per capita) is usually recorded in US dollars.

Germany has the largest GDP, followed by France, the United Kingdom, Italy and Spain. However, Monaco has the highest GDP per capita (US$163,026), followed by Liechtenstein (134,617), Luxembourg (107,476), Norway (99,558), Switzerland (79,052), Denmark (56,210) and Sweden (55,244). The lowest values are found in Kosovo (3,453), Albania (4,148), Bosnia and Herzegovina (4,446), FYR Macedonia (4,589), Serbia (5,189), Montenegro (6,183), Bulgaria (6,986) and Romania (7,942). Note that these are not average annual personal income figures. However, in countries where income inequalities are lower, and where shareholders and very rich people take fewer profits, the figure for GDP per capita is closer to that of the average personal income.

MAP 9.095 – GROSS DOMESTIC PRODUCT INCREASE, 2007–12
Constant 2005 US$
Source: The World Bank

This map shows the absolute increases in gross domestic product since the economic crisis started in 2007/08. The figures have all been converted to what are called 'constant 2005 US dollars' to eliminate any distortions due to inflation. There are 23 countries that experienced an absolute increase over the period to 2012. These were mostly in central Europe, with Germany, Turkey and Poland standing out. However, in relative terms the largest increase is observed in Kosovo, with its GDP growing by 25% between 2007 and 2012, followed by Albania (20%), Poland (18%), Turkey (16%) and Slovakia (10%). It is also worth noting that the economies of Switzerland, Norway and Sweden did not shrink overall during this period of massive economic slump.

The cartographic technique used to create these cartograms does not shrink away completely countries that should not be shown as the distortions created would be too severe. They would appear to be like black holes sucking in parts of the continent (see Chapter 1). Note that, because of the technique used to create this map, many of the countries that are shown as very small here did not in fact have very small increases in GDP but rather, as the next map shows, they experienced large declines.

MAP 9.096 – GROSS DOMESTIC PRODUCT DECLINE, 2007–12
Constant 2005 US$
Source: The World Bank

This map shows the absolute decline in gross domestic product in constant 2005 US dollars since the recent economic crisis began. The countries in the south of Europe stand out but there are also large decreases in GDP in the United Kingdom and the Republic of Ireland. Declines for some very small countries such as Iceland are also very prominent in this map. The largest absolute decline of GDP was experienced by Italy, followed by Greece, Spain, the United Kingdom and the Republic of Ireland. In relative terms, however, Greece experienced the highest decline in its GDP, shrinking by 20% between 2007 and 2012, followed by Latvia (13%), Croatia (8%), Italy (7%) and the Republic of Ireland (6%).

Decline in GDP is more obvious if a country is within the eurozone. Outside of the eurozone, a large part of such a decline can be concealed as the currency devalues. For example, part of the decline in the GDP of the UK is reflected in the fact that, in comparison with the euro and the dollar, the pound sterling is worth less now than it was. Constant US dollars are used here to mitigate these effects. It is also worth noting that this is not a map of falling household incomes. Incomes for most households can fall much faster than GDP but it is often the richest households and individuals that experience and/or can arrange smaller falls for themselves, as has occurred in the United Kingdom:

British workers' wages have suffered one of the biggest falls across Europe, according to House of Commons figures. The average hourly wage has fallen by 5.5% since 2010 – even more than austerity-hit Spain, which has seen a 3.3% drop in the same period.
(Sky News, 2013)

MAP 9.097 – CREDIT BY BANKING SECTOR, 2012

Source: The World Bank

This map shows the geographical distribution of the total domestic credit provided by the banking sector in Europe which, according to the latest data from the World Bank, was estimated to be approximately 28 trillion US dollars in 2012. The largest absolute figure is observed in the United Kingdom. The UK is followed by Germany, France, Italy and Spain. However, the country with the most sizeable domestic credit provided by its banking sector in 2012 was Cyprus (344% of its total GDP), followed by Spain (221%), the Netherlands (216%), the United Kingdom (210%) and Denmark (206%). The smallest figures were found in Kosovo (22% of GDP), FYR Macedonia (49%), Lithuania (52%), Slovakia (54%) and Romania (54%).

Note that there was a run on the banks in Cyprus in 2013, the year after the collation of data for this map. It is also worth noting how these lending figures for large countries are related to salaries, although the correlation is not that strong, as the UK does not lend the vast majority of domestic credit that is distributed across Europe but still dominates the banking pay league:

More British bankers earned more than one million euros (£860,000) each in 2011 than [in] the rest of the European Union (EU) put together, according to the European Banking Authority (EBA). Figures from the EU's banking regulator showed 2,346 bankers earned more than 1m euros in the UK, compared with 739 in the rest of the EU. In Germany [which had the second most] there were just 170.
(BBC News, 2013b)

MAP 9.098 – NUMBER OF LISTED DOMESTIC COMPANIES ON NATIONAL STOCK EXCHANGES, 2012

Source: The World Bank

According to the latest data from the World Bank, at the end of 2012 there was a total of 12,380 domestic companies listed in the national stock exchanges of Europe. About a quarter of these companies were in Spain, which also had the largest number (3,167), followed by the United Kingdom (2,179), Serbia (1,086), France (862) and Poland (844). However, it is also interesting to explore the number of listed companies in terms of their market value (see Map 9.099). Many of the companies in Spain are not worth as much as the average listed European company in terms of the arithmetic mean.

Only companies that have numerous shareholders were included in the data, which determines the size of each state on the map. Some private companies can be very large, employing thousands of people and making billions of pounds a year. Also, it is easier for private companies to be officially registered in a country other than that in which most of their work is based, than it is for publicly listed European companies to disguise their geographical location. Many private companies are registered in places like Monaco to avoid tax bills in those areas where they do most of their business and employ most of their staff. The most common reason for companies to be registered away from where they make their profits and carry out their work is to avoid tax.

Some of the largest companies operating in Europe may not be listed as domestic companies in European stock exchanges (or not listed at all) but may be headquartered in the United States, and they often they have their European base officially in countries like Ireland or Luxembourg where tax rates are particularly low (*Reuters*, 2013; *The Guardian*, 2011).

MAP 9.099 – MARKET CAPITALISATION OF LISTED DOMESTIC COMPANIES ON NATIONAL STOCK EXCHANGES, 2012

Source: The World Bank

The estimated market value of all listed 'domestic' companies expressed as their total share price at the end of 2012 was approximately 12 trillion US dollars. About a quarter of this total was found in the United Kingdom, which also had the highest absolute value, followed by France, Germany, Switzerland and Spain. There are four countries in which the total market value of listed companies in their stock exchange in 2012 was larger than their annual GDP. These are Switzerland with a total market value of listed companies equal to 170% of the country's GDP, followed by the United Kingdom (124%), Luxembourg (123%) and Sweden (106%). On the other hand, there are six countries where the market value of their listed companies is less than 10% of their GDP: Romania (9%), Lithuania (9%), Cyprus (9%), FYR Macedonia (6%), Slovakia (5%) and Latvia (4%).

This map, like the previous one, needs to be interpreted in the knowledge that many companies that appear to be domestic are officially registered elsewhere in order to avoid the payment of taxes. Ironically many of these so-called 'treasure islands' are sanctioned by Europe through the United Kingdom's government, which protects the status of jurisdiction in places such as the Channel Islands, the Isle of Man, the Cayman Islands and the Bahamas.

MAP 9.100 – STOCKS TRADED, 2012
Total value, current US$
Source: The World Bank

According to data from the World Bank, the total value of shares traded in all countries mapped in this atlas was just over 9 trillion US dollars. The largest value in 2012 was observed in the United Kingdom (approximately $2.5 trillion), followed by Germany, France and Italy. The United Kingdom also had the largest value, even when this was expressed as a percentage of GDP (102%), followed by Switzerland (101%), Spain (80%), Sweden (72%) and the Netherlands (57%). There are 20 countries where the total value of stocks traded is less than 10% of GDP, including the following eleven which have values of less than 1%: Slovenia, Croatia, Estonia, Serbia, Bulgaria, Malta, Lithuania, FYR Macedonia, Luxembourg, Slovakia and Latvia.

One reason why the UK has such a large share of the European trading market is that many companies trade shares in Europe through London even though they are declared as 'not domiciled' in the UK. Although this brings more financial business to the UK, when there is a financial crisis the UK's over-reliance on stock markets as a source of economic wealth becomes very clear. It is interesting to note that Switzerland appears to be similarly exposed – yet when the crisis hit Europe, Switzerland did not contract. Perhaps its banking sector is better regulated than that in the UK, or perhaps there are other factors making Switzerland more secure (such as gold, for example – see the next map).

MAP 9.101 – TOTAL RESERVES (INCLUDING GOLD), 2012
Current US$
Source: The World Bank

This map shows the geographical distribution of total reserves according to data from the World Bank for 2012. These comprise holdings of monetary gold, special drawing rights, reserves of International Monetary Fund (IMF) members held by the IMF, and holdings of foreign exchange under the control of monetary authorities. The total value in 2012 was approximately 1.4 trillion US dollars, of which about a third is found in Switzerland.

Famously, Harry Lime, Orson Wells' leading character in the 1949 film *The Third Man* declared that:

> *In Italy for thirty years under the Borgias they had warfare, terror, murder, bloodshed – but they produced Michelangelo, Leonardo da Vinci, and the Renaissance. In Switzerland they had brotherly love, 500 years of democracy and peace, and what did that produce? The cuckoo clock.*

Clearly, stability produced more than just a clock, while some countries that trade in money do so on a firmer foundation than others.

MAP 9.102 – FOREIGN DIRECT INVESTMENT, POSITIVE, 2012
Total net inflows
Source: The World Bank

This map and the next show the total net inflows (new investment inflows less disinvestment) of foreign direct investment (FDI) using data from the World Bank for 2012. The data mapped here comprises all acquisitions of a lasting management interest (10% or more of voting stock) in an enterprise operating in an economy other than that of the investor. It is the sum of equity capital, reinvestment of earnings, other long-term capital, and short-term capital as shown in the balance of payments (World Bank, 2013a). In 2012 nearly all countries mapped in this atlas had a positive net inflow (that is, the new investment was more than disinvestment). France had the largest net inflow, followed by the United Kingdom, Spain, the Republic of Ireland and Germany.

However, when looking at the total amounts as a proportion of GDP, the Republic of Ireland is at the top of the list, as the total net FDI inflow in 2012 represented 10.8% of its GDP. This is followed by Switzerland (7.8% of GDP), Estonia (4.8%), Sweden (4.5%) and Hungary (4.4%).

In three countries the total net inflow was negative (see the next map): the Netherlands had the largest negative net inflow, followed by Belgium and then Slovenia.

MAP 9.103 –FOREIGN DIRECT INVESTMENT, NEGATIVE, 2012
Total net inflows
Source: The World Bank

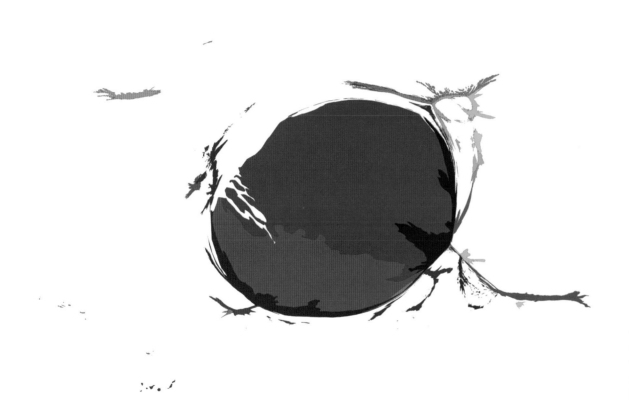

Foreign direct investment is a category of cross-border investment associated with a resident in one economy having control or a significant degree of influence on the management of an enterprise that is resident in another economy. As well as the equity that gives rise to control or influence, direct investment also includes investment associated with that relationship, including investment in indirectly influenced or controlled enterprises, investment in fellow enterprises (enterprises controlled by the same direct investor), debt (except selected debt), and reverse investment.

World Bank, 2014

When looking at these figures in relation to GDP, Belgium is top (3.0%), followed by the Netherlands (1.6%) and Slovenia (0.5%). However, there is considerable variation in FDI year by year; for example, if we consider the data for the previous year, 2011, all these three countries had significant positive net inflows.

The data used here is very volatile and subject to significant changes upon revision. These figures were accessed from the World Bank in July 2013, updated figures will be different and, of course, each later year's figures will also change significantly.

MAP 9.104 – PORTFOLIO EQUITY, POSITIVE, 2012
Total net inflows, BOP, current US$
Source: The World Bank

This map shows the total net inflows from equity securities, other than those recorded as direct investment, and includes shares, stocks and depository receipts as well as direct purchases of shares in local stock markets by foreign investors. Luxembourg has the largest inflow (relative to the size of its economy), followed by the Republic of Ireland, France, Italy and Switzerland.

Most striking on this map is the near economic collapse of Ireland. This money had to be drawn in because it was promised by law. A great deal of that money came from the United Kingdom in the form of loans. Following the crisis of 2008, the Irish government promised to cover all defaults by Irish banks, no matter how large they were. This was later viewed as madness, but it was also in the interest of the British, who did not want any doubt cast on the liquidity of their nearby banks, or fears raised over the safety of sterling.

In Ireland the market crash was described as beginning at 10 pm on 2 October 2008. It has been claimed that the precise moment the crash began was when Irish home-buyers saw the man from Ireland's Central Bank wheeled out on TV and he appeared to be incapable. The reaction was:

> ... they saw him and said, Who the fuck was that??? Is that the fucking guy who is in charge of the money??? That's when everyone panicked.
> Colm McCarthy, describing the response to a news item at 10 pm on Irish TV on 2 October 2008, quoted in Lewis, 2011, p 98

MAP 9.105 – PORTFOLIO EQUITY, NET INFLOWS, NEGATIVE, 2012
Total net inflows, BOP, current US$
Source: The World Bank

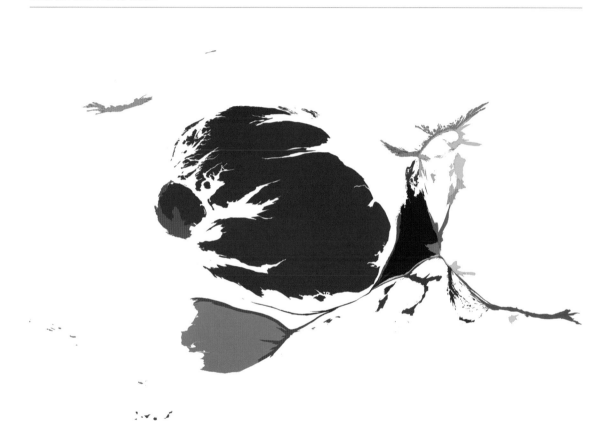

This map shows the countries where the total inflows from equity securities were smaller than the outflows and therefore the net value was negative in 2012 (see also the previous map). The largest absolute value is observed in the United Kingdom, followed by Portugal, Germany, Estonia, the Czech Republic and Greece.

A key reason for the large outflows from the UK during this year was the special loans that the UK was making to Ireland. Ireland was paying these back slowly, with interest, but the interest rate had to be reduced towards the end of 2012, presumably because the Irish government was finding it difficult to raise the money. The final disbursement of the loan was made on 26 September 2013 – the loan has to be paid back in 7.5 years (gov.uk, 2013; see under section 2 of the Loans to Ireland Act 2010: 1 April 2013 to 30 September 2013).

While the United Kingdom has been lending to Ireland and also to banks based in London to keep them afloat, the UK has seen larger falls in standards of living than have occurred in much of the European mainland:

The 5.5% reduction in average hourly wages since mid-2010, adjusted for inflation, means British workers have felt the squeeze more than those in countries which have been rocked by the eurozone crisis including Spain, which saw a 3.3% drop over the same period and Cyprus, where salaries fell by 3% in real terms. Only the Greeks, Portuguese and Dutch have had a steeper decline
(The London Standard, 2013)

The situation in 2013 remained precarious and these two maps (9.104 and 9.105) are likely to look very different within a year or two.

MAP 9.106 – NET ADJUSTED DISPOSABLE INCOME OF PRIVATE HOUSEHOLDS (PPCS), 2007

Source: European Commission, based on data from Eurostat, DG REGIO estimates, EQLS, Eurofound
Basemap: Hennig Projection Gridded Population Cartogram

Net adjusted disposable income of private households (PPCS), 2007
Index, EU-27=100

- <46
- 46–89
- 89–110
- 110–120
- >120

This map shows the geographical distribution of an index expressing the net adjusted disposable income across European regions in relation to the average value for the whole of the EU, which is equal to 100. The index mapped here encapsulates net disposable income including 'transfers in kind', reflecting benefits such as the varying provision of education, health care and other public services that are provided for free or below provision cost (European Commission, 2010). Two citizens of Europe will not have the same real disposable income, if one lives in an area where health care is provided free at the point of use and the other has to pay to gain access to such service. This index smooths out all those factors to show where the best-off people really are. What is seen is very much a core–periphery divide.

The highest value is found in *Luxembourg* (235.00), followed by *Inner London* (162.46) in the United Kingdom, *Hamburg* (147.72) in Germany, the French capital city region of *Île de France* (142.69) and the southeast region of the United Kingdom *Surrey, East and West Sussex* (142.55). In contrast, the lowest values are found in the Romanian region *Nord-Est* (23.08) and the Bulgarian regions *Severozapaden* (23.64), *Yuzhen Tsentralen* (23.87), *Severoiztochen* (24.85) and *Severen Tsentralen* (24.96).

MAP 9.107 – GROSS DOMESTIC PRODUCT (GDP) PER INHABITANT, 2010
Purchasing power standard (PPS), by NUTS 2 regions (% of EU-27 average, EU-27 = 100)
Source: Eurostat Regional Yearbook | Basemap: Hennig Projection Gridded Population Cartogram

The proportion of the population living in regions where the average GDP per inhabitant was less than 75% of the EU-27 average was 24.2%, while the proportion living in regions where this value was 125% or more of the EU-27 average was 18.4%; the proportion of the population in the mid-range (GDP per inhabitant ranging from 75% to less than 125%) was 57.4%.

European Commission, 2013d

GDP
% of the EU-27 average,
EU-27=100

 <53
53–82
82–97
 97–116
 >116

This map shows gross domestic product per inhabitant adjusted for the purchasing power standard (PPS) as a percentage of the overall EU average. The region with the highest value is *Inner London* (328% of EU average), the core region of the United Kingdom. It is followed by *Luxembourg* (266%), then by the Belgian capital city region of *Région de Bruxelles-Capitale/Brussels Hoofdstedelijk Gewest* (223%), by the German city region of *Hamburg* (203%), and the Norwegian capital city region of *Oslo og Akershus* (192%). The lowest values are observed in the Bulgarian regions *Severozapaden* (26%) and *Severen Tsentralen* (29%), in Romania's *Nord-Est* (30%) and *Yuzhen Tsentralen* (30%), and in *Severoiztochen* and *Yugoiztochen* (36%), both in Bulgaria. If regional data for Turkey had been available, then regions within Turkey may well have also been among the lowest values.

MAP 9.108 – CHANGE IN GROSS DOMESTIC PRODUCT (GDP) PER INHABITANT, 2008–10
Purchasing power standard (PPS), by NUTS 2 regions (percentage points difference between 2010 and 2008 in relation to the EU-27 average)
Source: Eurostat Regional Yearbook | Basemap: Hennig Projection Gridded Population Cartogram

GDP change 2008–10
Percentage points differences between 2010 and 2008; in relation to the EU-27 average

- <-2.8
- -2.8 – -0.6
- -0.6–1.2
- 1.2–2.7
- >2.7

In the two years following the worldwide financial crash of 2008, a total of 146 out of the 280 regions mapped here experienced a decrease in GDP as measured per inhabitant, when valued according to purchasing power standard (PPS). Many of these regions were in the south of Europe, but they can also be seen in the periphery of some central and northern European

countries, including *Groningen* in the Netherlands which experienced the largest decline (-12.6%), closely followed by *Iceland* (-11%), which is mapped as one region here (and stretched quite thin due to its very low population so it is hard to see). Other regions that experienced some of the faster falls in GDP following the crash included the Greek island region of *Ionia*

Nisia (-10.2%), the Finnish region *Etelä-Suomi* (-9.6%), Slovenia's *Zahodna Slovenija* (-8.3%) and *Drenthe* in the Netherlands (-7.5%). *Outer London* and *West Yorkshire* in the United Kingdom also experienced rapid falls, but not *Inner London*. At the other extreme, 25 regions experienced an increase of more than 5% in GDP per capita when measured in relation to the

EU average change. The Belgian region *Prov. Brabant Wallon* had the highest rise (13.5%), followed by the Polish regions *Mazowieckie* (12.5%) and *Dolnośląskie* (9.8%), the Danish region *Hovedstaden* (9.8%) and the capital city region of Slovakia, *Bratislavský Kraj* (8.9%).

10
ENVIRONMENT

MAP 10.109 – CARBON DIOXIDE EMISSIONS (KT), 2009
Source: The World Bank

Carbon dioxide levels in the atmosphere have broken through a symbolic mark. Daily measurements of CO_2 at a US government agency lab on Hawaii have topped 400 parts per million for the first time ... The last time CO_2 was regularly above 400ppm was three to five million years ago – before modern humans existed.

BBC News, 2013c

According to the latest data from the World Bank, the estimated carbon dioxide (CO_2) emissions produced by the burning of fossil fuels and the manufacture of cement in all countries mapped in this atlas was 4,101,932 kilotonnes (kt) in 2009. The largest share of this (about a fifth) was produced by Germany, followed by the United Kingdom (11.57%) and Italy (9.77%). However, when taking the total population of each state into account, Luxembourg has the highest level of emissions (20.3 metric tonnes per capita), followed by the Czech Republic and the Netherlands (10.3), while the lowest levels are observed in Albania (0.9), Turkey (3.9), Hungary, Croatia and Montenegro (each 4.9). The estimated level of world emissions of carbon dioxide is 4.7 metric tonnes per capita, while in the European Union it is 7.2 metric tonnes per capita.

Only in Albania and Turkey are emissions found to be lower than the global average. Lower levels of pollution are found only in areas where there is both very little highly polluting industry and where individual levels of material consumption are lower. Across all of Europe there is now an aim to reduce carbon dioxide pollution.

MAP 10.110 – NITROUS OXIDE EMISSIONS (KT OF CARBON DIOXIDE EQUIVALENT), 2010
Source: The World Bank

The levels of gases in the atmosphere that drive global warming increased to a record high in 2012. According to the World Meteorological Organization (WMO), atmospheric CO_2 grew more rapidly last year than its average rise over the past decade. Concentrations of methane and nitrous oxide also broke previous records. Thanks to carbon dioxide and these other gases, the WMO says the warming effect on our climate has increased by almost a third since 1990.

McGrath, 2013

This map shows the estimated emissions from agricultural biomass burning, industrial activities and livestock management across Europe. According to data from the World Bank, these were estimated to be approximately 324,884.90 kt of carbon dioxide equivalent. Germany has the largest volume (13% of the total), followed by France, Turkey, Poland and the United Kingdom.

Nitrous oxide emissions are presented numerically in terms of their equivalent effects to carbon dioxide pollution, but the map would be identical whatever units were used.

The Republic of Ireland has the highest level of emissions per capita (1.7), followed by Lithuania (1.5), Iceland (1.1), Finland (1.1) and Serbia (1.0). The lowest levels are observed in Malta (0.1), FYR Macedonia (0.2), Bosnia and Herzegovina (0.3), Switzerland (0.3) and Italy (0.3).

MAP 10.111 – METHANE EMISSIONS (KT OF CARBON DIOXIDE EQUIVALENT), 2010
Source: The World Bank

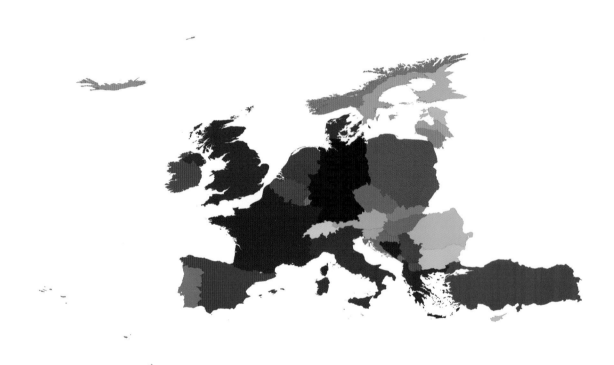

The importance of methane in the greenhouse effect is its warming effect. Even though it occurs in lower concentrations than carbon dioxide, it produces 21 times as much warming as CO_2. Methane accounts for 20% of the 'enhanced greenhouse effect'... Since the Industrial Revolution, the level of methane in the atmosphere has increased by about two and a half times.
BBC, 2009

This map shows the geographical distribution of an estimated total 638,239 kt of carbon dioxide equivalent emissions from human activities such as agriculture and from industrial methane production. France has the highest volume (and 13% of the total), followed by Turkey (12% of the total), Poland (10.2%), the United Kingdom (9.6%) and Germany (9.0%).

However, when the total population size is taken into account, Norway has the highest level of methane emissions (3.4 metric tonnes per capita), followed by the Republic of Ireland (3.0), Luxembourg (2.3), Estonia (1.7) and Poland (1.7). The lowest emissions are found in Malta (0.6 metric tonnes per capita), Italy (0.6), Switzerland (0.6), FYR Macedonia (0.7) and Germany (0.7).

MAP 10.112 – PERFLUOROCARBON GAS EMISSIONS (KT OF CARBON DIOXIDE EQUIVALENT), 2008
Source: The World Bank

Perfluorocarbons (PFCs) are from 5,700 to 10,000 times more powerful greenhouse gasses (depending on the exact type) than carbon dioxide, and have an atmospheric lifetime of up to 50,000 years.

Greenpeace, 2006

This map shows the estimated emissions stemming from perfluorocarbons (PFCs), which are used as a replacement for chlorofluorocarbons in manufacturing semiconductors, and are a by-product of aluminium smelting and uranium enrichment (World Bank, 2013b). The total estimated emissions in 2010 was 12,910 kt of carbon dioxide equivalent. The country with the largest volume is Norway (35% of the total), followed by Spain (14.3%) and Germany (8.5%).

The inequalities here are so great that there is no need to express these statistics per capita, as in the previous map, since to do so would produce astronomically large ratios of inequality in pollution levels from this particular source. Clearly while Norway, and to a lesser extent Iceland, continue to pollute to such an excess, other states are unlikely to see their levels as unacceptably high. It is also worth noting here that when there are such extreme differences as are found on this map, neighbouring countries can be unfairly represented as being larger than they really are in terms of the statistic, as occurs here for Sweden which is unduly stretched because it shares such a long border with Norway and because Norway has to be drawn so large.

MAP 10.113 – OTHER GREENHOUSE GAS EMISSIONS – HYDROFLUOROCARBONS, PERFLUOROCARBONS AND SULFUR HEXAFLUORIDE (KT OF CARBON DIOXIDE EQUIVALENT), 2010
Source: The World Bank

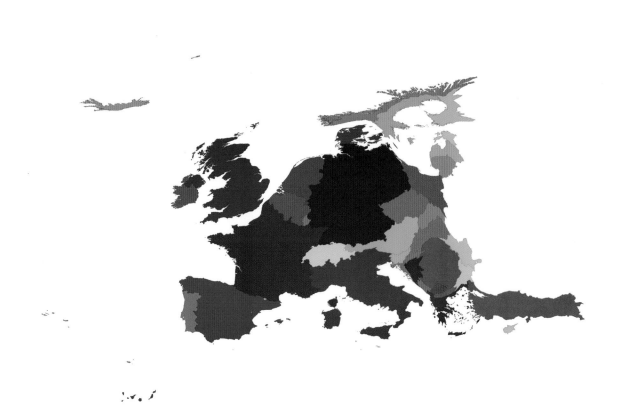

The EU launched its pioneering Emissions Trading Scheme (ETS) in 2005 ... All major industrial emitters of CO_2 are to be brought under the ETS eventually and the scheme will also include greenhouse gases other than CO_2 – nitrous oxide and perfluorocarbons.

BBC News, 2010

This map shows the geographical distribution of by-product emissions of hydrofluorocarbons (HFCs), perfluorocarbons (PFCs), and sulfur hexafluoride (SF6) in Europe. In 2010 there was estimated to be a total of 147,716 kt of carbon dioxide equivalent of these pollutants. Combining these three sources of pollution using this equivalence measure is one way of stating how damaging pollution from each source is, and of producing an overall aggregate.

Germany has the largest share of this total (about a fifth – 18%), followed by France (14.7% of the total), Italy (10.5%) and the United Kingdom (9.7%). However, when measured per capita, Serbia has the highest value per capita (1 metric tonne), followed by Latvia (0.7), Iceland (0.6), Austria (0.5) and Lithuania (0.4). The lowest values are observed in Croatia (0.02), Albania (0.03), Romania (0.04), Estonia (0.04) and Poland (0.07).

MAP 10.114 – SULFUR HEXAFLUORIDE GAS EMISSIONS (KT OF CARBON DIOXIDE EQUIVALENT), 2008
Source: The World Bank

Sulphur Hexafluoride is the most potent greenhouse gas evaluated by the Intergovernmental Panel on Climate Change. It is 23,900 times more powerful a greenhouse gas than carbon dioxide, and has an atmospheric lifetime of 3,200 years.

Greenpeace, 2006

This map shows the geographical distribution of an estimated 14,540 kt of carbon dioxide equivalent emissions of sulfur hexafluoride (SF6), which is used largely to insulate high-voltage electric power equipment (World Bank, 2013c). The largest share and nearly half of this total (44%) is produced in Germany, followed by Turkey (13%) and France (12%). Although this source is a relatively small part of the overall greenhouse gas emissions in Europe, it can be seen to be particularly skewed to these three countries, which between them contribute nearly three quarters of all of Europe's pollution from this source. Admittedly if other countries produced as much insulating material then they would appear larger and these countries smaller. It is also worth pointing out that insulating material reduces the loss of power from high-voltage equipment and so may reduce greenhouse emissions: if there is leakage from the network, more fossil fuels would need to be burnt to generate more electricity. Nevertheless if less energy was used overall, and more low-voltage power was generated locally, there would be less need for many of the materials whose production creates the pollution shown in this map.

MAP 10.115 – FOREST AREA (KM²), 2011
Source: The World Bank

Forests and agricultural land are important to climate change mitigation. Firstly because of the significance of their carbon stock and secondly because their exchange of greenhouse gases between the atmosphere and soils and vegetation can go both ways. Many human activities such as logging, grazing of livestock or ploughing, influence the exchange of greenhouse gases with the atmosphere and ultimately the carbon footprint of the sector. Both EU internal and international frameworks provide for the regulation of these sectors in terms of climate change.

European Commission, 2014b

According to the latest data from the World Bank, there was a total of 1,041,966 km² of forest area in all the countries mapped in this atlas. This figure excludes tree stands in agricultural production systems, so most of this is long-lasting 'natural' forest.

Nearly a third of all this forest area is found in Sweden (16%) and Finland (12%) when these two countries are combined (28%). When the area classified as forest is seen as a percentage of the total land area, in five countries more than half the land is classified as forest: Finland (73%), Sweden (69%), Slovenia (62%), Latvia (54%) and Estonia (52%). The lowest proportions are found in San Marino (0%), Iceland (0.3%), Malta (0.9%), the Netherlands (11%), the Republic of Ireland (11%) and the United Kingdom (12%).

MAP 10.116 – ENERGY USE (KT OF OIL EQUIVALENT), 2010
Source: The World Bank

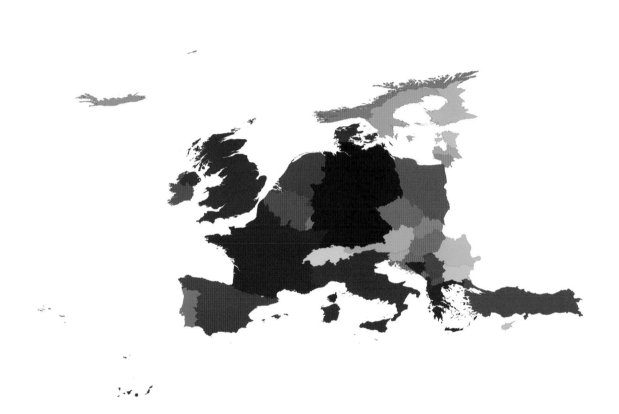

Energy use by household appliances such as washing machines, dishwashers, TVs and refrigerators can be reduced by 30% using the best available options and by 80% with advanced technologies. Energy use by office appliances can be reduced by 50–75% through a combination of power management and energy efficient computer systems.

Greenpeace International/European Renewable Energy Council, 2007, p 80

This map shows the geographical distribution of the total energy use in Europe (estimated to be approximately 1.9 million kt of oil equivalent for all Europeans). Germany has the highest value (and about 17% of the overall total), followed by France and the United Kingdom. However, the highest value per capita is found in Iceland, followed by Luxembourg, Finland, Romania and Norway. The lowest energy use per capita is found in Montenegro.

Often this energy is not primarily being used by households but by industry. Thus it is aluminium smelting in Iceland which propels that country to the top of the use list. Also, those countries that produce the most energy often use more energy. Iceland has access to geothermal sources and hydropower, and it is largely the oil equivalent of these two sources that is represented here for that country. In contrast, in France much more of the energy is nuclear, in Britain more comes from gas, and in Norway more is generated from oil.

MAP 10.117 – ENERGY PRODUCTION (KT OF OIL EQUIVALENT), 2010
Source: The World Bank

The European Commission adopted its second strategic energy review in November 2008. This addressed how the EU could reduce its dependency on imported energy, thereby improving its security of supply, as well as reducing its emissions of greenhouse gases.

Eurostat, 2013a

This map shows the spatial distribution of all energy produced in Europe, defined as 'all forms of petroleum (crude oil, natural gas liquids, and oil from non-conventional sources), natural gas, solid fuels (coal, lignite, and other derived fuels), and combustible renewables and waste' it also includes primary electricity generation (from both renewable and non-renewable sources), all converted into oil equivalents. The estimated total, according to the latest data from the World Bank at the time of writing (2010), was 1.1 million kt of oil equivalent. The largest producer of energy is Norway, where nearly a fifth of the total is produced, followed by the United Kingdom, France, Germany and the Netherlands.

Far more energy is produced in northern Europe than in the south. However, as we begin to see more solar power production across Europe, and also more wind power production (as currently in Denmark), we should expect to see the shape of this map change.

MAP 10.118 – ELECTRICITY PRODUCTION FROM RENEWABLE SOURCES (KWH), 2010
Source: The World Bank

MAP 10.119 – ELECTRICITY PRODUCTION FROM COAL SOURCES (KWH), 2010
Source: The World Bank

The next six maps show the geographical distribution of all electricity production from different sources in Europe. The first map shows the geographical distribution of all electricity production from renewable sources in Europe, using the latest data available from the World Bank. This includes all geothermal, solar, tides, wind, biomass and biofuels and hydroelectric production. Norway is the largest producer, followed by Germany and Spain, each producing 10% of the total electricity from renewable sources in Europe. When looking at production in relation to the population size of each country, however, Iceland is at the top of the list with 53,374 kWh per capita, followed by Norway (23,827), Sweden (8,658), Austria (5,343) and Switzerland (4,709). The lowest per capita production is found in Cyprus (84), Kosovo (87), Poland (283), Lithuania (303), Hungary (303) and the United Kingdom (409).

The second map and the maps on the next two pages show the geographical distribution of electricity production from other sources across Europe. (Note that states like Andorra, Liechtenstein, Monaco, San Marino and the Vatican do not produce any energy, and so are not mentioned in the commentary in relation to these maps.)

Looking at production from coal sources, the highest production of electricity from ▶

MAP 10.120 – ELECTRICITY PRODUCTION FROM HYDROELECTRIC SOURCES (KWH), 2010
Source: The World Bank

MAP 10.121 – ELECTRICITY PRODUCTION FROM NATURAL GAS SOURCES (KWH), 2010
Source: The World Bank

coal sources per capita is found in Estonia (8,460 kWh), followed by the Czech Republic (4,729), Poland (3,669), Serbia (3,565) and Germany (3,401). A number of states have no production from coal sources, including Albania, Iceland, Cyprus, Lithuania, Luxembourg, Malta and Switzerland.

Iceland has the highest production per capita of electricity from hydroelectric sources (39,136 kWh), followed by Norway (24,231), Sweden (6,988), Montenegro (4,427) and Switzerland (4,040). Malta and Cyprus produce no electricity from hydroelectric sources, and it is very low in Denmark (3 kWh per capita), the Netherlands (3.4) and Belgium (18).

Luxembourg has the highest electricity production from natural gas sources relative to its population (4,460 kWh per capita), followed by the Netherlands (4,094), the Republic of Ireland (3,282), Italy (2,335) and the United Kingdom (2,307). At the other end of the scale, Cyprus, Iceland, Kosovo, Malta and Montenegro have zero production.

Fifteen countries use nuclear power to produce electricity. The highest production both in absolute terms and in relation to its population is France (7,772 kWh per capita). Sweden has the second highest production per capita (6,332), followed by Belgium (4,347), Finland (4,292) and Switzerland (3,358).

▶

MAP 10.122 – ELECTRICITY PRODUCTION FROM NUCLEAR SOURCES (KWH), 2010
Source: The World Bank

MAP 10.123 – ELECTRICITY PRODUCTION FROM OIL SOURCES (KWH), 2010
Source: The World Bank

Other countries that produce electricity from nuclear sources are (in descending order of per capita production): Slovenia, Czech Republic, Slovakia, Bulgaria, Hungary, Germany, Spain, the United Kingdom, Romania and the Netherlands.

Looking at the map of electricity production from oil sources, it is worth noting that Cyprus has the highest value in relation to its population (6,089 kWh per capita),

followed by Malta (5,060), Greece (507), Spain (328) and Italy (295) – oil is a source of electricity production typically found in island economies. The lowest values per capita are found in Montenegro (zero), Albania (0.3 kWh per capita), Latvia (1.0), Luxembourg (1.9) and Norway (6.0).

MAP 10.124 – FOSSIL FUEL ENERGY CONSUMPTION, 2010
Source: The World Bank

The use of renewable energy sources is seen as a key element in energy policy, reducing the dependence on fuel imported from non-EU countries, reducing emissions from fossil fuel sources, and decoupling energy costs from oil prices.

Eurostat, 2013b

This map shows the geographical distribution of the estimated total fossil fuel energy consumption in Europe in 2010, based on the latest data available from the World Bank. The country with the highest consumption was Germany, followed by the United Kingdom, Italy, France and Spain. However, if the fossil fuel energy consumption is examined as a percentage of the total energy consumption in each country, then Malta is seen to have the highest figure (99.89%). Malta is the most densely populated state in Europe and so has less space available to generate energy (per person) than other areas, although it could create and use more solar power. In terms of reliance on fossil fuels it is followed by Cyprus, the Netherlands, Poland, Bosnia Herzegovina and Greece (all above 90%). In contrast, Iceland has the lowest percentage (17.5%) and Sweden the second lowest (34%). A more detailed picture can be found in the next map which shows the distribution of fossil fuel energy as a percentage of all energy consumption.

MAP 10.125 – DISTRIBUTION OF FOSSIL FUEL ENERGY AS A PERCENTAGE OF ALL ENERGY CONSUMPTION, 2010

Source: The World Bank | Basemap: Population Cartogram

The primary source of the increased atmospheric concentration of carbon dioxide since the pre-industrial period results from fossil fuel use ...

Intergovernmental Panel on Climate Change, 2007

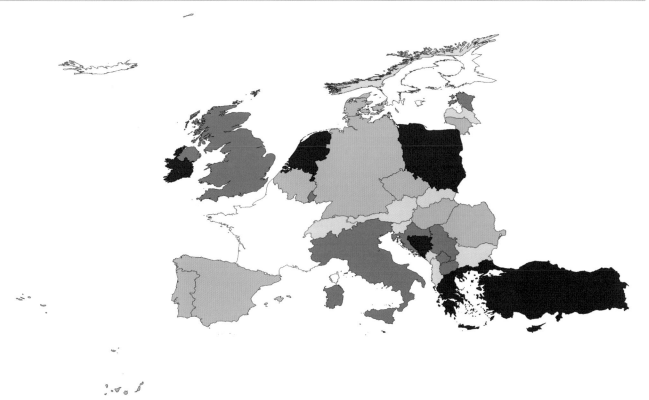

Fossil fuel energy consumption as % of total

- <50
- 50–73
- 73–79
- 79–88
- >88

FOSSIL FUEL ENERGY CONSUMPTION AS % OF TOTAL

TOP 5		BOTTOM 5	
Malta	99.9%	Iceland	17.5%
Cyprus	95.2%	Sweden	34.1%
Netherlands	93.8%	Finland	48.9%
Poland	92.2%	France	49.9%
Bosnia and Herzegovina	91.5%	Switzerland	51.5%

MAP 10.126 –COMBUSTIBLE RENEWABLES AND WASTE, COMPRISING SOLID BIOMASS, LIQUID BIOMASS, BIOGAS, INDUSTRIAL WASTE AND MUNICIPAL WASTE (KT OF OIL EQUIVALENT), 2010
Source: The World Bank

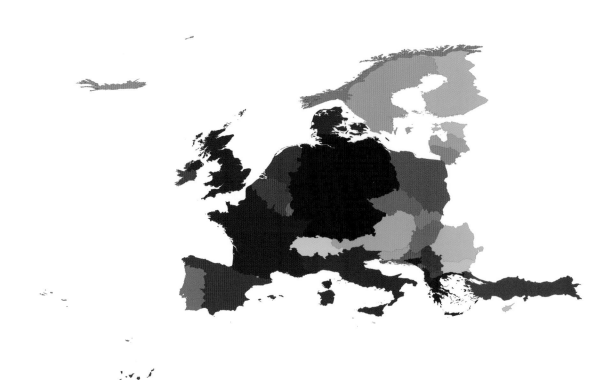

The EU aims to get 20% of its energy from renewable sources by 2020. Renewables include wind, solar, hydro-electric and tidal power as well as geothermal energy and biomass. More renewable energy will enable the EU to cut greenhouse emissions and make it less dependent on imported energy. And boosting the renewables industry will encourage technological innovation and employment in Europe.

European Commission, 2013e

According to data from the World Bank, in 2010 the total combustible renewables and waste energy use in Europe was approximately 140,498 kt of oil equivalent. This map shows the geographical distribution of this across Europe. The largest share of the total (21%, just over a fifth) was in Germany, followed by France (11%). However, in relative terms the country with the highest share (as a percentage of its total energy use) is Latvia (29.2%), followed by Sweden (23.2%), Finland (22.6%), Denmark (18.6%) and Austria (17.8%). The next map shows the thematic mapping of these percentages for all countries.

MAP 10.127 – DISTRIBUTION OF COMBUSTIBLE RENEWABLES AND WASTE AS A PERCENTAGE OF ALL ENERGY USE, 2010
Source: The World Bank | Basemap: Population Cartogram

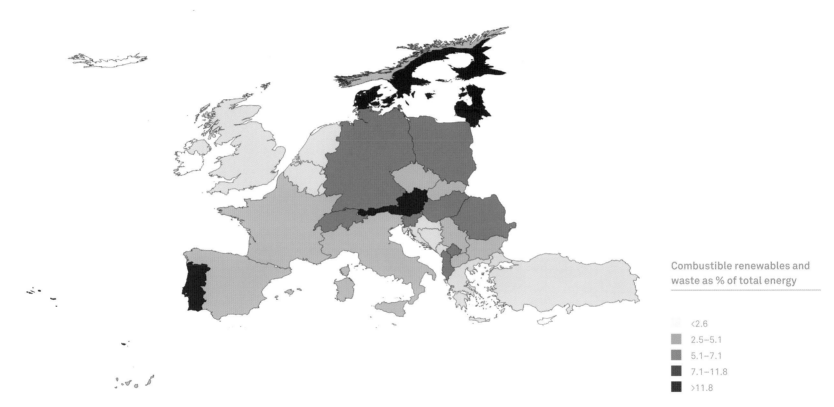

Combustible renewables and waste as % of total energy

- <2.6
- 2.5–5.1
- 5.1–7.1
- 7.1–11.8
- >11.8

COMBUSTIBLE RENEWABLES AND WASTE ENERGY USE AS % OF TOTAL

TOP 5		BOTTOM 5	
Latvia	29.2%	Malta	0%
Sweden	23.2%	Iceland	0.02%
Finland	22.6%	Cyprus	1.8%
Denmark	18.6%	Ireland	2.5%
Austria	17.8%	Bosnia and Herzegovina	2.8%

MAP 10.128 – TOTAL ANNUAL FRESHWATER WITHDRAWALS (BILLION M³), 2011
Source: The World Bank

Currently about 70% of the world's freshwater withdrawals are for agriculture, 16% are for energy and industry and 14% are for domestic purposes. Recent work suggests that unless we change our historic approach to how we use water, we could face a 40% gap by 2030 between global demand and what can sustainably be supplied.

Waughray, 2010

According to data from the World Bank there was an estimated total of 292 billion m³ of annual freshwater withdrawals from all countries mapped in this atlas. This total comprises withdrawals by agriculture and industry (including total withdrawals for irrigation and livestock production) and for direct industrial use (including withdrawals for cooling thermoelectric plants) as well as withdrawals for domestic use.

Italy has the largest volume of water being withdrawn, followed by Turkey, Spain, Germany and France. However, when taking the total resident population into account, Estonia has the highest volume of freshwater withdrawals per capita, followed by Greece, Bulgaria, Portugal and Lithuania. The lowest volume per capita is observed in Bosnia and Herzegovina. Whether the level of freshwater withdrawal in a country is problematic depends very much on how much rainfall that country receives. Using up sources stored in underground aquifers often creates problems, which could include salination in the near future.

MAP 10.129 – TOTAL RENEWABLE INTERNAL FRESHWATER RESOURCES (BILLION M³), 2011

Source: The World Bank

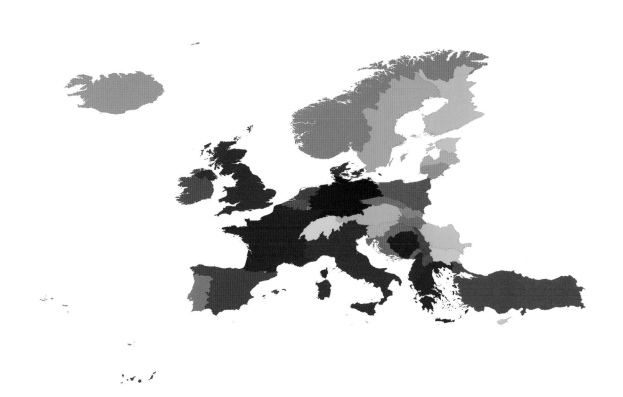

Water is an essential commodity upon which all life on Earth depends. For most nations, economic development is inextricably linked to the availability and quality of freshwater supplies. Although everyone uses water on a daily basis, we often take this vital commodity for granted – particularly in regions with a natural abundance of water. We forget that, in many regions, the availability of water is a matter of life and death.

United Nations Environment Programme, 2008

According to data from the World Bank in 2011 there was an estimated total of 2,400 billion m³ of renewable internal freshwater resources (such as internal river flows and groundwater from rainfall) in all countries mapped in this atlas. Norway has the largest share (16% of the total), followed by Turkey, France, Italy and Sweden. However, when taking the population size into account, Iceland has by far the largest volume per capita, followed by Norway, Finland, Sweden and the Republic of Ireland. The smallest volume per capita is found in Malta.

  A country that is relatively small on this map (such as Italy), but where extraction is shown to be larger than average on the previous map, will potentially have more problems with water access in future.

MAP 10.130 – TERRESTRIAL AND MARINE PROTECTED AREAS, 2010
% of total territorial area
Source: The World Bank | Basemap: Population Cartogram

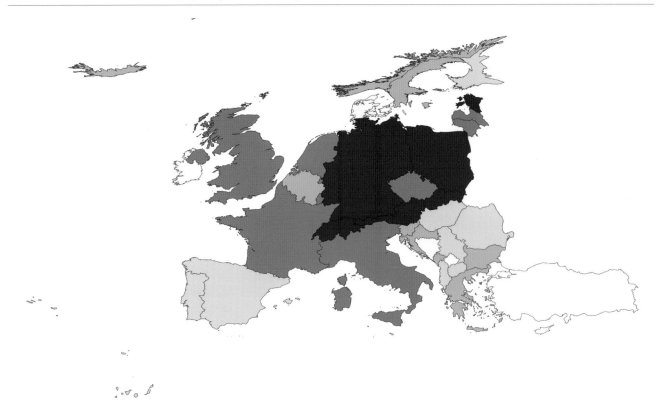

Terrestrial and marine
protected areas as % of total
territorial area, 2010

	<4.5
	4.5–8.5
	8.5–13.2
	13.2–20.0
	>20.0

This map shows terrestrial and marine protected areas. The shading shows the percentage of the total territorial area in each of the states mapped in this atlas. The terrestrial areas include 'scientific reserves with limited public access, national parks, natural monuments, nature reserves or wildlife sanctuaries, protected landscapes, and areas managed mainly for sustainable use' (World Bank, 2013d). The marine areas include 'intertidal or subtidal terrain and overlying water and associated flora and fauna and historical and cultural features – that have been reserved by law or other effective means to protect part or all of the enclosed environment' (World Bank, 2013e). Monaco has the highest percentage (98.0%), followed by Liechtenstein (42.4%), Germany (42.3%), Switzerland (24.8%), Slovakia (23.1%), Austria (22.9%) and Estonia (22.5%). The lowest percentages are observed in Bosnia and Herzegovina (0.6%), the Republic of Ireland (1.2%), Malta (1.6%) and Turkey (1.9%).

MAP 10.131 – PROJECTED CHANGE IN THE NUMBER OF TROPICAL NIGHTS BETWEEN 1961–90 AND 2071–2100

Source: European Commission, based on data from CLM scenario A1B, JRC-IES, REGIO-GIS
Basemap: Hennig Projection Gridded Population Cartogram

The EU has declared an objective of limiting the rise in temperature to 2°C. The IPCC (Inter-governmental Panel on Climate Change) has prepared climate forecasts under several possible future scenarios for 2070–2099. According to the IPCC A1B scenario, temperatures will rise by 3–5°C in Europe as compared with the average for 1961–1990.

European Commission, 2010, p 118

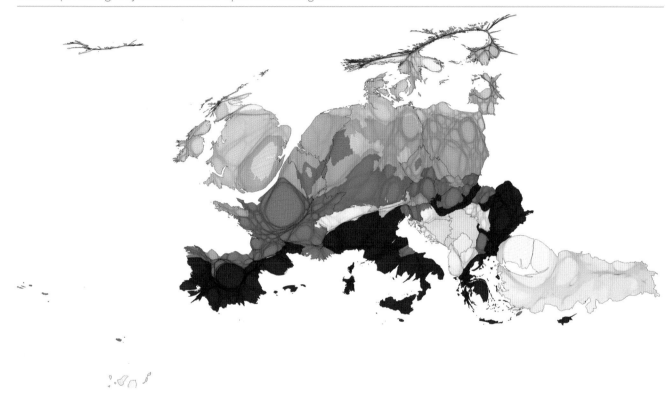

Projected change in number of tropical nights between 1961–1990 and 2071–2100

	<0.05
	0.05–0.83
	0.83–1.53
	1.53–5.02
	>5.02

This map shows the projected change in the number of days with a minimum temperature of over 20°C during the summer months, drawing on data put together by the European Commission (2010). The region with the highest rise in the number of projected tropical nights using this definition is the Spanish Balearic region *Illes Balears* with a projected increase of 9.6, followed by the Spanish regions *Región de Murcia* (8.9) and *Extremadura* (8.7) and the Italian island regions of *Sicilia* (8.6) and *Sardegna* (8.4). In contrast, there are 94 regions with a projected value of less than one, mostly in northern Europe. The region with the lowest projected value (0.001) is *North Eastern Scotland* in the United Kingdom.

Tropical nights are not particularly comfortable nights to sleep through. Rooms can be air-conditioned to make sleeping more comfortable but that in turn uses up energy that produces pollution which adds to global warming. Air-conditioning units also warm up the air for everyone else in the city!

MAP 10.132 – VULNERABILITY OF EUROPEAN REGIONS TO CLIMATE CHANGE
NUTS 2 regions

Source: European Commission, based on data from JRC, Eurostat, EFGS, Oxford Economics, Nordregio, ICIS Maastricht University, REGIO-GIS | Basemap: Hennig Projection Gridded Population Cartogram

The severity of the impact of climate change will vary across the EU according to geophysical vulnerability, the natural and human capacity to adapt, and the level of economic development. In the face of these variations, it is crucial for regions to plan an adaptation strategy most appropriate for them.

European Commission, 2010, p 118

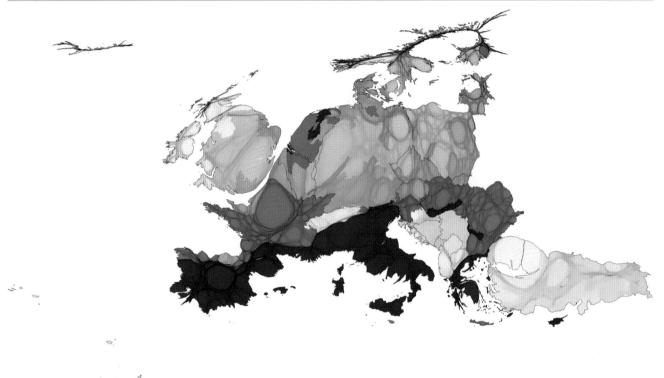

Vulnerability to climate change
Index score between
0 = low vulnerability and
100 = high vulnerability

- <6
- 6–19
- 19–29
- 29–56
- >56

This map shows the geographical distribution of an index expressing how vulnerable European regions are to climate change from both an environmental and a socio-economic point of view. The composite index, taking values from 0 to 100, is based on estimates of several factors: the total number of people in each region who are expected to be affected by increases in river floods; the total population living below 5 metres above sea level; the regional gross value added in agriculture and fisheries and in tourism and summer tourism; expected changes in precipitation and temperature; and an estimate of the impact of the total territory of mountainous areas in each region.

The regions with the highest index are mostly found in southern and eastern Europe. The most vulnerable region is *Extremadura* in western Spain where the index takes its maximum possible value of 100, followed by the Greek regions *Ionia Nisia* (90.94) and *Thessalia* (88.54), and the Portuguese regions *Algarve* (87.78) and *Alentejo* (86.33). In contrast, the lowest value of zero is observed in the United Kingdom region *Islands and Highlands*, with the second lowest index recorded *North Eastern Scotland* (1.05). The Republic of Ireland region of *Border, Midland and Western* has the third lowest value (2.74), with *Northern Ireland* (3.65) and *Devon* (3.87) in the United Kingdom coming fourth and fifth respectively.

11

SOCIAL COHESION

MAP 11.133 – INDIVIDUALS LIVING BELOW THE NATIONAL POVERTY LINE, 2000–12
Income below 60% of the median for EU member states
Source: The World Bank and Eurostat; data for most recent year available used for each country

Today, as the economic crisis has planted its roots, millions of Europeans live with insecurity, uncertain about what the future holds. This is one of the worst psychological states of mind for human beings and we now see a quiet desperation spreading among Europeans, resulting in depression, resignation and loss of hope for their future.

International Federation of Red Cross and Red Crescent Societies, 2013, p 2

This map shows the spatial distribution of the number of individuals living in relative poverty, defined as having an income below the official poverty line of the country they live in. According to the latest data from the World Bank and Eurostat, the total number of people living in poverty for all countries is 109,387,770. This is approximately 18% of the total population in Europe, as defined in this atlas. The highest absolute number is observed in Turkey, followed by Germany, Italy, the United Kingdom and Spain. However, in relative terms the largest proportion of the total population living in poverty is observed in Kosovo (29.7%), followed by Turkey (26.0%), Bulgaria (22.3%), Romania (22.2%) and Spain (21.8%). The smallest percentages are observed in Iceland (9.2%), Serbia (9.2%), Montenegro (9.3%), the Czech Republic (9.8%) and Norway (10.5%).

MAP 11.134 – POVERTY HEAD COUNT AT $2 A DAY (PPP), 2004–08

Source: The World Bank and Eurostat; data for most recent year available used for each country

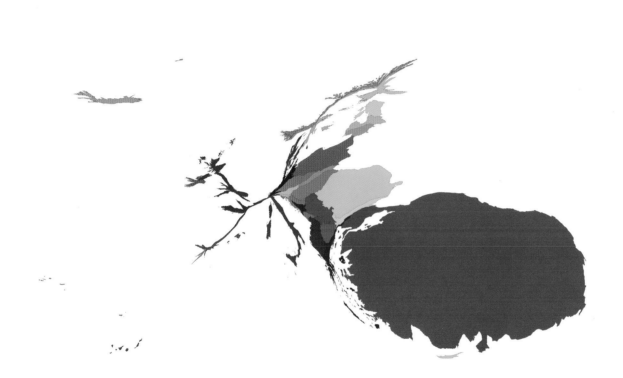

Five years ago it would have been unimaginable; so many millions of Europeans lining up for food in soup kitchens, receiving food parcels at home or being referred to social groceries ... Former middle class citizens living in trailers, tents, railway stations or in shelters for the homeless, hesitating to go to the Red Cross, Red Crescent and other organizations to ask for help.

International Federation of Red Cross and Red Crescent Societies, 2013, p 9

According to the latest data from the World Bank there are an estimated 4 million people in Europe living on the equivalent of less than US$2 a day at 2005 international prices, when prices are made comparable using established purchasing power parity (PPP) ratios. This is a measure that makes it possible to compare prices in different countries – for example to compare the cost of a meal that might cost $2 in the United States with the cost of a similar meal in another country. Approximately 3.5 million of these 4 million lowest-paid people live in Turkey. While these 'poorest of the poor' have a near-subsistence lifestyle, those who work on the land may in fact have better access to basic foodstuffs than would be available in a US city for $2. Romania has the second highest absolute number of the poorest of the poor, followed by FYR Macedonia, Albania and then Poland. In relative terms, however, FYR Macedonia has the highest proportion of very poor people as a percentage of its total population (9.1%), followed by Turkey (4.7%), Albania (4.2%), Romania (1.8%) and Estonia (1.5%).

MAP 11.135 – GINI INDEX OF INCOME INEQUALITY

Source: Eurostat and World Bank, various years between 1999 and 2012; most recent available values used here
Basemap: Population Cartogram

Income inequality changes
the way people interact
with other members of
their society and engage in
society itself ... People in
European countries with
higher levels of inequality
are less likely to help each
other in acts of altruism.

The Equality Trust, 2014

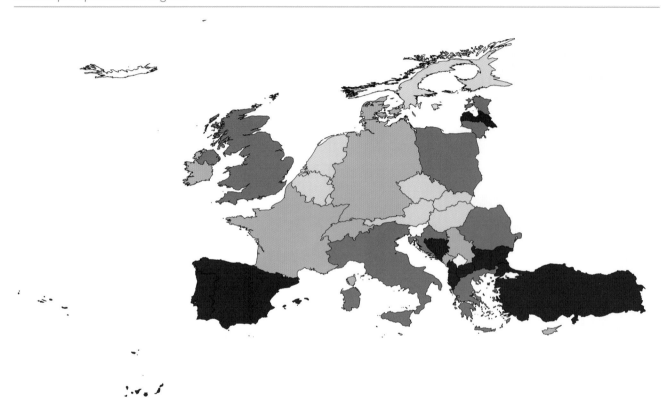

Gini index

	<23.8
	23.8–27.4
	27.4–30.8
	30.8–33.5
	>33.5

This map shows the different values of an index of income inequality known as the Gini index. The shading shows the extent to which the distributions of income within each country deviate from a perfectly equal distribution. The index can range from a minimum value of 0, representing perfect equality, to 100 implying perfect inequality.

FYR Macedonia is most inequitable and has the highest value (43.6) – which is largely why it also has the highest proportion of very poor people found in any country in Europe (see the previous map). It is followed in descending order by Turkey (40.0), Bosnia and Herzegovina (36.2), Latvia (35.9) and Bulgaria (35.1). At the other

extreme, Norway has the lowest Gini value in Europe (22.9); relatively low values are also found in in Iceland (23.6), Slovenia (23.8), Sweden (24.4), the Czech Republic (25.2), Slovakia (25.7), the Netherlands (25.8) and Finland (25.9). Among the richer European countries, Spain and Portugal, followed by the United Kingdom, are most unequal

when inequality is measured by the Gini index. When it is measured by the amount taken by the best-off 1% the United Kingdom is found to be most unequal.

MAP 11.136 – INCOME SHARE HELD BY THE MOST AFFLUENT 20%, 2000–12

Source: Eurostat and World Bank; data for most recent year available used for each country
Basemap: Population Cartogram

Overall levels of health are far worse in more economically unequal societies. Research suggests that life expectancy is longer and rates of adult mortality, infant mortality, mental illness and obesity are lower in more equal societies.

The Equality Trust, 2014

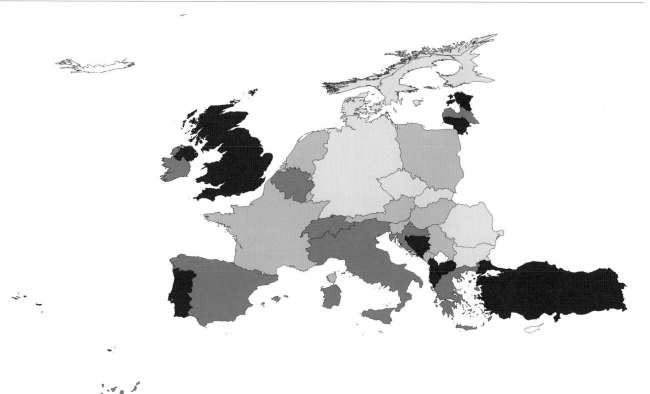

Income share held by most affluent 20%

- <37.2
- 37.2–40.9
- 40.9–42.1
- >42.1

This map shows the income share held by the top fifth income quintile (top 20%) of the population in each country. The highest value, and hence the greatest level of inequality by this measure, is in FYR Macedonia, where the most affluent 20% of the population received nearly half the income of the country (48.9%). In other words, the best-off fifth receive almost 2.5 times the mean average income in that country. Turkey has the second highest value by this measure of inequality (46.0%), followed by Portugal (45.9%), Lithuania (44.4%) and the United Kingdom (44.0%). The lowest values of income inequality by this measure are observed in Denmark (35.8%), Romania (36.1%), Slovakia (36.2%), the Czech Republic (36.2%) and Sweden (36.6%). Here the best-off fifth received a little more, on average, than 1.75 times the average income in the country.

This is an easier measure to understand than the Gini index (see the previous map), but it only considers part of the inequality distribution. It is not affected by how unequal are the lives of the other 80% of people. It is also not influenced by how much inequality there is within the best-off 20%.

MAP 11.137 – INCOME SHARE HELD BY THE LEAST AFFLUENT 20%, 2000–12

Source: Eurostat and World Bank; data for most recent year available used for each country
Basemap: Population Cartogram

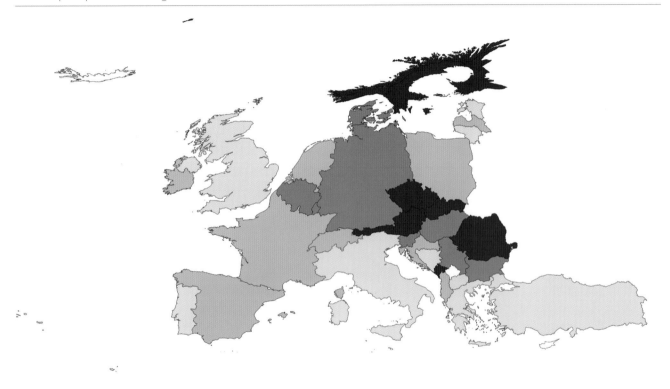

FIVE EUROPEAN COUNTRIES WITH THE HIGHEST 20:20 RATIO
(BEST-OFF:WORST-OFF SHARES)

FYR Macedonia	10.0
Turkey	8.3
Portugal	8.0
United Kingdom	7.2
Lithuania	6.7

FIVE EUROPEAN COUNTRIES WITH THE LOWEST 20:20 RATIO
(BEST-OFF:WORST-OFF SHARES)

Czech Republic	3.5
Slovakia	3.6
Finland	3.8
Norway	3.9
Sweden	4.0

Income share held by least affluent 20%

- <6.8
- 6.8–8.1
- 8.1–8.5
- >8.5

This map depicts the income share held by the poorest fifth of the population in each country. The highest value is observed in the Czech Republic (10.2%), where the poorest fifth are the best-off in Europe, although they still exist on half the mean average income in that country. It is followed by Slovakia (10.1%), Finland (9.6%), Norway (9.6%) and Sweden (9.1%). The lowest values of income received by the poorest fifth are found in FYR Macedonia (4.9%), Turkey (5.5%), Portugal (5.8%), the United Kingdom (6.1%) and Italy (6.5%). In Italy the poorest fifth are managing to exist on just a third of the mean average income.

It is interesting to combine this measure with that shown on the previous map, particularly if the share of income held by the highest 20% is divided by that of the lowest 20%. The two tables on this page show the five most equal and five most unequal countries in Europe on the basis of this measure.

MAP 11.138 – VULNERABLE EMPLOYMENT, 2011
Unpaid family workers and own-account workers as percentage of total employment
Source: The World Bank

We see emerging vulnerable groups of working poor contacting the Red Cross or Red Crescent for assistance at the end of the month, facing the dilemma of buying food or paying their utility bills – with the risk of being cut off if they do not, or evicted if unable to pay mortgages.

International Federation of Red Cross and Red Crescent Societies, 2013, p 2

According to the latest data from the World Bank, in 2011 there was an estimated total of 37,491,586 people working as unpaid family workers or own-account workers as a percentage of total employment across all the countries mapped in this atlas. The highest absolute number, and about a fifth of the overall total, is found in Turkey, followed by Italy, the United Kingdom, Poland, Romania and Germany. In Germany in recent years, unemployment has fallen while precarious and temporary employment rates have risen. In relative terms, the highest proportion of people in vulnerable employment, as a percentage of all the workforce in each country, is found in Turkey (33.0%), followed by Romania (31.5%), Greece (28.7%) and Serbia (26.6%). The smallest percentages are found in Estonia (4.6%), Norway (5.1%), Denmark (5.5%) and Luxembourg (5.9%). The proportion of all workers in vulnerable employment in relation to the total workforce in all countries mapped here is 13%. Recently a new term has been coined, the *precariat* (Standing, 2011), to describe the growing numbers of vulnerably employed people in Europe.

MAP 11.139 – POPULATION AT RISK OF POVERTY AFTER SOCIAL TRANSFERS, 2008

Source: European Commission, 2010; DE 2008 data Microcensus – DESTATIS | Basemap: Hennig Projection Gridded
Population Cartogram

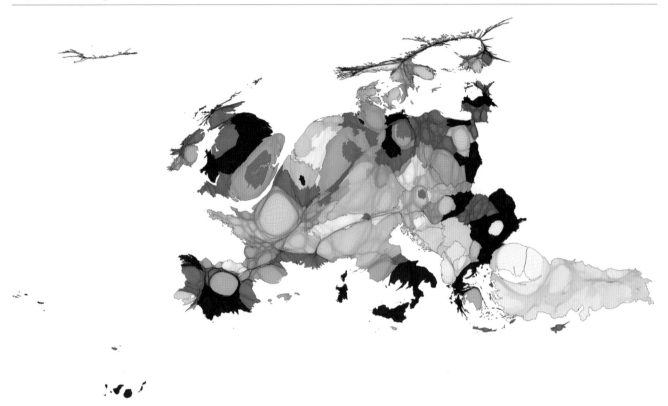

The relative number of
people with income which
puts them at risk of poverty
(less than 60% of national
median disposable income)
differs not only between
Member States but also
between regions within
Member States. In several
Member States, including
in the UK, Spain, Italy,
Germany and Poland,
the relative number is
twice as large in the least
prosperous regions as in the
most prosperous.

European Commission, 2010, p 117

**Population at risk of poverty
after social transfers, 2008**
% of total population

- <8.5
- 8.5–12.4
- 12.4–15.7
- 15.7–20.4
- >20.4

This map is a population gridded
cartogram showing the number of people
who live on an income (adjusted for
household size and composition) that
is less than that of 60% of the national
median. It should be noted that the data
used here is mainly for 2008 and in some
cases earlier (going back to 2005 for
Portugal, for example), and therefore

the map does not reflect the impact of
the severe global and European financial
crisis and recession.

The region with the highest poverty
rate (41.1%) is the Spanish region *Ciudad
Autónoma de Ceuta*, located in north
Africa. This is followed by *Extremadura*
(38.4%), also in Spain; the Italian regions
Campania (37.9%) and *Sicilia* (37%); and

the Romanian region *Sud-Vest Oltenia*
(36.1%). The lowest percentages are
observed in *Provincia Autonoma Trento*
(4.9%) in Italy, *Jihozápad* (5.8%) and
Praha (6.1%) in the Czech Republic, the
Romanian capital region of *Bucureşti-Ilfov*
(6.5%), and the Spanish region *Comunidad
Foral de Navarra Severovýchod* (6.8%).

MAP 11.140 – UN HUMAN POVERTY INDICATORS, 2007

UN Human Poverty Index 2 (for developed countries)

Source: European Commission, 2010; based on data using UN methodology, DG REGIO calculations and Eurostat data | Basemap: Hennig Projection Gridded Population Cartogram

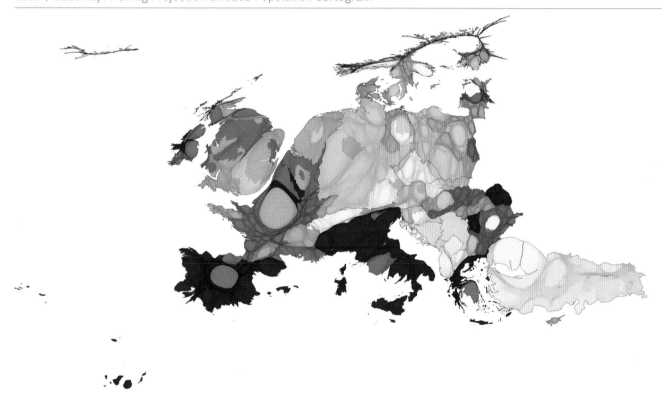

Social inclusion policies, both at EU and national levels, tend to focus on specific groups of disadvantaged and vulnerable people (such as lone mothers, elderly people living alone, migrants, homeless people, ethnic minorities and people with disabilities). One of the Europe 2020 headline targets is to lift at least 20 million people out of the risk of poverty and exclusion.

European Commission, 2010, p 187

UN Human Poverty Index 2, 2007

0 = low levels of human poverty
100 = high levels of human poverty

- <11.0
- 11.0–18.6
- 18.6–27.7
- 27.7–40
- >40

This map is a representation of the UN Human Poverty indicator by region. This particular composite indicator is based on the share of population aged 25–64 with a record of low educational attainment, the total number of long-term unemployed people as a proportion of the labour force, the probability of not living to 65 at birth, and the percentage of population with an at-risk-of-poverty income.

The five regions with the highest poverty index are all in Portugal: the island region *Região Autónoma dos Açores* has the top value of 100, followed by *Norte* (95.5), *Centro* (92.7), *Região Autónoma da Madeira* (92.0) and *Alentejo* (91.5). The lowest value of 0 is recorded in the Czech capital city region of *Praha*. Other areas in the 'bottom five' include the Czech regions *Jihozápad* (2.9), *Severovýchod* (4.1) and *Střední* Čechy (4.3), and the Slovakian capital city region of *Bratislavský Kraj* (4.7).

MAP 11.141 – INTERNET USERS, 2011
Source: The World Bank

The internet habits of different countries and socio-economic groups vary significantly. About a fifth of the EU population have never used the internet.
Eurostat, 2013c

Internet users are people with access to the worldwide network. This map shows the areas of countries stretched so that they are drawn in proportion to the spatial distribution of the population with access to the internet. The largest number of internet users is in Germany, followed by France, the United Kingdom, Italy and Turkey. In relative terms, however, Iceland is at the top of the list, with 95 internet users per 100 people, closely followed by Norway (93%), the Netherlands (92%), Sweden (91%), Luxembourg (91%) and Denmark (90%). If this very high figure for Iceland is correct, this implies that some children under the age of 4, and very elderly people, must all be internet users. However, it may be that these people are living in households that have internet access but they may not make use of it themselves. The lowest numbers of internet users as a proportion of the total population are found in Montenegro (40%), Turkey (42%), Serbia (42%), Romania (44%) and Albania (49%). It is interesting to note how these figures compare with the total estimated proportion of internet users in all countries mapped in this atlas, which is 68%.

MAP 11.142 – FIXED BROADBAND INTERNET SUBSCRIBERS, 2011
Source: The World Bank

A large majority of Europeans have used the internet in 2013. It has become important for daily life, education, work and participation in society and enables people to access information and services at any time from any place. Most internet users search for information and news, consult wikis, participate in social networks and buy products online.

Eurostat, 2013c

According to the latest data from the World Bank in 2011, there were approximately 150 million people across all countries mapped in this atlas with a broadband internet subscription being paid for by someone in their household, potentially giving everyone in the household access to high-speed internet. This represents approximately 25% of all people living in the countries mapped. In absolute terms, the largest number of people with access to fast internet is in Germany, followed by France, the United Kingdom, Italy and Spain. In relative terms, however, the highest share of broadband internet subscribers as a proportion of the total population is in Liechtenstein (71.6%), followed by Monaco (44.2%), Switzerland (39.9%), the Netherlands (38.7%) and Denmark (37.6%). The lowest percentages are in Albania (3.9%), Montenegro (8.2%), Bosnia and Herzegovina (9.7%) and Turkey (10.2%).

MAP 11.143 – BROADBAND CONNECTIONS IN HOUSEHOLDS, BY NUTS 2 REGIONS, 2011

Source: Eurostat Regional Yearbook, 2013 | Basemap: Hennig Projection Gridded Population Cartogram

Efforts have been made to expand both the geographic reach and the speed of broadband internet across the EU and by 2011 around two thirds (67%) of all households in the EU-27 had broadband internet access at home – a share that rose to 72% in 2012. The relative importance of broadband internet access grew at an average annual rate of 11.4% within the EU-27 from 2007 to 2012 ...

European Commission, 2013d

Households with a broadband connection

%

 <41

41–61

61–73

73–80

>80

This map shows the high percentage of households enjoying high-speed broadband internet access across all European regions by 2011. The highest percentage is observed in Iceland (92%), which is a single NUTS 2 region on its own. It is followed by a total of 87 regions with percentages that are above the EU-27 average (67%). These are found in Germany (in 14 regions), the Netherlands (12 regions), the United Kingdom (11), Belgium (10), Sweden (8), Norway (7), Austria (6), France (6), Denmark (5), Spain (2), Hungary, the Republic of Ireland, the Czech Republic, Luxembourg and Malta (each with 1).

The smallest proportion of households with access to high-speed broadband is in the Romanian region of *Nord-Est* (17%). A total of 24 areas are mapped here showing households with a broadband internet connection below 50%. These least well-served areas are in Bulgaria, Romania, Greece, Italy and in the United Kingdom (in Northern Ireland), in Turkey, Serbia and FYR Macedonia (the last three are each mapped as a single regions), and all have a percentage less than 50%. Note that the areas shaded grey, indicating missing data, probably include some places with very low connection rates (in South East Europe), as well as others with very high rates (in Switzerland).

MAP 11.144 – SECURE INTERNET SERVERS, 2011
Source: The World Bank

Altogether, Switzerland has around 1,440,000 square feet of data-center space. While that is far less than is available in countries like the U.S. and Germany, it's a lot relative to Switzerland's population of eight million.

Juskalian, 2014

According to World Bank data for 2011, there is a total of 418,897 internet servers using encryption technology across all countries mapped in this atlas. Following revelations made in the summer of 2013 about encryption having been broken by various security services and possibly by other agencies, these services may not be completely secure, but are probably running to a high specification. The United Kingdom has the highest absolute number of servers – nearly a quarter – followed by Germany, the Netherlands, France and Switzerland. In relative terms, the highest number of servers per person is observed in Liechtenstein (7,667 per million people), followed by Iceland (3,064), Monaco (2,906), the Netherlands (2,880) and Denmark (2,242). The smallest ratios, when access is measured in relative terms, are found in Albania (18.3 per million people), Serbia (27.2), Bosnia and Herzegovina (28.4), FYR Macedonia (41.1) and Romania (67.2). As a comparison, for every server in Romania there are 114 in Liechtenstein, per person!

MAP 11.145 – TELEPHONE LINES, 2011
Source: The World Bank

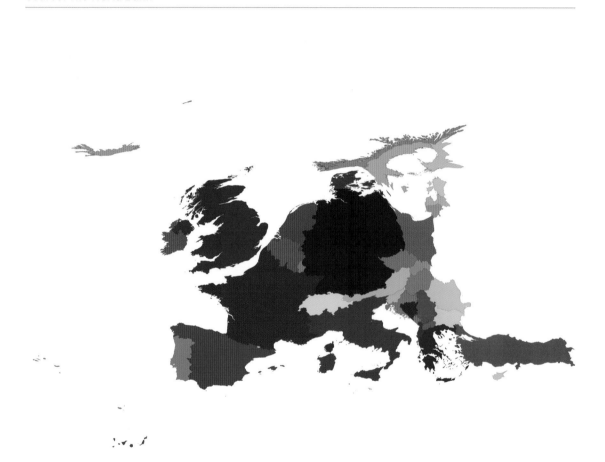

The price of telecommunications fell between 2000 and 2010 in many EU Member States. Price reductions were most apparent for national long-distance calls and international calls (represented here by calls to the United States). Across the EU, the average price of a national long-distance call almost halved between 2000 and 2010, with most of this reduction occurring by 2005, as the average price fell 5% between 2005 and 2010.

Eurostat, 2012a

This map shows the total number of fixed telephone lines in working order to be found across Europe. According to the latest data from the World Bank there were approximately 255 million fixed telephone lines in all the countries mapped here. In absolute terms, Germany has the largest number, followed by France, the United Kingdom, Italy and Spain. In relative terms, the highest number of lines per inhabitant is found in Monaco (125 per 100 people), followed by France (63), Germany (also 63), Switzerland (60) and Iceland (59). In contrast, the lowest number of fixed telephone lines in relation to the population is found in Albania (10 per 100 people), Poland (18), the Slovak Republic (19), Finland (20), FYR Macedonia and Turkey (both 21). It is noteworthy that Finland is to be found within the bottom five countries. It is also interesting to note that the number of fixed telephone lines has become less important over the years due to the proliferation of mobile cellphones (see the next map) and, more recently, to the advent of alternative internet-based communications (such as Skype).

MAP 11.146 – MOBILE CELLPHONE SUBSCRIPTIONS, 2011
Source: The World Bank

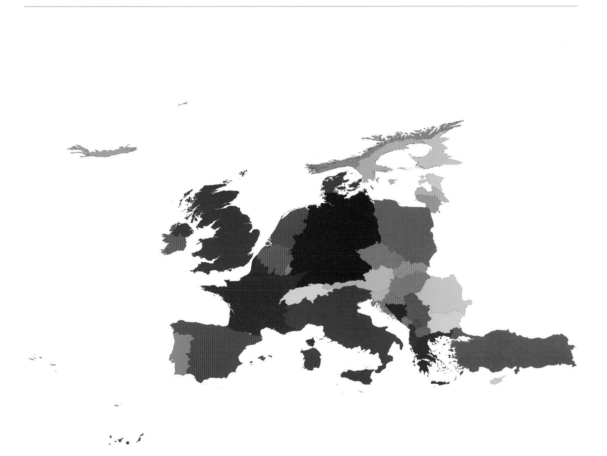

The average number of mobile phone subscriptions per 100 inhabitants stood at 125 in the EU-27 in 2009 ... It surpassed parity (100) in 24 of the EU Member States, where there were more subscriptions than inhabitants.

Eurostat, 2012a

According to the latest data from the World Bank, there were approximately 736 million mobile cellphone subscriptions in working order across all the countries mapped in this atlas in 2011. This means that there were approximately 120 subscriptions per 100 people! This could be because someone has two SIM cards in one phone, and that would count as two subscriptions; or a number of SIM cards might be used in various devices, for example. Also, many people keep a pay-as-you-go cellphone in their car in case of emergency, and another which they use more regularly; or they may have an old phone that still has access, and a new one from another provider. Others may have one phone provided by their work, and another for personal use ... and so on. However, given that many people still have no cellphone subscription, it is likely that the data includes many subscriptions that are, in practice if not on record, inoperative. In absolute terms, the largest number of subscribers is in Germany, followed by Italy, the United Kingdom and Turkey. In relative terms the highest number of cellphone subscriptions per 100 people is in Montenegro (185), followed by Finland (166), Italy (157), Austria (155) and Lithuania (151). The lowest relative numbers are in Andorra (75), Bosnia and Herzegovina (85), Turkey (89), Monaco (90) and France (95).

MAP 11.147 – MOTOR VEHICLES, 2012
Source: The World Bank

In 2011 the stock of vehicles at EU level continued to fall for the second year, the decrease compared to 2010 is only 0.3% but 21.5% compared to 2006. The highest increase in stock of vehicles can be found in Latvia (5.8%), after a decrease in 2010 (9.2%); Finland had the second highest increase (3.5%). The highest decrease can be observed in Romania (7.9%) which is lowering its stock of vehicles for the third year in a row; Greece follows Romania with a drop of 5.3% after a steady increase since 2006.

Eurostat, 2012b

This map shows the spatial distribution of the European fleet of cars, buses and all road-going freight vehicles (excluding motorbikes) across all countries mapped in this atlas. According to the latest data from the World Bank, the estimated total was approximately 300 million. Some 258 million of these are passenger cars (see the next map). About 186 million are found in five countries: the largest number in Germany (15.6% of all vehicles in Europe are found here), followed by Italy (13.8%), France (12.6%), the United Kingdom (10.9%) and Spain (9.0%). When taking population into account, however, San Marino is at the top of the list, with 1,263 vehicles per 1,000 people, followed by Monaco (863), Liechtenstein (750), Iceland (745) and Luxembourg (738). Interestingly, some of the highest numbers of cars, buses and other road vehicles per person are recorded in some of the smallest countries, where one might expect that people would not need a car to get around the small area.

The countries with the least vehicles per 1,000 people are Albania (124), Turkey (155), FYR Macedonia (155), Bosnia and Herzegovina (214) and Romania (235).

MAP 11.148 – PASSENGER CARS, 2012
Source: The World Bank

Passenger cars accounted for 84.1% of inland passenger transport in the EU-27 in 2011, with buses and coaches (8.8%) and railways, trams and metros (7.1%) both accounting for less than a tenth of all traffic (as measured by the number of inland passenger-kilometres travelled by each mode).
Eurostat, 2013d

This map shows the geographical distribution of all cars 'intended for the carriage of passengers and designed to seat no more than nine people (including the driver)' in Europe. According to the most recent data from the World Bank (2012), the total number is estimated to be approximately 258 million. In absolute terms, Germany has the highest number, followed by Italy, France, the United Kingdom and Spain. In relative terms, however, the country with the highest number of passenger cars per 1,000 people is San Marino (1,139), followed by Liechtenstein (750), Monaco (732), Luxembourg (665), Iceland (643), Italy (602) and Malta (579). The lowest numbers in relation to population size are found in Albania (92 per 1,000 people), Turkey (103), Bosnia and Herzegovina (119), FYR Macedonia (138) and Romania (201). Clearly in San Marino, even if everyone were able to drive, including all children, at least a seventh of all cars could not be driven at any one time. In practice, in households in the richest European countries there are more cars than there are adults who can drive them.

MAP 11.149 – RAILWAY LINES (TOTAL ROUTE-KM), 2011

Source: The World Bank

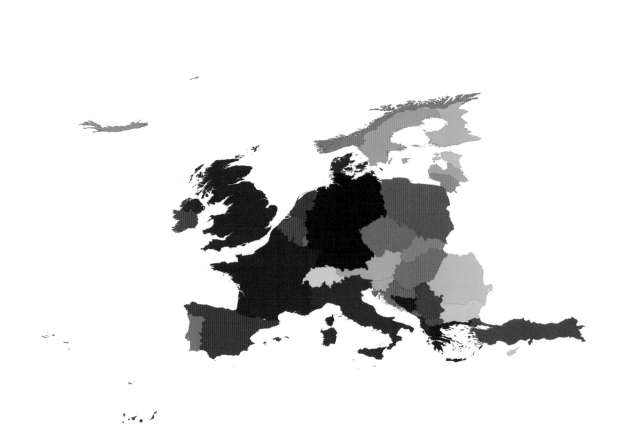

More than 70.0% of all rail travel (national and international combined) in the EU-28 was accounted for by the four largest EU Member States (note that neither Cyprus nor Malta has a railway network), with France and Germany together accounting for approximately 43% of national rail travel within the EU-28 and around 63% of international rail travel. In 2012, the number of international passenger-kilometres travelled by passengers in France was more than twice the level for Germany (in 2010) which in turn recorded a figure that was more than twice as high as that for the United Kingdom.

Eurostat, 2013e

According to the latest data from the World Bank (2011), the railway lines available for train services in all countries mapped in this atlas amount to a length of approximately 260,000 km. This map shows how the total length is distributed across countries. Germany has the longest available railway route (33,708 km), closely followed by France (33,608) and the United Kingdom (31,471).

However, in relation to population it is interesting to note that Finland has the highest number of rail-metres per person (1.09), followed by Sweden (1.05), Latvia (0.92), the Czech Republic (0.91) and Norway (0.92). At the other end of the scale is Turkey (0.12 rail-metres per person), Albania (0.14), the Netherlands (0.22), Greece (0.23) and Bosnia and Herzegovina (0.27). The following states have no railway lines at all: Andorra, Cyprus, Iceland, Kosovo, Liechtenstein, Malta, Montenegro, San Marino and the Vatican.

MAP 11.150 – NUMBER OF US DOLLAR BILLIONAIRES
Source: Kroll, 2013

According to *Forbes Magazine*, in 2013 there were 1,426 billionaires worldwide having a combined wealth of US$ 5,431,810,000,000, including 288 billionaires in Europe. This map shows what a Europe shaped by billionaires would look like if every billionaire were treated as equal, and everyone else had no value at all. You may be surprised to see how many billionaires favour living in Sweden in comparison to its relatively small population of non-billionaires.

There are 22 countries with at least one billionaire. Germany has the highest number (58), followed by Turkey (43), the United Kingdom (37), France (24) and Italy (23). However, when taking total population size into account, Monaco is top of the list (3 billionaires, when the total population is 33,000 people), followed by Cyprus (3 billionaires; total population 860,000), Switzerland (14 billionaires; population 8 million), Sweden (14 billionaires; population 9.5 million) and Norway (6 billionaires; population 5 million).

Worldwide the average billionaire has $3.8 billion. Given this average, Europe's 288 billionaires have a combined wealth of $1.01 trillion. As a comparative example, their wealth is the equivalent of the current value of Europe's largest and richest city: London – so those 288 people effectively own assets that are equal to all the buildings in Greater London. And that number could all easily fit within one jumbo jet – although they could not all fly business class if they did!

MAP 11.151 – HOMICIDES PER 100,000 INHABITANTS, 2005

Source: European Commission, 2010; OECD, Eurostat, WHO, UN-CTS-10, Bundeskriminalamt (Germany),
Federal Police (Belgium) | Basemap: Hennig Projection Gridded Population Cartogram

Homicide rate, 2005
Homicides per 100,000
inhabitants

	<0.56
	0.56–0.99
	0.99–1.45
	1.45–2.08
	>2.08

This map shows the geographical pattern of homicide rates as reported across NUTS 2 regions (and in some instances NUTS 1 regions). The highest rate (11.8 homicides per 100,000 people) is observed in *Lithuania* when it is mapped as a single region. The second highest rate (8.6) is in the French island region *Corse* (Corsica), followed by *Estonia* (8.4),

the Swedish region *Småland med* Öarna (6.6), and *Latvia* (5.5 – but note that this last statistic also includes serious attempts at murder as well as actual homicides). The Spanish city region on the north coast of Africa, *Morroco Ciudad Autónoma de Melilla*, and the Finnish island region *Åland* each have a rate of 0. Other regions with very low rates include

Itä-Suomi (0.2) and *Pohjois-Suomi* (0.2) in Finland, *Noord-Nederland* (0.3) in the Netherlands, and *Marche* (0.3) in Italy.

Not all deaths that might be classified as homicides are classified that way. For example, in the *North West* region of the United Kingdom, which has the highest recorded murder rate in that country, the deaths of cockle-pickers on a beach in

that region were all recorded as murder because the gang in charge of the pickers was found to be negligent. Similarly, hundreds of elderly people killed by one doctor, Harold Shipman, were all classified as murders. If Shipman had not been caught they would not have been recorded as murders.

MAP 11.152 –STANDARDISED DEATH RATE FROM SUICIDE FOR POPULATION UNDER 65, 2006–08
Source: European Commission, 2010 (Eurostat, DG REGIO) | Basemap: Hennig Projection Gridded
Population Cartogram

In ten regions – Lithuania, three Hungarian regions, Bretagne, Itä-Suomi in Finland and four Belgian regions – the rate is above 20 per 100 000 people. By contrast, 30 regions, all those in Greece, 6 in Spain and Italy, Flevoland in the Netherlands, Cyprus, Outer London, Norte in Portugal and Bucureşti-Ilfov in Romania, had rates below 5.

European Commission, 2010, p 79

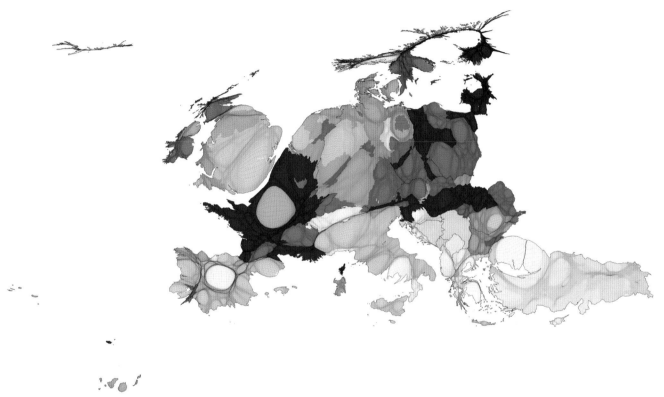

Standardised death rate from suicide for population under 65, 2006–08

Deaths per 100,000 inhabitants

	<3.4
	3.4–6.6
	6.6–9.4
	9.4–12.9
	>12.9

This map shows the standardised death rate (deaths per 100,000 inhabitants) from suicide across European regions. The highest rate is observed in *Lithuania* (28.2), followed by *Észak-Alföld* (26.4) and *Dél-Alföld* (25.1) in Hungary, the French region *Bretagne* (23.5), and *Itä-Suomi* in Finland (22.5). The lowest rates are found in the Greek regions *Kentriki Makedonia* (2.1), *Attiki* (2.1), *Notio Aigaio* (2.4) and *Sterea Ellada* (2.6); and the Spanish region *Cantabria* (2.8). It should be noted, however, that early evidence suggests the rates in Greece are likely to have risen due to the severe economic recession (Economou et al, 2011), and this may be the case in other countries severely affected by the crisis. There is evidence already from Spain and Ireland of rising rates there. There has been speculation for many years as to why France has such high rates of suicide (Farber, 1979).

MAP 11.153 – EU HUMAN DEVELOPMENT INDEX, 2007

Source: European Commission, 2010; based on data from Eurostat, DG REGIO | Basemap: Hennig Projection Gridded Population Cartogram

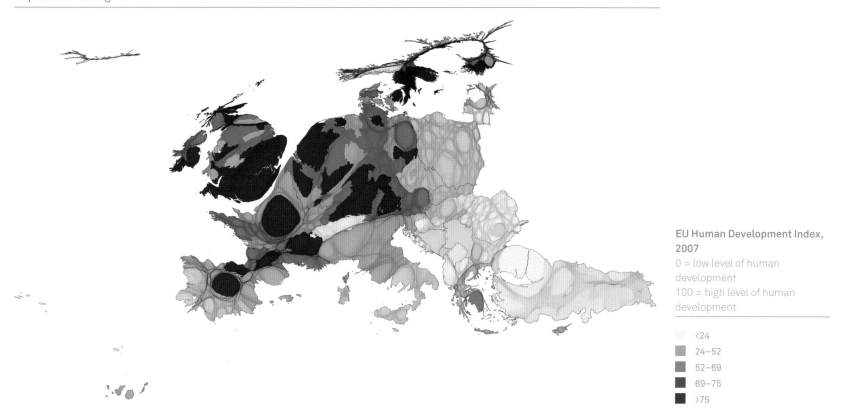

EU Human Development Index, 2007

0 = low level of human development
100 = high level of human development

- <24
- 24–52
- 52–69
- 69–75
- >75

This map shows the geographical distribution at regional level of the EU Human Development Index ranging from 0 to 100. This combined index is based on three indicators: the life expectancy of people in good health; net adjusted household income per head; and level of educational attainment of the population aged 25–64. These three indicators are combined, building on the work of Professor Amartya Sen on human development, which also provided the conceptual foundation for the United Nations Development Index. The higher the index, the better off people are said to be. In Europe the index tends to be heavily influenced by the distribution of high incomes, because variations in education and health are lower than those found worldwide.

The United Kingdom's capital city region *Inner London* has the highest value of 100, followed by the *Surrey, East and West Sussex* region (93.64). The Swedish capital city region of *Stockholm* is third with an index of 93.25, followed by *Berkshire, Buckinghamshire and Oxfordshire* (92.43) in the United Kingdom and *Utrecht* (92.43) in the Netherlands. The bottom five regions are all in Romania: *Sud-Est* with a value of 0, *Sud-Muntenia* (0.15), *Nord-Est* (0.50), *Nord-Vest* (2.36) and *Sud-Vest Oltenia* (2.71).

12

POLICY

DIAGRAM 12.01 – MONEY FLOW IN THE EUROPEAN UNION (%)

Where does the European Union get its money from, and how does it spend it? With an annual budget of over €122bn, the EU is an economic power in its own right, more significant than many countries. So, how do those finances break down?

Rogers, 2012b

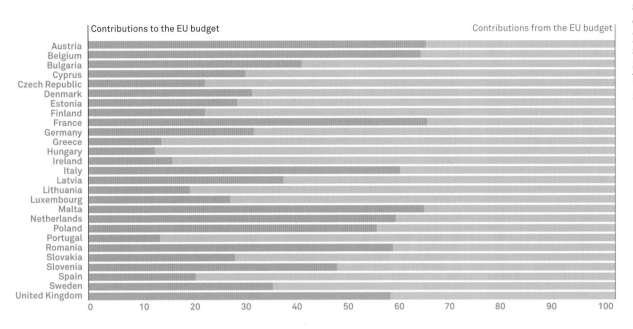

Contributions to the EU budget

Contributions from the EU budget

Austria
Belgium
Bulgaria
Cyprus
Czech Republic
Denmark
Estonia
Finland
France
Germany
Greece
Hungary
Ireland
Italy
Latvia
Lithuania
Luxembourg
Malta
Netherlands
Poland
Portugal
Romania
Slovakia
Slovenia
Spain
Sweden
United Kingdom

0   10   20   30   40   50   60   70   80   90   100

As noted in the above quote, the European Union can be seen as an economic power in its own right. However, it is also important to highlight that the total EU budget is very small when compared with the sum of all the national budgets of member states. In 2011 the total EU budget was €140 billion, whereas the total budget of all EU member states was €6,300 billion – 50 times bigger (European Commission, 2014c).

This chapter focuses on current EU member states (at the time of compiling the data for the atlas) and explores the distribution of EU policy and in particular the geographical distribution of the EU budget. The EU budget aims to promote the policy priorities agreed by all member states through a multi-annual spending plan known as the 'Financial Framework', which specifies the EU expenditure over a fixed period for specified categories. The last financial framework covered the period 2007–13 and ensured a certain planning security for the main areas of the common political goals of the EU. At the time of writing, tense negotiations are under way for the forthcoming Multiannual Financial Framework 2014–20.

The contributions to the EU budget by each country are based on economic power: each EU member state contributes to the budget a percentage of its value added tax (VAT) receipts and 1% of its gross national income (GNI). But because of various rebates the EU's overall budget represents approximately 1% of the gross national income of all member states.

The graph here shows the total payments and contributions by country. It demonstrates one other, often less discussed, aspect of the EU: that although some of the wealthier countries pay quite large sums into the EU budget (depending on their GDP) they also receive quite large payments from it. For example, the largest contributors, such as France, Germany and the United Kingdom, are also those in receipt of the largest payments from the EU budget. In 2010, for example, nine countries paid more in total into the EU budget than they received from it; the remaining 18 countries received more than they contributed (European Commission, 2014c; Rogers, 2012b).

MAP 12.154 – NET PAYMENTS INTO THE EU BUDGET
Source: European Commission, 2012

€ million

Germany	8.9
United Kingdom	5.4
France	5.06
Italy	4.16
Netherlands	1.7

This map highlights the nine countries that pay more into the EU budget than they receive from it. Germany is the biggest net contributor, with €8.9 billion more going into than coming out of the budget. It is followed by the United Kingdom with €5.4 billion, then France and then Italy. When looking at the net contributions in terms of GDP Germany remains at the top of the list with its net contributions representing 0.35% of its GDP in 2010, followed by Sweden (0.33% of its GDP), then the United Kingdom (0.31%) and the Netherlands (0.29%). By a third way of ranking, when taking into account the total population of the net contributors, Sweden is at the top of the list with an estimated net contribution of €125.05 per inhabitant, followed by Germany (€108.59) and the Netherlands (€103.49).

MAP 12.155 – NET PAYMENTS RECEIVED FROM THE EU BUDGET

Source: European Commission, 2012

TOP 5 NET RECIPIENTS

€ million

Poland	8.48
Spain	4.25
Greece	3.65
Belgium	2.85
Hungary	2.78

This map shows the countries where the difference between payments into the EU budget and the total budget spending from the EU to projects within the country is negative. In other words, these countries benefit most from EU membership in terms of net payments received. Poland is the biggest net receiver. Here the difference between paying into the EU budget and spending within the country is €8.48 billion. Spain is the second biggest receiver (€4.25 billion), followed by Greece (€3.65 billion). However, if these figures are seen as a proportion of each country's GDP, then the order changes: Lithuania has the highest proportion (4.98%), followed by Estonia (4.77%) and Latvia (3.80%). Finally, when considered in relation to the population of each country, then Luxembourg is at the top (€2,612 per inhabitant), followed by Estonia (€525.38) and Lithuania (€428.75). It should be noted, however, that the large sizes of Luxembourg and Belgium in this map are to a great extent explained by the central role they play in EU administration.

DIAGRAM 12.02 – THE EU BUDGET BY SPENDING CATEGORY (€ BILLION)
Source: European Commission, 2012

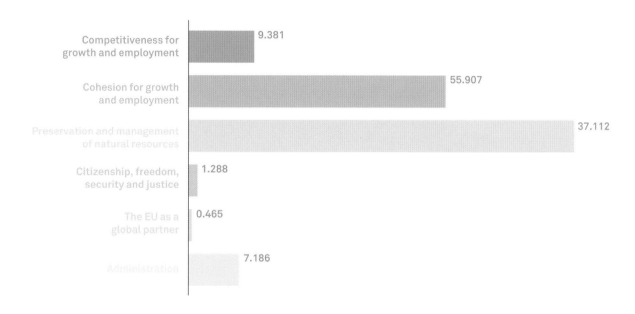

The EU budget focuses on bringing growth and jobs, tackling climate change, migration, cross-border crime and other challenges that affect us all. It helps boost prosperity, for example by better interconnecting Europeans through energy, transport and ICT infrastructure, by supporting less well-off regions to create growth and jobs both there and in the rest of the EU, and by pooling our efforts in areas like research. It is also about securing our own food supply. And finally, it is about making the EU's size count in the world – just as the US and China make their size count, and pooling our efforts to help the world's poorest people.

European Commission, 2014c

This graph shows the focus, in terms of policy priorities, of current EU spending. These individual fields of spending are distributed very differently amongst the member states, as the following maps show. Preservation and management of natural resources includes farm subsidies, but increasingly these are being geared towards paying farmers to better manage the land, to leave strips fallow, hedgerows intact, introduce buffer zones (especially around rivers), create ponds and so on. What is called 'Pillar 2' of the Common Agricultural Policy is currently being 'greened' to make it compulsory for farmers to better conserve their land if they are to continue to receive payments.

MAP 12.157 – SPENDING ON COMPETITIVENESS FOR GROWTH AND EMPLOYMENT
Source: European Commission, 2012

The expenditure allocated under 'Competitiveness for growth and employment' is at the heart of the drive to turn the EU into a smart, sustainable and inclusive economy delivering high levels of employment, productivity and social cohesion.

European Commission, 2013f

This map shows how the €9.38 billion spent on 'competitiveness for growth and employment' is distributed across member states. This spending category includes 'research and innovation, education and training, trans-European networks, social policy, economic integration and accompanying policies' (European Commission, 2013f). In absolute terms, the largest amount is received by Germany (€1.60 billion), followed by France (€1.31 billion) and the United Kingdom (€0.93 billion). However, when the size of each country's economy is considered, then Lithuania is at the top of the list with the amount spent there representing 0.44% of that country's GDP, followed by Estonia (0.28%) and Luxembourg (0.25%). The smallest percentages are observed in Romania (0.04% of GDP), Italy (0.04%) and Poland (0.05%). If total spending is explored in relation to the total population, then Luxembourg is at the top of the list (€204.00 spent per inhabitant), followed by Belgium (€75.09 per inhabitant) and Denmark (€44.54). The smallest figures are observed in Romania (€2.55 per inhabitant), Poland (€4.84) and the Czech Republic (€8.38).

MAP 12.158 – SPENDING ON COHESION FOR GROWTH AND EMPLOYMENT

Source: European Commission, 2012

Every household in the French region of Auvergne now has access to high-speed broadband thanks to a project co-financed by the European Regional Development Fund.

European Commission, 2013f

Spending under this category includes the 'convergence of the least developed EU countries and regions, EU strategy for sustainable development outside the least prosperous regions, inter-regional cooperation. Cohesion policy helps poorer regions and countries catch up and connect to the Single Market' (European Commission, 2013f). A total of €37.11 billion was spent under this category across the EU. The largest amount, and just over a fifth of this total amount, was received by Poland (€7.78 billion), followed by Spain (€5.12 billion) and Germany (€3.00 billion). However, when considering the total size of the economy then the three Baltic states are at the top of the list: Estonia (where EU spending represents 3.95% of its GDP), followed by Lithuania (3.28%) and Latvia (2.82%). The lowest percentages are observed in Denmark (0.02%), the Netherlands (0.03%) and Austria (0.05%). When total EU spending is looked at in relation to each country's population then Estonia is at the top of the list (€435.38 per inhabitant), followed by Lithuania (€282.18) and Portugal (€277.07). The lowest figures are observed in Denmark (€12.18), the Netherlands (€14.03) and Belgium (€18.70).

MAP 12.159 – SPENDING ON PRESERVATION AND MANAGEMENT OF NATURAL RESOURCES

Source: European Commission, 2012

EU funding enabled the transformation of a damaged farm building in the city of Międzychód (Poland) into an environmental education centre attracting more than 8 000 visitors every year.

European Commission, 2013f

Spending under this category represents the largest proportion of the total EU budget and includes 'the common agricultural policy, common fisheries policy, rural development and environmental measures' (European Commission, 2013f). This map shows how the total €55.9 billion is spent across EU member states. In absolute terms, the largest amounts are spent in France (€9.85 billion), Spain (€7.03 billion) and Germany (€6.94 billion). However, when the total size of national economies is considered, the highest value as a proportion of total GDP is observed in Lithuania (1.97%), followed by Bulgaria (1.59%) and Latvia (1.57%). The lowest values are in Luxembourg (0.14%), the Netherlands (0.19%) and Belgium (0.19%). If the total size of the population in each country is taken into account, the member state with the highest amount spent per person is the Republic of Ireland (€389.54 per inhabitant), followed by Greece (€258.14) and Denmark (€208.90). The lowest figures per person are in Malta (€55), the United Kingdom (€63.56) and Belgium (€64.44).

MAP 12.160 – SPENDING ON CITIZENSHIP, FREEDOM, SECURITY AND JUSTICE
Source: European Commission, 2012

The Commission proposed a set of concrete and practical measures to tackle human trafficking, including prevention, protection and support of the victims, as well as prosecution of the traffickers.

European Commission, 2013f

This map shows the distribution of the total €1.22 billion spent on 'justice and home affairs, border protection, immigration and asylum policy' as well as 'public health, consumer protection, culture, youth, information and dialogue with citizens' (European Commission, 2012). The highest amount in absolute terms is observed in Italy (€0.16 billion), followed by the Netherlands (€0.14 billion) and Belgium (€0.14 billion).

However, when GDP is taken into account, Malta is at the top of the list with the total amount spent there representing 0.16% of the country's GDP, followed by Lithuania (0.06%) and Bulgaria (0.05%). The smallest percentages are observed in Germany (0.003%), the United Kingdom (0.003%) and Spain (0.005%).

When the total size of the population is taken into account, Luxembourg has the highest amount spent per inhabitant (€26.00), closely followed by Malta (€25.00), with Belgium coming third (€13.24). The lowest values are observed in Romania (€0.69 per inhabitant), Germany (€1.02) and the United Kingdom (€1.04).

MAP 12.161 – SPENDING ON EU AS A GLOBAL PLAYER
Source: European Commission, 2012

Public support for humanitarian aid has gone up in the EU in spite of the economic crisis: a Eurobarometer survey showed that 88% of European citizens believe it is important for the EU to continue funding humanitarian aid.
European Commission, 2013f

This area *'covers all external action [foreign policy] by the EU'* (European Commission, 2013f). It is the least significant in terms of total spending compared with the other categories, but it is also the most geographically skewed. This map shows how the €0.46 billion spent under this category is distributed across EU member states. It is interesting to note that there were only 10 countries where there was any spending at all under this category. The largest amount was in Romania, where more than half of the total amount was spent (€0.28 billion), followed by Bulgaria (€0.14 billion) and Poland (€0.02 billion). When the size of national economies is taken into account, then Bulgaria is at the top of the list, with the total amount spent there representing 0.4% of that country's GDP, followed by Romania (0.22%) and Estonia (0.02%). Bulgaria is also at the top of the list when population size is considered, with an expenditure of €18.94 per inhabitant, followed again by Romania (€12.93) and Estonia (€3.07).

MAP 12.162 – SPENDING ON ADMINISTRATION
Source: European Commission, 2012

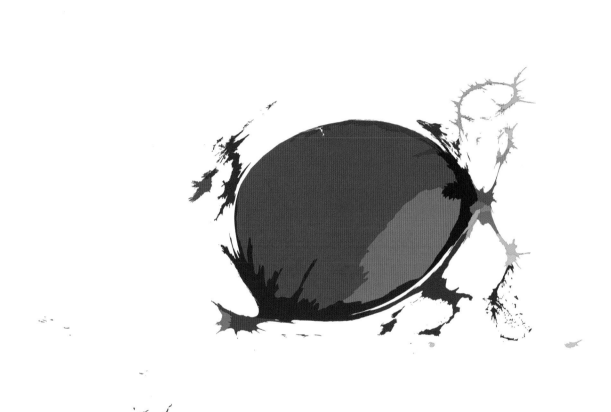

The European Ombudsman directly helped over 22,000 individuals by dealing with their complaints, replying to questions or offering advice.
European Commission, 2013f

A total of €7.18 billion was spent on *'running the EU'*, which includes *'the administrative expenditure of all the European institutions, pensions and EU-run schools for staff members' children [European Schools]'*. This map is dominated by Belgium (where €4.29 billion is spent) and Luxembourg (total €1.34 billion spent). This is not surprising given that Belgium is the headquarters of key EU institutions such as the European Commission and the European Parliament, while Luxembourg is the location of many of the remaining key European institutions such as the European Court of Justice and Eurostat. Luxembourg has the highest amount spent as a proportion of its GDP (3.33%), followed by Belgium (1.21%) and Malta (0.13%). The smallest percentages are observed in Austria (0.007%), Germany (0.007%) and the United Kingdom (0.008%).

It is also interesting to explore how much is spent in relation to the total population of each country. Luxembourg has by far the highest amount, with €2,692 per inhabitant, followed by Belgium (€397.57) and Malta (€20.00). At the other extreme, the smallest amounts are observed in Poland (€0.83 per inhabitant), Romania (€1.06) and the Czech Republic (€1.80).

MAP 12.163 – SEVENTH FRAMEWORK PROGRAMME, AVERAGE FUNDING PER HEAD
Index EU-27=100
Source: European Commission, 2010b; DG RTD, DG REGIO calculations | Basemap: Hennig Projection Gridded
Population Cartogram

The 7th Research
Framework Programme
(FP7) has a budget of
some EUR 50 billion for
the period 2007–2013. Its
objective is to help to make
the EU the leading research
area in the world through
supporting research
excellence wherever
it takes place.

European Commission, 2010

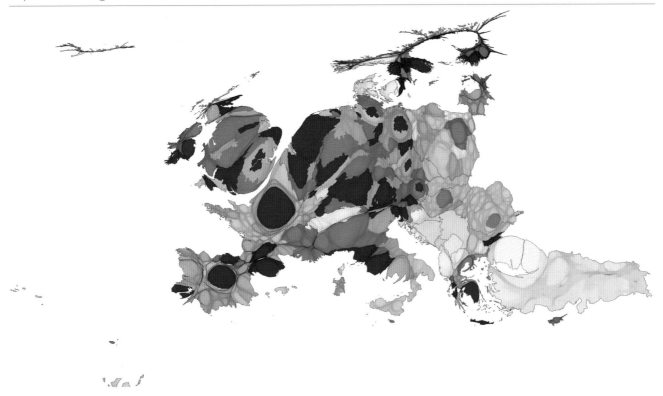

Seventh Framework Programme
Average funding per head

- <1
- 1–14
- 14–43
- 43–115
- >115

This cartogram has drawn upon it a thematic map of an index representing average EU Seventh Framework funding per head in relation to the overall average value for the EU. This funding is used to promote research activities across EU regions. The British region *Berkshire, Buckinghamshire and Oxfordshire* has the highest value – over six times that of the

EU average (index value 625, with the EU=100). It is followed by the Belgian region *Prov. Vlaams-Brabant* (605), *Inner London* (597), the Belgian capital city *Région de Bruxelles-Capitale / Brussels Hoofdstedelijk* (559), and the German region in Bavaria *Oberbayern* (505). At the other end of the distribution, there are eleven regions with an index of 0: five

are in Denmark, three in Poland, one in France, one in Greece and one in Bulgaria. An index of 0 may mean that a region contains no universities, or universities that have received almost none of this funding from the Commission.

MAP 12.164 – POTENTIAL INCREASE IN GDP PER HEAD BY RAISING THE EMPLOYMENT RATE OF POPULATIONS AGED 20–64 TO 75%, 2007

Source: European Commission, 2010b; Eurostat, DG REGIO calculations | Basemap: Hennig Projection Gridded Population Cartogram

Europe 2020 is the EU's growth strategy with five ambitious objectives – on employment, innovation, education, social inclusion and climate/energy – to be reached by 2020.

European Commission, 2013g

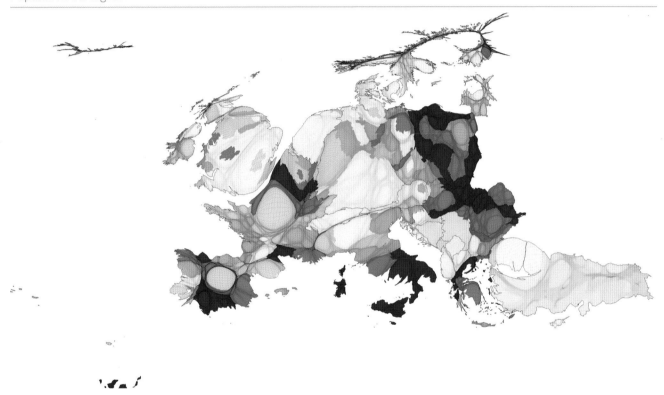

Potential increase in GDP per head from raising employment rate, 20–64, to 75%, 2007

% change

- 0
- 0–4.2
- 4.2–7.6
- 7.6–14.5
- >14.5

This cartogram shows the geographical distribution across European regions of the estimated potential increase in GDP per head from raising the employment rate of populations aged 20–64 to 75%, which is one of the key targets of the Europe 2020 strategy (European Commission, 2010). This target can be achieved by significantly reducing unemployment and increasing the participation of the economically inactive population in the labour market. (People looking after their own children are classified as inactive, along with the sick, and many higher education students who do not also have a job.)

The highest estimated percentage change resulting from reaching this target is found in the region of *Campania* (55.3%), followed by the island region *Sicilia* (52.8%), *Calabria* (50.4%) and *Puglia* (45.1%), all in Italy; these are followed by the Spanish region *Ciudad Autónoma de Ceuta* (43.5%). Most of the regions with high percentages are found in southern and eastern Europe. On the other hand, there are 85 regions with high employment rates where the percentage change value is 0; these are mostly found in northern and western Europe. The estimated increase of GDP per head for the whole of the EU is 6%. In places where not many gains can be made there may already be more people having to be in paid work than would really like to be if they had the choice.

MAP 12.165 – THE LISBON INDEX, 2008 (AVERAGE SCORE BETWEEN 0 AND 100)

Source: European Commission, 2010b; Eurostat, DG REGIO | Basemap: Hennig Projection Gridded Population Cartogram

The Lisbon Strategy, launched in 2000, can be described as an ambitious project aimed at developing a coordinated European approach in the field of economic, employment and social policy.

Rodriguez et al, 2010, p 29

The Lisbon Index, 2008

- <22
- 22–45
- 45–63
- 63–75
- >75

This map presents the geographical distribution of the Lisbon Index, showing how close an EU region is to the following targets:

- *85% for employment rate for men aged 15–54*
- *64% for employment rate for women aged 15–54*

- *64% for employment rate for women aged 15–54*
- *50% employment rate for people aged 55–64*
- *10% employment secured by early school leavers aged 18–24*
- *85% of people aged 20–24 attaining secondary educational level education as a minimum*

- *2.5% of lifelong learning participation among people aged 25–64*
- *2% for business expenditure in R&D as a proportion of GDP*
- *1% for government, higher education and non-profit expenditure in R&D as a proportion of GDP*

(European Commission, 2010)

The index can take values ranging from 0 (for the region that is furthest away from the targets) to a maximum of 100 (meaning that all targets have been reached); the index for the whole of the EU in 2008 was equal to 68. There are three regions where the index has this maximum value of 100: *Östra Mellansverige* and *Västsverige* in Sweden, and *Länsi-Suomi* in Finland.

MAP 12.166 – CHANGE IN THE LISBON INDEX, 2000–08 (PERCENTAGE POINT CHANGE)

Source: European Commission, 2010b; Eurostat, DG REGIO | Basemap: Hennig Projection Gridded Population Cartogram

Change in Lisbon Index,
2000–08

	<0
	0 – +5
	+5 – +10
	+10 – +15
	>+15

This map shows the percentage point change in the Lisbon Index (see also the previous map) between 2000 and 2008. The overall change in the index for the whole of the EU was 11% (European Commission, 2010). The biggest change is observed in the French island region of *Corse* (42.1% increase), followed by the Spanish regions *País Vasco* (36.3%),

Cantabria (30.6%), *Comunidad Foral de Navarra* (29.9%) and *Galicia* (28.7%). At the other end of the scale, 32 regions experienced a reduction in the index, most of these in eastern Europe, but also in northern Europe and in the United Kingdom.

The highest negative percentage point change is observed in the Danish region

Syddanmark (–22.4%), followed by *Sjælland* (–21%) and *Nordjylland* (–18.3%), also in Denmark, the UK region *Cumbria* (–16%), and the Romanian region *Sud-Est* (–14.2%). These tend to be areas where employment rates have fallen and/or where participation in lifelong learning and further training declined in the years immediately prior to the economic

crash of 2008 and in that crash year. It is very likely that more up-to-date data will reveal a far worse picture of areas falling behind. Many of the fast gains in employment experienced in Spain, southern France, much of Italy, parts of Greece and in the Baltic states, as well as on *Clydeside* and *Tyneside* in the United Kingdom, are likely to have been reversed.

13

CONCLUSION

MAP 13.167 – EUROPE AT NIGHT
Source: NASA

One's destination is never a place, but a new way of seeing things.

Goodreads, 2013*

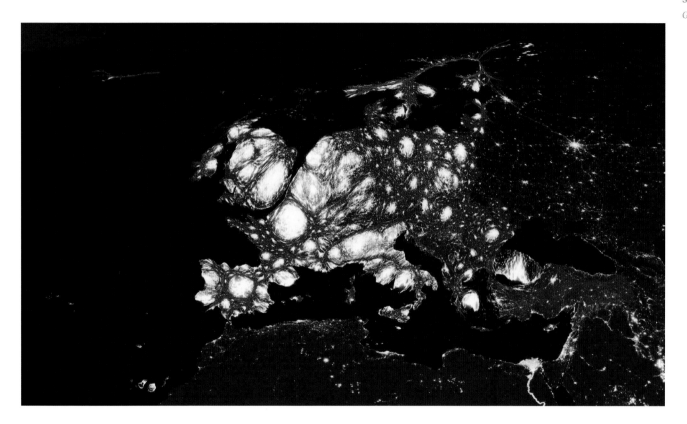

This atlas presents a cartographic story of contemporary Europe, adopting a new visual approach to exploring European human geography and identity. The aim of the atlas is to show Europe as a whole, concentrating first on where most Europeans are, and then on how they differ from each other.

The map above shows all the large cities of Europe. Each is drawn to the size of its population, but the strength of the colour shows how much light is emitted from each city and from across the countryside of the continent. The most wasteful cities in terms of energy use are to the north and west. On this map, areas outside of the current

European boundaries are also shown, to give an idea of the continent's immediate context. The Nile delta is clear to see, as is Moscow to the east. From this it is clear to see that outside of Europe, people are far less wasteful of energy – often they have less to waste.

There are thousands of people, mostly from Africa and Asia, risking their

* This quote is attributed to Henry Miller, but in fact it is a rewording and refinement (appearing in Goodreads, 2013) of the original quote which is as follows: 'One's destination is never a place, but rather a new way of looking at things' (Miller, 1957, p 25).

lives each year to reach this very affluent continent. According to 'The migrants files', a project set up by a pan-European consortium of journalists joining forces to calculate accurately and report the deaths of emigrants seeking refuge in Europe, there have been at least 13,703 migrants (including 46 babies and 388 children) who died trying to enter Europe since 2000 (journalismfund.eu, 2014). This work (which includes maps of these tragic deaths) highlights the responsibilities of Europe to live up to the underpinning ideals discussed in Chapter One. Not only do these deaths put many of the issues highlighted in this atlas into a far more important perspective, they also show how lucky people are to be born and live in this continent.

Overall, the collection of demographic, social, economic and environmental maps and diagrams presented here can be used to inform debate about prospects for the future of European identity. These images also raise questions about the feasibility of different future 'projects for Europe' (Guibernau, 2011). They raise the issue of 'whether Europe is becoming more united in cultural and social terms or whether, on the contrary, greater divisions are emerging among EU member states' (Guibernau, 2011, p 35). They can also be used to inform the many debates about other current issues, some of which are briefly discussed in the introductory chapter or touched on throughout the rest of the atlas. We can only hope that in the future, this current decade will become known as the era in which the switch to sustainable growth began, when social cohesion developed from the economic crisis, and as a time when old divisions, national stereotypes and local conflicts became a thing of the past.

The maps presented in this atlas show how Europe and its people can be seen as one entity, moving towards becoming a European people, united in diversity. At the same time, they highlight very important, and sometimes extreme, social and spatial disparities and inequalities, which call for socially and environmentally sustainable action. Considerable effort has been expended recently to put in place and to implement cohesion policies at the European level, aimed at correcting imbalances and ameliorating inequalities. Examples of such policies include the European Social Fund, the European Regional Development Fund and the Cohesion Fund (European Commission, 2013). But are these enough? Do we need more and/or better policies of this kind? Is there a need for more European top-down policies, or more devolved powers to regions and local communities?

In order to achieve sustainable growth in Europe, in terms of both environmental issues and issues of social cohesion, it is crucial, first, to ensure that Europeans move away from a 'nation-state mentality' towards a 'European people mentality'. Old nationalisms can appear a little ridiculous when they are viewed dispassionately. For example, there are no truly 'British birds': there are of course birds found in Britain, but most of them are found elsewhere in Europe too, and what happens to the birds depends on what happens in more than one country and they also move across national borders. It is also a debatable point as to which looks the most eccentric: English Morris dancing outfits, Greek traditional folk costumes, or German lederhosen – yet in many ways traditional European costumes are similar. In fact there are a huge number of ways in which people living in different parts of Europe are living very similar lives. Often the real differences are not found across national borders but between villages and cities, or between rich and poor quarters of a town. And the rich quarters of Europe are all more similar to each other than to the poorer areas that are nearer to them.

However, there are some signs of wider thinking and the expression of feelings of solidarity within Europe (Sassatelli, 2009; Cinnirella, 2011; Friedman and Thiel, 2012; Kohli et al, 2012; Moes, 2012), despite the revival of national stereotypes (Müller, 2012) and the rise of far right, national populism and xenophobia (Doxiadis and Matsaganis, 2012; Zonderop, 2012). At the same time, and from a more practical point of view, there are attempts to strengthen the feeling of pan-European citizenship and political action through the strengthening of institutions such as the European Parliament which, as noted in its promotion campaign for the 2014 elections, 'never had as much power to shape Europe' (European Parliament, 2013).

We hope the work presented in this social atlas (written by three European geographers whose first languages are Greek, English and German respectively) will do more to enhance feelings of social cohesion and solidarity amongst the people of Europe. We have tried to achieve this by highlighting important disparities and inequalities and, at the same time, reminding Europeans how much we have in common, and the potential for what can be achieved if we move away from a 'nation-state mentality' and work, rather, towards a socio-economically and environmentally sustainable common European future.

The continent does not appear so large when it is viewed in the context of this atlas, when all its peoples are given equal prominence. We hope that by viewing these maps the reader will have begun to see a different Europe: a Europe of cities rather than states; a continent of people rather than power; and one of hope rather than decline. After all, where else in the world is there such complexity, coherence and communality?

REFERENCES

Almunia, J. (2013) 'European and global perspectives for competition policy', European Commission, available from: http://europa.eu/rapid/press-release_SPEECH-13-250_en.doc (accessed 2 May 2013).

Ballas, D. and Dorling, D. (2013) 'The geography of happiness', in S. David, I. Boniwell and A. Conley Ayers (eds) *The Oxford handbook of happiness*, Oxford: Oxford University Press, pp 465–81.

Ballas, D., Lupton, R., Kavroudakis, D., Hennig, B., Yiagopoulou, V., Dale, R. and Dorling, D. (2012) *Mind the gap: Education inequality across EU regions*, Network of Experts in Social Sciences Education and Training (NESSE) report for the European Commission, Brussels, ISBN: 978-92-79-25980-7 (http://ec.europa.eu/education/news/20120914docs_en.htm)

Barro, R.J. and Lee, J.W. (2013) 'A new data set of educational attainment in the world, 1950–2010', *Journal of Development Economics*, vol 104, pp 184–98; dataset available from: www.barrolee.com/

BBC (2009) 'Climate change: methane', available online from: www.bbc.co.uk/climate/evidence/methane.shtml (accessed 17 March 2014).

BBC News (2010) 'EU climate package explained', 29 April, available from: www.bbc.co.uk/news/10086349 (accessed 17 March 2014).

BBC News (2013a) 'Zadar: One Square Mile of Croatia', 27 April, available from: www.bbc.com/news/world-radio-and-tv-22294290 (accessed 7 May 2013).

BBC News (2013b) 'EU: More UK bankers paid above 1m euros', available from: www.bbc.co.uk/news/23321835

BBC News (2013c) 'Carbon dioxide passes symbolic mark, 10 May', available from: www.bbc.co.uk/news/science-environment-22486153 (accessed 17 March 2014).

Beracochea, E., Weinstein, C. and Evans, D. (2011) *Rights-based approaches to public health*, New York: Springer.

Bombay Sarvodaya Mandal/Gandhi Book Centre (2014) *Essence of democracy*, online document, available from: www.mkgandhi.org/momgandhi/chap72.htm (accessed 16 March 2014).

Carroll, L. (2011) 'If Google is in Ireland for tax reasons, why are most of its profits in Bermuda?', *The Guardian*, available from: www.theguardian.com/business/ireland-business-blog-with-lisa-ocarroll/2011/mar/24/google-ireland-tax-reasons-bermuda

Cinnirella, M. (2011) 'Towards a European identity? Interactions between the national and European social identities manifested by university students in Britain and Italy', *British Journal of Social Psychology*, vol 36, no 1, pp 19–31.

Corrente (2013) 'Russell Brand vs. Jeremy Paxman: the full transcript', available from: www.correntewire.com/russell_brand_vs_jeremy_paxman_the_full_transcript (accessed 1 November 2013).

Dorling, D. (2013) *Population 10 Billion*, London: Constable.

Dorling, D. and Thomas, B. (2011) *Bankrupt Britain: An atlas of social change*, Policy Press, Bristol.

Dorling, D., Newman, M. and Barford, A. (2008) *The atlas of the real world*, London: Thames and Hudson.

Doxiadis, A. and Matsaganis, M. (2012) 'National populism and xenophobia in Greece', Counterpoint UK (online), Creative Commons: http://counterpoint.uk.com/wp-content/uploads/2013/01/507_CP_RRadical_Greece_web-1.pdf (accessed 11 October 2013).

Economou, M. et al (2011) 'Increased suicidality amid economic crisis in Greece', *The Lancet*, vol 378, p 1459

The Equality Trust (2014) 'How does inequality affect the individual, society and the economy?', available from: www.equalitytrust.org.uk/about-inequality/effects (accessed 17 March 2014).

Ernest Mandel Internet Archive (2005) 'Karl Marx: Historical Materialism', available from: www.ernestmandel.org/en/works/txt/1990/karlmarx/2.htm (accessed 16 April 2013).

Eurofound (2012) 'Women in the labour market', available online from: www.eurofound.europa.eu/areas/industrialrelations/dictionary/definitions/womeninthelabourmarket.htm (accessed 6 March 2014).

European Commission (2010) *Investing in Europe's future: Fifth report on economic, social and territorial cohesion*, available from: http://ec.europa.eu/regional_policy/sources/docoffic/official/reports/cohesion5/index_en.cfm

European Commission (2012a) 'How the EU works', online document, available from: http://europa.eu/about-eu/ (accessed 23 February 2012).

European Commission (2012b) 'The history of the European Union', available from: http://europa.eu/about-eu/eu-history/index_en.htm (accessed 22 February 2012).

European Commission (2012c) 'Report highlights major geographic disparities in education', online document, available from: http://europa.eu/rapid/press-release_IP-12-960_en.htm?locale=en (accessed 15 June 2013)

European Commission (2013a) 'Report on health inequalities: gaps in life expectancy and infant mortality narrow across the EU', online document, available from: http://europa.eu/rapid/press-release_IP-13-823_en.htm?locale=en

European Commission (2013b) 'Enlargement', online document, available from: http://ec.europa.eu/enlargement/policy/conditions-membership/index_en.htm (accessed 9 May 2014).

European Commission (2013c) 'Education statistics at regional level', online document, available from: http://epp.eurostat.ec.europa.eu/statistics_explained/index.php/Education_statistics_at_regional_level (accessed 14 March 2014)

European Commission (2013d) Eurostat Regional Yearbook 2013, Luxembourg: Publications Office of the European Union, available from: http://epp.eurostat.ec.europa.eu/cache/ITY_OFFPUB/KS-HA-13-001/EN/KS-HA-13-001-EN.PDF

European Commission (2013e) 'Renewable energy', online document, available from: http://ec.europa.eu/energy/renewables/index_en.htm (accessed 17 March 2014).

European Commission (2013f) 'Financial Programming and Budget', online document, available from: http://ec.europa.eu/budget/financialreport/contents/index_en.html (accessed 18 March 2014).

European Commission (2013g) 'Europe 2020 initiatives', online document, available from: http://ec.europa.eu/social/main.jsp?langId=en&catId=956 (accessed 18 March 2014).

European Commission (2013h) 'European Regional Development Fund', online document, available from: http://ec.europa.eu/regional_policy/thefunds/regional/index_en.cfm

European Commission (2014a) 'Enterprise and industry', online document,, available from: http://ec.europa.eu/enterprise/initiatives/mission-growth/index_en.htm (accessed 6 March 2014).

European Commission (2014b) 'Climate action: forests and agriculture', 12 March, online document, available from: http://ec.europa.eu/clima/policies/forests/index_en.htm (accessed 17 March 2014).

European Commission (2014c) 'EU: Budget myths and facts, European Commission', online document, available from: http://ec.europa.eu/budget/explained/myths/myths_en.cfm#1of15

European Parliament (2013) 'Act, React, Impact', European Elections 2014 promotions campaign video, available in all EU official languages from: www.youtube.com/user/EuropeanParliament?feature=watch

Eurostat (2012a) 'Telecommunication statistics', online document, available from: http://epp.eurostat.ec.europa.eu/statistics_explained/index.php/Telecommunication_statistics (accessed 17 March 2014).

Eurostat (2012b) 'Road freight transport by vehicle characteristics', online document, available from: http://epp.eurostat.ec.europa.eu/statistics_explained/index.php/Road_freight_transport_by_vehicle_characteristics (accessed 17 March 2014).

Eurostat (2013a) 'Energy production and imports', online document, available from: http://epp.eurostat.ec.europa.eu/statistics_explained/index.php?title=Energy_production_and_imports&stable=1 (accessed 17 March 2014).

Eurostat (2013b) 'Energy', online document, available from: http://epp.eurostat.ec.europa.eu/portal/page/portal/energy/introduction (accessed 17 March 2014).

Eurostat (2013c) 'Internet use statistics – individuals', online document, available from: http://epp.eurostat.ec.europa.eu/statistics_explained/index.php/Internet_use_statistics_-_individuals (accessed 17 March 2014).

Eurostat (2013d) 'Passenger transport statistics', online document, available from: http://epp.eurostat.ec.europa.eu/statistics_explained/index.php/Passenger_transport_statistics (accessed 14 March 2014).

Eurovision (2013) 'Eurovision Song Contest 2013 Grand Final', online document, available from: http://www.eurovision.tv/page/history/by-year/contest?event=1773 (accessed 10 June 2013).

Food and Water Watch Europe (2014) 'Agriculture Frequently Asked Questions', online document, available from: https://www.foodandwaterwatch.org/europe/agriculture/faq/ (accessed 6 March 2014).

Farber, M.L. (1979) 'Suicide in France: some hypotheses', *Suicide and Life Threatening Behavours*, vol 9, no 3, pp 154–62.

Fontevecchia, A. (2011) 'The largest U.S. companies with big European exposure', *Forbes Magazine*, available from: www.forbes.com/sites/afontevecchia/2011/11/09/defensive-stocks-like-coke-and-ge-far-from-immune-to-europe/

Friedman, R. and Thiel, M. (2012) *European identity and culture: Narratives of transnational belonging*, Surrey: Ashgate.

Gastner, M.T. and Newman, M.E.J. (2004) 'Diffusion-based method for producing density equalizing maps', *Proc. Natl. Acad. Sci. USA*, vol 101, pp 7499–504.

Google (2014a) Result of a google search with terms 'synonyms for professional', available from: google.co.uk (accessed 14 April 2014).

Google (2014b) Result of a google search with terms 'synonyms for elementary', available from: google.co.uk (accessed 14 April 2014).

Goodreads (2013) Henry Miller quotes, available from: https://www.goodreads.com/quotes/133768-one-s-destination-is-never-a-place-but-a-new-way (accessed 20 September 2013).

gov.uk (2013) 'Bilateral loan to Ireland', online document, available from: www.gov.uk/government/publications/bilateral-loan-to-ireland

Greenpeace (2006) 'Other gases', 16 March, online document, available from: www.greenpeace.org/international/en/campaigns/climate-change/science/other_gases/ (accessed 17 March 2014).

Greenpeace International/European Renewable Energy Council (2007) *Energy [r]evolution: a sustainable world energy outlook*, available from: www.greenpeace.org/international/Global/international/planet-2/report/2007/1/energyrevolution-2007.pdf

Guibernau, M. (2011) 'Prospects for a European identity', *International Journal of Politics, Culture, and Society*, vol 24, no 1, pp 31–43.

Hennig, B.D. (2013) *Rediscovering the world: Map transformations of human and physical space*, Heidelberg/New York/Dordrecht/London: Springer.

Hicks, R.D. (ed) (1972) *Diogenes Laertius, Lives of Eminent Philosophers*, Cambridge, MA: Harvard University Press (first published 1925), available online under a Creative Commons Attribution-ShareAlike 3.0 United States License from: www.perseus.tufts.edu/ hopper/text?doc=Perseus Perseus%3Atext%3A1999.01.0258% 3Abook%3D5%3Achapter%3D1

Intergovernmental Panel on Climate Change (2007) 'Human and Natural Drivers of Climate Change', online document, available from: https://www.ipcc.ch/publications_and_data/ar4/wg1/en/spmsspm-human-and.html (accessed 17 March 2014).

International Federation of Red Cross and Red Crescent Societies (2013) *Think differently: Humanitarian impacts of the economic crisis in Europe*, Geneva: IFRC, available from: www.ifrc.org/PageFiles/134339/1260300-Economic%20crisis%20Report_EN_LR.pdf

Jasper, J.M. (1997) *The art of moral protest: Culture, biography and creativity in social movements*, Chicago, The University of Chicago Press.

journalismfund.eu (2014) 'The migrants files', available from: www.journalismfund.eu/migrants-files (accessed 23 April 2014).

Juskalian, R. (2014) 'For Swiss Data Industry, NSA Leaks Are Good as Gold', *The MIT Technology Review*, 18 March, available from: www.technologyreview.com/news/525546/for-swiss-data-industry-nsa-leaks-are-good-as-gold/

Kohli, M. et al (2012) 'European identity in times of crisis: Sociological perspectives on identification with Europe in turbulent times', Workshop 11–12 June 2012, detailed programme available from: www.eui.eu/seminarsandevents/index.aspx?eventid=75961 [accessed 11 October 2013]

Kroll, L. (2013) *Mapping the wealth of the world's billionaires*, available from: http://www.forbes.com/sites/luisakroll/2013/03/09/mapping-the-wealth-of-the-worlds-billionaires/ (accessed 12 September 2013).

Krugman, P. 'On the political economy of permanent stagnation', online document, available from: http://krugman.blogs.nytimes.com/2013/07/05/on-the-political-economy-of-permanent-stagnation/

Lev, M. and Dorling, B. (1983) *Rising five*, Oxford: Pre-school Playgroup Association.

Lewis, M. (2011) *The meltdown tour*, London: Boomerang.

London Evening Standard (2013) 'UK workers suffer sharp wage fall', available from: www.standard.co.uk/panewsfeeds/uk-workers-suffer-sharp-wage-fall-8755998.html

Lu, L. and Gilmour, R. (2004) 'Culture and conceptions of happiness: Individual oriented and social oriented SWB', *Journal of Happiness Studies*, vol 5, no 3, pp 269–91.

Mason, P. (2014) 'If Transnistria is the next flashpoint between Putin and the west, how should Europe react?', *The Guardian*, 1 April, available from: www.theguardian.com/commentisfree/2014/apr/01/transnistria-putin-west-europe-dniester-river-moldova

Mason, R. (2014) 'Dole queue for young would go from London to Edinburgh, research shows', *The Guardian*, available from: www.theguardian.com/society/2014/mar/04/dole-queue-young-stretch-london-edinburgh (accessed 6 March 2014).

McGrath, M. (2013) 'Concentrations of warming gases break record', BBC Science and Environment, 6 November, online document, available from: www.bbc.co.uk/news/science-environment-24833148 (accessed 17 March 2014).

McKee, M., Pomerleaua, J., Robertson, B.A., Pudulec, I., Grinbergac, D., Kadziauskiened, K., Abaraviciuse, A. and Vaaskf, S. (2000) 'Alcohol consumption in the Baltic Republics', *Journal of Epidemiology & Community Health*, vol 54, pp 361–6, doi: 10.1136/jech.54.5.361

Mill, J.S. (1974) *On liberty*, London, Penguin.

Miller, H. (1957) *Big Sur and the oranges of Hieronymus Bosch*, New York: New Directions Publishing Corporation.

Moes, J. (2012) 'Imagining Europe: Conceptualizations of Europe in a supra-national perspective across social groups and networks', online document, available from: www.imagining.eu (accessed 11 October 2013).

Mossialos, E., Permanand, G., Baeten, R. and Hervey, T (eds) (2010) *Health systems governance in Europe: the role of European Union law and policy*, Cambridge: Cambridge University Press, also available online from: www.euro.who.int/en/about-us/partners/observatory/studies/health-systems-governance-in-europe-the-role-of-eu-law-and-policy

Moore, J. (2014) 'Considering Europe: Students in continental shift', *The Independent*, 14 March, available from: www.independent.co.uk/student/study-abroad/considering-europe-students-in-continental-shift-8160026.html

Müller, J. (2012) 'Europe's perfect storm: The political and economic consequences of the Eurocrisis', *Dissent*, no 4, Fall, pp 47–53, doi: 10.1353/dss.2012.0089

Murphy-Lejeune, E. (2002) *Student mobility and narrative in Europe: The new strangers*, London: Routledge.

Official Journal of the European Union (2007) Charter of Fundamental Rights of the European Union, 14 December, 2007/C 303/01, available from: http://fra.europa.eu/sites/default/files/charter-of-fundamental-rights-of-the-european-union-2007-c_303-01_en.pdf (accessed 28 April 2013).

Rechel, B., Grundy, E., Robine, J.M., Cylus, J., Mackenbach, J.P., Knai, C. and McKee, M. (2013) 'Ageing in the European Union', *The Lancet*, vol 381, no 9874, pp 1312–22.

Reher, D.S. (1998) 'Family ties in Western Europe: persistent contrasts', *Population and Development Review*, vol 24, pp 203–34.

Reuters (2013) 'Factbox: Apple, Amazon, Google and tax avoidance schemes', online document, available from: http://in.reuters.com/article/2013/05/22/eu-tax-avoidance-idINDEE94L07Z20130522

Ringold, D., Orenstein, M.A. and Wiklens, E. (2005) *Roma in an expanding Europe: Breaking the poverty cycle*, Washington DC: The World Bank.

Rodriguez, R. et al (2010) 'The Lisbon Strategy 2000–2010: an analysis and evaluation of the methods used and results achieved', Directorate General for Internal Policies, European Parliament, available from: www.europarl.europa.eu/document/activities/cont/201107/20110718ATT24270/20110718ATT24270EN.pdf

Rogers, S. (2012a) 'Healthcare spending around the world, country by country', *The Guardian*, 30 June.

Rogers, S. (2012b) 'EU budget 2010: what does the European Union spend and where does the money come from?', 26 January, available from: www.theguardian.com/news/datablog/2012/jan/26/eu-budget-european-union-sp

RTE (2014) Bono addressing delegates at the European People's Party Congress, Dublin, 7 March 2014, available from: www.rte.ie/news/player/2014/0307/20540276-bono-addressesdelegates-at-the-european-peoples-party-congress-indublin/

Sassatelli, M. (2009) *Becoming Europeans: Cultural identity and cultural policies*, Palgrave: New York.

Schlesinger, P. and Foret, F. (2006) 'Political roof and sacred canopy? Religion and the EU Constitution', *European Journal of Social Theory*, vol 9, pp 59-81.

Schoch, R. (2007) *The secrets of happiness: Three thousand years of searching for the good life*, London: Profile Books.

Sky News (2013) 'Wages: UK workers in Europe's bottom four', available at: http://news.sky.com/story/1127184/wages-uk-workers-in-europes-bottom-four

Smith, H. (2010) 'Greek comrade', *European Voice*, available online from: https://www.europeanvoice.com/article/imported/greek-comrade/67685.aspx (accessed 16 March 2014).

Standing, G. (2011) *The precariat: The new dangerous class*, Bloomsbury: London.

Stiglitz, J.E., Sen, A., Fitoussi, J.-P. et al (2009) 'Report by the Commission on the Measurement of Economic Performance and Social Progress', available from: www.stiglitz-sen-fitoussi.fr/documents/rapport_anglais.pdf (accessed 2 May 2013).

Tiberius, V. (2004) 'Cultural differences and philosophical accounts of wellbeing', *Journal of Happiness Studies*, vol 5, no 3, pp 293–314.

Traynor, I. (2013) 'Austerity pushing Europe into social and economic decline, says Red Cross', available from: www.theguardian.com/world/2013/oct/10/austerity-europe-debt-red-cross

Twitter (2013) Volonteurope, European Year of Citizenship tweet #volonteurope #axsolidaridad, available from: https://twitter.com/Volonteurope/status/340448995052777472 (accessed 3 March 2014).

Uchida, Y., Norasakkunkit, V. and Kitayama S. (2004) 'Cultural constructions of happiness: Theory and empirical evidence', *Journal of Happiness Studies*, vol 5, no 3, pp 223–39.

United Nations (2013) 'International Human Development Indicators', available from: http://hdr.undp.org/en/statistics/

United Nations Environment Programme (2008) 'Vital water graphics: an overview of the state of the world's fresh and marine waters', available from: www.unep.org/dewa/vitalwater/article2.html (accessed 17 March 2014).

Van Stekelenburg, J. (2012) 'The Occupy Movement: Product of this time', *Development*, vol 55, no 2, pp 224–31.

Veenhoven, R. (1993) *Happiness in nations: Subjective appreciation of life in 56 nations 1946–1992*, Rotterdam: Erasmus University Press.

Warnes, A.M., Friedrich, K., Kellaher, L. and Torres, S. (2004) 'The diversity and welfare of older migrants in Europe', *Ageing and Society*, vol 24, pp 307–26, doi:10.1017/S0144686X04002296

Waughray, D. (2010) 'Why worry about water? A quick global overview', *The Guardian*, 10 November, available from: www.theguardian.com/sustainable-business/freshwater-risk-water-demand-sustainability

Weeks, J. (2013) 'The faux European recovery and youth unemployment', *Social Europe Journal*, available from: http://www.social-europe.eu/2013/12/youth-unemployment-faux-recovery (accessed 6 March 2014).

WHO Regional Office for Europe (2014a) *HIV/AIDS*, online document, available from: www.euro.who.int/en/health-topics/communicable-diseases/hivaids/hivaids (accessed 15 March 2014).

WHO Regional Office for Europe (2014b) *Alcohol use*, online document, available from: www.euro.who.int/en/health-topics/disease-prevention/alcohol-use, online document (accessed 15 March 2014).

Wikiquote (2014) Dag Hammarskjöld, available from: http://en.wikiquote.org/wiki/Dag_Hammarskj%C3%B6ld (accessed 14 March 2014).

Wilde, O. (1891) *The soul of man under socialism*, available online from: www.marxists.org/reference/archive/wilde-oscar/soul-man/ (accessed 16 March 2014).

World Bank (2013a) 'Foreign direct investment, net inflows (BoP, current US$)', available from: http://data.worldbank.org/indicator/BX.KLT.DINV.CD.WD (accessed 29 July 2013).

World Bank (2013b) 'PFC gas emissions (thousand metric tons of CO2 equivalent', online document, available from: http://data.worldbank.org/indicator/EN.ATM.PFCG.KT.CE (accessed 28 July 2013).

World Bank (2013c) 'SF6 gas emissions', online document, available from: http://data.worldbank.org/indicator/EN.ATM.PFCG.KT.CE (accessed 28 July 2013).

World Bank (2013d) 'Terrestrial protected areas (% of total land area)', available from: http://data.worldbank.org/indicator/ER.LND.PTLD.ZS (accessed 29 July 2013).

World Bank (2013e) 'Marine protected areas (% of territorial waters)', available from: http://data.worldbank.org/indicator/ER.MRN.PTMR.ZS (accessed 29 July 2013).

World Bank (2014) 'What is the difference between Foreign Direct Investment (FDI) net inflows and net outflows?', online document, available from: https://datahelpdesk.worldbank.org/knowledgebase/articles/114954 (accessed 17 March 2014).

Worldmapper (2009) 'Worldmapper: The world as you've never seen it before', available from: http://worldmapper.org/ (accessed 3 September 2013).

YouTube (2013) 'Channel 4 News: Nigel Farage visits Bulgaria', available from: www.youtube.com/watch?v=kuxksNkmFiw#t=650 (accessed 25 October 2013).

Zonderop, Y. (2012) *The Roots of Contemporary Populism in the Netherlands*, Counterpoint UK (online), Creative Commons, available from: http://counterpoint.uk.com/wp-content/uploads/2013/01/507_CP_RRadical_DutchEnglish_web.pdf (accessed 11 October 2013).

APPENDIX: SOURCES OF DATA

The maps and diagrams in this atlas were created using data from the sources listed below. It should be noted that it was not always possible to obtain data for all countries (and especially for Andorra, Kosovo, Liechtenstein, Monaco, San Marino or the Vatican City). In these cases and in order to create the *country cartogram maps* (see Chapter One) the data were either estimated based on available statistics for a neighbouring country that was deemed to be of similar socio-economic profile (more information is provided in the detailed notes for each individual map below), or a zero value was entered when there were no suitable data that could be used for the estimation and at the same time the estimated value would have been too small to have any visible impact on the cartogram creation result (this mostly applies to missing data for the Vatican City).

Sources of data and websites

Barro-Lee educational attainment dataset: www.barrolee.com

CIA World Factbook: www.cia.gov/library/publications/the-world-factbook

Esri ArcGIS software maps database: www.esri.com

European Regional Yearbook 2013: http://epp.eurostat.ec.europa.eu/portal/page/portal/publications/regional_yearbook

European Union Fifth Report on Economic, Social and Territorial Cohesion: http://ec.europa.eu/regional_policy/sources/docoffic/official/reports/cohesion5/index_en.cfm

European Union Statistics on Income and Living Conditions (EU-SILC): http://epp.eurostat.ec.europa.eu/portal/page/portal/microdata/eu_silc

European Values Survey: www.europeanvaluesstudy.eu

Eurostat database: http://epp.eurostat.ec.europa.eu/portal/page/portal/statistics/search_database

Eurovision Song Contest: www.eurovision.tv

Forbes Magazine data on 'the world's billionaires': www.forbes.com/sites/luisakroll/2013/03/09/mapping-the-wealth-of-the-worlds-billionaires

Guardian data blog on health spending by country: https://docs.google.com/spreadsheet/ccc?key=0AonYZs4MzlZbdHMzaGRuOWFVQjZEWmJJb2JnNEZIREE#gid=0

International Labour Organisation (ILO): www.ilo.org/global/statistics-and-databases/lang--en/index.htm

National Aeronautics and Space Administration (NASA) MODIS sensor: http://modis.gsfc.nasa.gov

Socio-Economic Data and Applications Center (SEDAC) of the Columbia University, New York: http://sedac.ciesin.columbia.edu/data/collection/gpw-v3

Wikipedia data on Romani people: http://en.wikipedia.org/wiki/Romani_people

The Vatican City State website: www.vaticanstate.va

The World Bank: http://data.worldbank.org

World Directory of Minorities: www.minorityrights.org/?lid=1873&tmpl=printpage #peoples

World Health Organization (WHO): www.who.int/research/en

WorldClim Global Climate Data: http://worldclim.org

Detailed list of sources of data for all tables, maps and diagrams

Table 1: Eurostat, data for 2012 except for Albania (2011), Andorra (2011), Monaco (2005); data for the Vatican from Vatican City State website.

Figure 2: Eurostat, data for 2012 except for Albania (2011), Andorra (2011), Monaco (2005); data for the Vatican City from Vatican City State website.

Figure 3: Gridded Population of the World, 2013.

Figure 4: Gridded Population of the World, 2013; Esri ArcGIS software database topographical data.

Figure 5: Gridded Population of the World, 2013; NASA MODIS sensor.

Figure 6: Gridded Population of the World, 2013; WorldClim.

Figure 7: Gridded Population of the World, 2013; WorldClim.

Figure 8: WorldClim.

Maps 2.001–2.013: Eurostat (population data presented in Table 1); European Values Survey, 2008.

Map 2.014: 'Romani diaspora' in Wikipedia; World Directory of Minorities.

Maps 2.015–2.019: Eurovision Song Contest, 2013.

Population pyramids, pp 34–39: Eurostat, data for 2012, except for Albania (2011 and 2007) and Andorra (2011).

Maps 3.020–3.023: Eurostat, data for 2012, except for Turkish regions (2011).

Map 3.024: The World Bank, data for 2010.

Maps 3.025–3.026: The World Bank, data for 2000 and 2010.

Maps 4.027–4.030: Eurostat population data for 2012, except for Albania (2011) and Andorra (2011); Barro-Lee educational attainment dataset (2013), data for 2010, but missing for Andorra (estimated using the rates for Spain), Bosnia and Herzegovina, FYR Macedonia and Montenegro

(estimated using the rates for Serbia), Liechtenstein (estimated using the rates for Switzerland), Monaco (estimated using the rates for France), San Marino (estimated using the rates for Italy) or the Vatican City.

Maps 4.031–4.032: Eurostat, data for 2010.

Map 4.033: Gridded Population of the World, 2013; Eurostat, data for enrolments school year 2009/2010, except for Estonia, Cyprus, Latvia, Lithuania, Malta, Iceland, Liechtenstein, Switzerland, the FYR Macedonia and Turkey, 2009; Greece and Luxembourg, 2008; data at NUTS 2 regional level except for Germany and the UK (NUTS 1 regions) and Switzerland (national level).

Map 4.034: Gridded Population of the World, 2013; Eurostat, data for 2010.

Map 4.035: Gridded Population of the World, 2013; Eurostat, data for 2010, except for Estonia, Cyprus, Latvia, Lithuania, Luxembourg, Malta, Iceland, Liechtenstein, Switzerland, the FYR Macedonia and Turkey, 2009; Greece, 2008; Vlaams Gewest (BE2), 2007; Région Wallonne (BE3), 2001; data at NUTS 2 level, except for Germany and the UK (NUTS 1

regions), and Greece, the Netherlands, Switzerland and Croatia (national level).

Map 4.036: Gridded Population of the World, 2013; Eurostat, data for 2010, except for Hamburg (DE6), 2008; Brandenburg (DE4), 2007; Mecklenburg-Vorpommern (DE8), 2005; data at NUTS 2 regional level except for Finland (national level).

Map 5.037: Eurostat, data for 2012, except for Albania (2011 and 2007) and Andorra (2011); ILO, data for 2010 on economic activity by age and sex for all countries except Andorra (estimated using the activity rates for Spain), Kosovo (estimated using the activity rates for Serbia), Liechtenstein (estimated using the activity rates for Switzerland), Monaco (estimated using the activity rates for France).

Maps 5.038–5.043: Eurostat, unemployment and youth (less than 25 years) unemployment data for 2012 for all countries except the following for which unemployment and youth unemployment rate data obtained from the World Bank were applied on economically active population data obtained from the ILO in order to estimate the total numbers:

Albania, Bosnia and Herzegovina, FYR Macedonia, Kosovo, Montenegro and Serbia. No data for Andorra, Liechtenstein, Monaco or the Vatican City.

Maps 5.044–5.045: Eurostat, data for 2012.

Map 5.046: Eurostat, data for 2007 and 2012.

Map 5.047: Eurostat, data for 2008 except for the regions of Bulgaria (2007), Poland (2007), Sweden (2007) and Slovenia (2007).

Maps 6.048–6.050: Eurostat and ILO data on age structure, labour force and economic activity rate (see note on Map 5.037). CIA World Factbook data on labour force by category (agriculture, industry and services) for years 2005 (Greece, France, the Netherlands), 2007 (Cyprus, United Kingdom), 2007 (Belgium and Luxemburg), 2008 (Bosnia and Herzegovina, Iceland, Norway, Sweden), 2009 (Bulgaria, Czech Republic, Portugal, Slovakia, Slovenia, Spain), 2010 (Albania, Andorra, Estonia, San Marino, Liechtenstein, Poland, Romania, Serbia, Switzerland, Turkey), 2011 (Denmark, Finland, Germany, Hungary, Ireland, Italy,

Malta, Montenegro), 2012 (Austria, FYR Macedonia, Lithuania). No data for Monaco (estimated using data for France), Kosovo (estimated using data for Serbia) or the Vatican City.

Maps 6.051–6.059: Eurostat population data for 2012, except for Albania (2011) and Andorra (2011); EU-SILC data for 2011 except for Ireland (2009).

Map 6.060: Eurostat, data for 2010, except for Greece and the UK (2009); Cyprus, Latvia, Lithuania, Luxembourg, Malta and Poland (2008); data at NUTS 2 regional level except for Belgium, Slovenia, Norway, Switzerland and FYR Macedonia (national level).

Map 6.061: Eurostat, data for 2010, except for Greece and the Netherlands (2009); data at NUTS 2 regional level except for Croatia and Switzerland (national level).

Maps 6.062–6.064: Eurostat, data for 2010, except for Bulgaria, Greece and the Netherlands (2009); data at NUTS 2 regional level except for Croatia (national level).

Maps 7.065 and 7.066: Eurostat, data for 2007, except for Belgium (2006) and Ireland (2006).

Maps 7.067: Eurostat population data for 2012, except for Albania (2011) and Andorra (2011); Health data from WHO (2010), no data for Kosovo (estimated using data for Serbia) and Liechtenstein (estimated using data for Switzerland).

Maps 7.068–7.071: Eurostat population data for 2012, except for Albania (2011) and Andorra (2011); Health data from WHO (2008), no data for Kosovo (estimated using data for Serbia) or Liechtenstein (estimated using data for Switzerland).

Maps 7.072–7.074: Eurostat, data for 2008–10 at NUTS 2 level except for Scotland (NUTS 1), Denmark (national level), Slovenia (national level) and Croatia (national level).

Map 7.075: WHO, data for 2010 (obtained via The Guardian blog; also see notes and abbreviations); No data for Kosovo (estimated using data for Serbia), Liechtenstein (estimated using data for Switzerland) or the Vatican City (estimated using data for Italy).

Map 7.076: Eurostat, 2010, except for the Netherlands and Sweden (2009). Greece, France, Italy, the Netherlands, Slovakia, Finland, FYR Macedonia and Turkey: professionally active physicians; Ireland and Portugal: licensed physicians; Cyprus: Eurostat estimate. Data at NUTS 2 regional level except for Germany, and England and Wales (NUTS 1 level), and Belgium and Ireland (national level).

Map 7.077: WHO, data for 2009 except for Belgium (2010), Cyprus (2008), France (2010), Iceland (2010), Malta (2010), Spain (2010), FYR Macedonia (2008), United Kingdom (2010). No data for Ireland (estimated using data for the UK), Italy (estimated using data for France), Kosovo (estimated using data for Serbia), Latvia (estimated using data for Lithuania), Monaco (estimated using data for France), Portugal (estimated using data for Spain), San Marino (estimated using data for Italy), Liechtenstein (estimated using data for Switzerland) or the Vatican City.

Map 7.078: WHO data for 2009 except for Austria (2010), Cyprus (2008), France (2010), Iceland (2010), Ireland (2010), Malta (2010), Sweden (2007), FYR Macedonia (2008), United Kingdom (2010). No data for Albania (estimated using data for FYR Macedonia), Kosovo (estimated using data for Serbia), Latvia (estimated using data for Lithuania), Liechtenstein (estimated using data for Switzerland), the Netherlands (estimated using data for Sweden), San Marino (estimated using data for Italy), Slovakia (estimated using data for the Czech Republic) or the Vatican City (estimated using data for Italy).

Map 7.079: WHO data for 2009 except for Austria (2010), France (2010), Iceland (2010), Ireland (2010), Malta (2010), Spain (2010), FYR Macedonia (2010). No data for Albania (estimated using data for FYR Macedonia), Bulgaria (estimated using data for FYR Macedonia), Denmark (estimated using data for the Netherlands), Greece (estimated using data for Italy), Lithuania (estimated using data for Latvia), Liechtenstein (estimated using data for Switzerland), Norway (estimated using data for the Netherlands) or the United Kingdom (estimated using data for the Netherlands).

Map 7.080: Eurostat, 2010 except for Greece (2009), United Kingdom (2009), Iceland (2007) and the Netherlands (2002). Data at NUTS 2 regional level except for Germany (NUTS 1 regions).

Map 7.081: WHO data for 2011. No data for Bosnia and Herzegovina (estimated using data for Serbia), Cyprus (estimated using data for Greece), Kosovo (estimated using data for Serbia), Liechtenstein (estimated using data for Switzerland), Monaco (estimated using data for France), Montenegro (estimated using data for Serbia), San Marino (estimated using data for Italy), FYR Macedonia (estimated using data for Serbia). The following countries had WHO estimates of <0.1% and a value of 0.1% (among adults aged 15–49) was assumed to estimate the total numbers: Croatia, Czech Republic, Hungary, Lithuania, Serbia, Slovakia, Slovenia, Turkey.

Map 7.082: WHO data for 2005. No data for Kosovo (estimated using data for Serbia), Liechtenstein (estimated using data for Switzerland), Monaco (estimated using data for France), Montenegro (estimated using data for Serbia), Italy (estimated using data for San Marino) or the Vatican City.

Maps 8.083–8.093: Eurostat (population data presented in Table 1); European Values Survey, 2008.

Map 9.094: World Bank, data for 2012 except for Andorra, Liechtenstein, Monaco and San Marino (2007). No data for the Vatican City.

Maps 9.095–9.096: World Bank, data for 2012. No data for Andorra, Liechtenstein, Monaco and San Marino.

Map 9.097: World Bank, data for 2012. No data for Andorra (estimated using data for Spain), Liechtenstein (estimated using data for Switzerland), Monaco (estimated using data for France), San Marino (estimated using data for Italy).

Map 9.098: World Bank, 2012. No data for Albania, Andorra, Bosnia and Herzegovina, Kosovo, Liechtenstein, Monaco, San Marino or the Vatican City.

Map 9.099: World Bank, 2012. No data for Albania (estimated using data for Serbia), Andorra (estimated using data

for Spain), Bosnia and Herzegovina (estimated using the data for Serbia), Kosovo (estimated using the data for Serbia), Liechtenstein, Monaco, San Marino or the Vatican City.

Map 9.100: World Bank, 2012. No data for Albania, Andorra, Bosnia and Herzegovina, Kosovo, Liechtenstein, Monaco, San Marino or the Vatican City.

Map 9.101: World Bank, data for 2012. No data for Andorra, Liechtenstein, Monaco or the Vatican City.

Maps 9.102 and 9.103: World Bank, data for 2012. No data for Andorra, Cyprus, Monaco, Montenegro, Norway, Romania, San Marino, Serbia, Slovakia or the Vatican City.

Maps 9.104 and 9.105: World Bank, data for 2012: No data for Andorra, Bosnia and Herzegovina, Cyprus, Liechtenstein, Monaco, Montenegro, Norway, Romania, San Marino, Serbia, Slovakia or the Vatican City.

Map 9.106: European Commission Fifth Report on Economic, Social and Territorial Cohesion using data from Eurostat, DG REGIO estimates, EQLS, Eurofound. Net adjusted disposable income expressed in PPCS includes 'transfers in kind', including services such as education, health care and other public services that are provided for free or below provision cost. EU-27 = 17,606 PPCS/inhabitant.

Map 9.107: Eurostat Regional Yearbook, data for 2010; data at NUTS 2 regional level (except for Turkey (national level).

Map 9.108: Eurostat Regional Yearbook, data for 2008 and 2010 (percentage points difference between 2010 and 2008; in relation to the EU-27 average); data at NUTS 2 regional level (except for Turkey (national level).

Map 10.109: World Bank, data for 2009. No data for Kosovo, San Marino and the Vatican.

Maps 10.110, 10.111 and 10.113: World Bank, data for 2010. No data for Andorra, Kosovo, Liechtenstein, Monaco, Montenegro, San Marino or the Vatican City.

Map 10.112 and 10.114: World Bank, data for 2008. No data for Andorra, Kosovo, Liechtenstein, Monaco, Montenegro, San Marino or the Vatican City.

Map 10.115: World Bank, data for 2011. No data for Kosovo or the Vatican City.

Maps 10.116 and 10.117: World Bank, data for 2010. No data for Andorra, Liechtenstein, Monaco, San Marino or the Vatican City.

Maps 10.118–10.124: World Bank, data for 2010. No data for Andorra, Liechtenstein, Monaco, San Marino or the Vatican City.

Map 10.125: Eurostat population data for 2012, except for Albania (2011) and Andorra (2011); fossil fuel energy data for 2010 from the World Bank (no data for Andorra, Liechtenstein, Monaco, San Marino or the Vatican City).

Map 10.126: World Bank, data for 2010. No data for Andorra, Kosovo, Liechtenstein, Monaco, Montenegro, San Marino or the Vatican City.

Map 10.127: Eurostat population data for 2012, except for Albania (2011) and Andorra (2011); combustible renewables and waste data for 2010 from the World Bank (no data for Andorra, Liechtenstein, Monaco, San Marino or the Vatican City).

Map 10.128: World Bank, data for 2011. No data for Andorra, Kosovo, Liechtenstein, Monaco, San Marino or the Vatican City.

Map 10.129: World Bank, data for 2011. No data for Kosovo, Liechtenstein, Monaco, Montenegro, San Marino or the Vatican City.

Map 10.130 Eurostat population data for 2012, except for Albania (2011) and Andorra (2011); terrestrial and marine protected areas data for 2010 from the World Bank (no data for Kosovo, San Marino or the Vatican City).

Map 10.131: Data from the European Commission Fifth Report on Economic, Social and Territorial Cohesion (Climate Limited-area Modelling scenario A1B, JRC-Institute for Environment and Sustainability, REGIO-GIS).

Map 10.132: Data from the European Commission Fifth Report on Economic, Social and Territorial Cohesion (JRC, Eurostat, EFGS, Oxford Economics, Nordregio, ICIS Maastricht University, REGIO-GIS).

Map 11.133: Eurostat/EU-SILC data for 2011, except for the following countries for which the most recent available data from the World Bank was used (year in brackets): Albania (2008), Bosnia and Herzegovina (2007), FYR Macedonia (2006), Serbia (2010), Turkey (2010). No data for Andorra, Liechtenstein, Monaco, San Marino or the Vatican City.

Map 11.134: Most recent available World Bank data for the following countries (year in brackets): Albania (2008), Bosnia and Herzegovina (2007), Bulgaria (2007), Croatia (2008), Estonia (2004), Hungary (2007), Latvia (2009), Lithuania (2008), FYR Macedonia (2010), Montenegro (2010), Poland (2011), Romania (2011), Serbia (2010), Slovakia (2009), Slovenia (2004), Turkey (2010). There were no reported data for any of the other countries.

Map 11.135: Eurostat population data for 2012, except for Albania (2011) and Andorra (2011); most recent available Eurostat Gini index data (year in brackets) for the following countries: Austria (2011), Belgium (2011), Bulgaria (2011), Croatia (2011), Cyprus (2011), Czech Republic (2011), Denmark (2011), Estonia (2011), Finland (2012), France (2011), Germany (2011), Greece (2011), Hungary (2012), Iceland (2011), Ireland (2011), Italy (2011), Latvia (2012), Lithuania (2011), Luxembourg (2011), Malta (2011), the Netherlands (2011), Norway (2011), Poland (2011), Portugal (2011), Romania (2011), Slovakia (2011), Slovenia (2011), Spain (2011), Sweden (2011), Switzerland (2011), United Kingdom (2011); most recent available Gini index data from the World Bank (year in brackets) for the following countries: Albania (2008), Bosnia and Herzegovina (2007), FYR Macedonia (2010), Montenegro (2010), Turkey (2010). No data for Andorra, Kosovo, Liechtenstein, Monaco, San Marino or the Vatican City.

Maps 11.136 and 11.137: Eurostat population data for 2012, except for Albania (2011) and Andorra (2011); most recent available income shares data from the World Bank (year in brackets): Albania (2008), Austria (2000), Belgium (2000), Bosnia and Herzegovina (2007), Bulgaria (2007), Croatia (2008), Czech Republic (1996), Denmark (1997), Estonia (2004), Finland (2000), France (1995), Germany (2000), Greece (2000), Hungary (2007), Ireland (2000), Italy (2000), Latvia (2009), Lithuania (2008), Luxembourg (2000), FYR Macedonia (2010), Montenegro (2010), the Netherlands (1999), Norway (2000), Poland (2011), Portugal (1997), Romania (2011), Serbia (2010), Slovakia (2009), Slovenia (2004), Spain (2000), Sweden (2000), Switzerland (2000), Turkey (2010), United Kingdom (1999). No data for Andorra, Cyprus, Iceland, Kosovo, Liechtenstein, Malta, Monaco, San Marino or the Vatican City.

Map 11.138: World Bank data for 2011. Missing data for Albania (estimated using data for Serbia), Andorra, Kosovo (estimated using data for Serbia), Montenegro (estimated using data for Serbia), Liechtenstein, Monaco, San Marino and the Vatican City.

Map 11.139: Data from the European Commission Fifth Report on Economic, Social and Territorial Cohesion for 2008 (Germany, 2008 data from microcensus – DESTATIS; France, 2007 data; Portugal, based on Household Budget Survey data 2005; the Netherlands, CBS 2007, UK, data from the Households Below Average Income 2007/09; all other data from EU-SILC).

Map 11.140: Data from the European Commission Fifth Report on Economic, Social and Territorial Cohesion for 2007 (based on UN methodology, DG REGIO calculations and Eurostat data).

Maps 11.141 and 11.142: Data from the World Bank for 2011; no data for Kosovo or the Vatican City.

Map 11.143: Eurostat Regional Yearbook 2013 data for 2011 except for FYR Macedonia and Turkey (2010), Serbia (2009), Northern Ireland (UKN) (2008), Åland region (FI20), 2007; data at NUTS 2 regional level except for Germany, Greece, France, Poland and the United Kingdom (NUTS 1 regional level) and Slovenia, Serbia and Turkey (national data).

Maps 11.144 – 11.146: World Bank data for 2011; no data for Kosovo or the Vatican City.

Maps 11.147 and 11.148: World Bank data for 2012; no data for Andorra, Kosovo or the Vatican City.

Map 11.149: World Bank data for 2011; no data (or not applicable) for Andorra, Cyprus, Iceland, Kosovo, Liechtenstein, Malta, Monaco, Montenegro, San Marino or the Vatican City.

Map 11.150: *Forbes Magazine* (Kroll, 2013).

Map 11.151: Data from the European
Commission Fifth Report on
Economic, Social and Territorial
Cohesion for 2005 (OECD, Eurostat,
WHO, UN-CTS-10, Belgian Federal
Police, Bundeskriminalamt); Latvia
data include attempts; Albania, data
for 2004.

Map 11.152: Data from the European
Commission Fifth Report on Economic,
Social and Territorial Cohesion for
2006–08 (Eurostat, DG REGIO).

Map 11.153: Data from the European
Commission Fifth Report on
Economic, Social and Territorial
Cohesion for 2007. Method based on
life expectancy in good health, net
adjusted household income per head,
high and low educational attainment
of population aged 25–64 (Eurostat,
DG REGIO).

Diagrams 12.01 and 12.02 and
Maps 12.154–12.162: European
Commission, 2012.

Map 12.163: Data from the European
Commission Fifth Report on
Economic, Social and Territorial
Cohesion (DG RTD, DG REGIO
calculations).

Map 12.164: Data from the European
Commission Fifth Report on
Economic, Social and Territorial
Cohesion for 2007 (Eurostat, DG
REGIO calculations).

Map 12.165: Data from the European
Commission Fifth Report on
Economic, Social and Territorial
Cohesion for 2008 (Eurostat, DG
REGIO calculations).

Map 12.166: Data from the European
Commission Fifth Report on
Economic, Social and Territorial
Cohesion for 2000–08, percentage
point change (Eurostat, DG REGIO
calculations).

Map 13.167: NASA MODIS sensor.

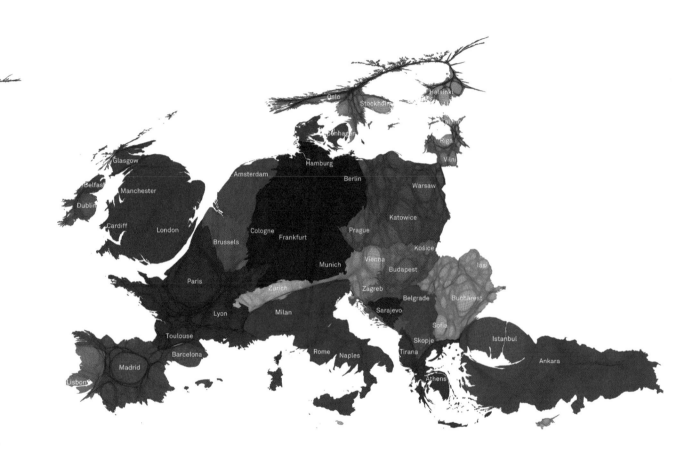

Glasgow
Belfast
Manchester
Dublin
Cardiff
London
Paris
Toulouse
Barcelona
Madrid
Lisbon
Brussels
Amsterdam
Hamburg
Berlin
Cologne
Frankfurt
Munich
Zurich
Lyon
Milan
Rome
Naples
Oslo
Stockholm
Copenhagen
Helsinki
Tallinn
Riga
Vilnius
Warsaw
Katowice
Prague
Košice
Vienna
Budapest
Zagreb
Belgrade
Sarajevo
Sofia
Skopje
Tirana
Athens
Bucharest
Iași
Istanbul
Ankara